"Jeffrey Lipshaw combines acute legal and philosophical analysis with prodigious legal experience to explain to us both how lawyers do think and how they should think. He makes clear why lawyering needs a fundamental transformation, and starts us down the path to achieving it. Anyone perplexed or angered by the role of lawyers and lawyering in modern society should read this book."

Professor Barry Schwartz, author of "Why We Work" and
co-author of "Practical Wisdom"

"Jeffrey Lipshaw draws on long experience, first in corporate legal practice, then in teaching, to offer a unique and invaluable guide to legal reasoning: its use in practice and, more importantly, its limits. I would advise all law students who are considering a career in transactional law to read it right away."

Professor Brian Bix, University of Minnesota, USA

"Professor Jeffrey Lipshaw, who practiced law for more than 26 years, has written a great and timely book—calling to mind Karl Llewellyn's efforts to champion 'the grand tradition' of law as against 'the formal style.' Lipshaw leads the reader to recognize that if lawyering is to have any real value, it must shed its narrow self-image as weaponized reason, and achieve self-awareness to understand its language within broader moral, social, and philosophical contexts. It must in short understand itself as not merely a technical profession, but a liberal arts vocation. This is a distinctive and learned book with a breezy earnest style all its own. Law students should read this after the 1L year, lawyers and academics at any time, and judges right away."

University Distinguished Professor Pierre Schlag,
University of Colorado, USA

Beyond Legal Reasoning: A Critique of Pure Lawyering

The concept of learning to "think like a lawyer" is one of the cornerstones of legal education in the United States and beyond. In this book, Jeffrey Lipshaw provides a critique of the traditional views of "thinking like a lawyer" or "pure lawyering" aimed at lawyers, law professors, and students who want to understand lawyering beyond the traditional warrior metaphor. Drawing on his extensive experience at the intersection of real world law and business issues, Professor Lipshaw presents a sophisticated philosophical argument that the "pure lawyering" of traditional legal education is agnostic to either truth or moral value of outcomes. He demonstrates pure lawyering's potential both for illusions of certainty and cynical instrumentalism, and the consequences of both when lawyers are called on as dealmakers, policymakers, and counselors.

This book offers an avenue for getting beyond (or unlearning) merely how to think like a lawyer. It combines legal theory, philosophy of knowledge, and doctrine with an appreciation of real-life judgment calls that multi-disciplinary lawyers are called upon to make. The book will be of great interest to scholars of legal education, legal language, and reasoning as well as professors who teach both doctrine and thinking and writing skills in the first-year law school curriculum; and for anyone who is interested in seeking a perspective on "thinking like a lawyer" beyond the litigation arena.

Jeffrey Lipshaw is a professor at Suffolk University Law School and former company general counsel. He writes on contract theory, business judgment, legal education, and jurisprudence. His most recent publication uses business law to reassess the influence of Kant's epistemology on Hans Kelsen.

Beyond Legal Reasoning:
A Critique of
Pure Lawyering

Jeffrey Lipshaw

Routledge
Taylor & Francis Group

LONDON AND NEW YORK

First published 2017
by Routledge
2 Park Square, Milton Park, Abingdon, Oxon OX14 4RN

and by Routledge
711 Third Avenue, New York, NY 10017

Routledge is an imprint of the Taylor & Francis Group, an informa business

British Library Cataloguing in Publication Data
A catalogue record for this book is available from the British Library

Library of Congress Cataloging in Publication Data
A catalog record for this book has been requested

ISBN: 978-1-138-22130-7 (hbk)
ISBN: 978-1-315-41081-4 (ebk)

Typeset in Galliard
by Keystroke, Neville Lodge, Tettenhall, Wolverhampton

Printed and bound in Great Britain by
TJ International Ltd, Padstow, Cornwall

To Alene, who liked the title.

Contents

Acknowledgments

I gratefully acknowledge comments and the willingness to read all or portions of the manuscript of the following: Hilary Allen, Brian Bix, Ray Campbell, Alan Childress, Rebecca Curtin, Josh Fershee, Joe Franco, David Haig, Stephen Hicks, John Infranca, Anna Ivey, Kristi Jobson, Sardiaa Leney, Alene Franklin Lipshaw, Michael Madison, Steve McJohn, Betsy Munnell, Frank Pasquale, Tracey Riley, John Henry Schlegel, Ilene Seidman, Steven D. Smith, David Soutter, Richard Wright, and five anonymous Routledge reviewers.

When I interviewed to be a law professor after twenty-six years in practice and business, I frequently got the question, "Why?" The pithy response I finally developed was that I had always been a scholar, but my law career got in the way for a long time. That was true. The person who most influenced me when I was an undergrad at Michigan was my teaching fellow in Kenneth Lockridge's survey course on United States history, Andy Achenbaum. Andy went on to a distinguished career as a historian and gerontologist at Michigan and Houston, and has remained a lifelong friend. I really did want to be a historian like Andy, but I also wanted not to be poor anymore. So I went to law school.

After I read Susan Neiman's *Evil in Modern Thought*, I found her email at the Einstein Forum in Berlin, and sent her a note with a bunch of questions. She responded quickly and graciously. I ended up organizing a speaking tour for her in Indianapolis in 2004 while the evil of September 11 was still fresh. We have maintained a correspondence and friendship ever since. Her work is both "but for" and proximate cause of this book.

My friend and colleague, Associate Dean Pat Shin, helped arrange the sabbatical leave and research stipends that gave me the time and space to write. My research assistant, Rochella Davis, went through the entire text, checked the citations, and gave me valuable comments.

I have been developing the ideas incorporated in this book for some time. Although I have never presented them in precisely this form, many of them have appeared in earlier work. The last part of Chapter 3 and Chapters 4 through 7 are based upon or incorporate portions of articles that have previously appeared in Volume 10:2 of the *Berkeley Business Law Journal*, Volume 45 of the *Connecticut Law Review*, Volume 116 of the *Penn State Law Review*, Volume 95 of the *Minnesota Law Review*, Volume 41 of the *Seton Hall Law Review*, Volume 19 of the *Southern California Interdisciplinary Law Journal*, Volume 56 of the *Cleveland State Law Review*, Volume 78 of the *Temple Law Review*, and Volume 37 of the *University of Toledo Law Review*.

Finally, I happen to have been married for going on thirty-seven years to one of the smartest people I know. Alene read the manuscript and found more mistakes than I care to admit. For an almost saintly ability to put up with me, she deserves the dedication.

Jeff Lipshaw
Cambridge, Massachusetts
September 2, 2016

Preface

This book is the culmination of a drum I have been beating for over ten years, from before I had any hope of being a law professor, much less writing this book.

Up until 2005, I was the general counsel of a Fortune 850 company listed on the New York Stock Exchange. The early 2000s were golden years to be running legal affairs in a public company *not* doing the dastardly deeds of an Enron, WorldCom, or Tyco. Without having to manage scandal, we got to deal with the fascinating governance issues that the legislative, regulatory, and business backlash generated: Sarbanes-Oxley, the revised New York Stock Exchange governance rules in the listing requirements, and the rise of shareholder activism, including proxy advisors and commentators like Institutional Shareholder Services and Nell Minow's firm, The Corporate Library.

One of the inanities (in my humble opinion) of Sarbanes-Oxley I had to manage was the required designation of one or more board members as "Audit Committee Financial Experts." Imagine the reaction of a well-to-do certified public accountant or a former chief financial officer being trotted out publicly as the board member assigned to be the point person for discovering any financial shenanigans of the Enron variety. It wasn't that they refused to be so designated; it was more "misery loves company." Hence the reaction was, "If I'm going to be designated, I want Joe to be designated too, so I'm not out there exposed all by myself." Well, Joe had been a chief executive officer , but not a financial person, even though the chief financial officer reported to him. That was the loophole we used to designate Joe and almost everybody else on the board as an Audit Committee Financial Expert.

At some point, it dawned on me how tenuous the relationship was between the presumed objective of the statute and the regulations and the hand-holding and other wasted time I was spending to get this all done. We had to work through compliance with the various requirements under Sarbanes-Oxley, the required certifications of financial statements under Sections 302 and 906, and the vetting of the board for compliance with the new independence requirement of the New York Stock Exchange. I came to feel the same way about many of the governance requirements, largely for the reasons Roberta Romano catalogued in her exhaustive article on quack corporate governance.[1]

My take on the whole regulatory mess was more ethereal than Professor Romano's. What you really wanted in a board member was the Corporate Right Stuff: intellectual independence, commitment, wisdom, and the courage to make tough calls. Some prophylactic rules, like barring directors with direct conflicting financial interests or with family ties to management, made sense as a negative assurance. Even that, however, was an underdetermined approach. There really was no way of screening out someone, say a sorority sister or one's long-time golf partner, who was as likely as a family member to be non-independent. From the standpoint of positive assurance, there was simply no way to articulate rules of law, whether by legislation, regulation, or case decision, that captured the essence of the Corporate Right Stuff. There might well be a norm against which you would measure it, but it was going to be social or moral and not legal. I wrote a law review article about that, much of which now makes me cringe, despite the fact that it's been downloaded almost 1,000 times on the Social Science Research Network.

At the time I was also consuming vast amounts of Enlightenment and other philosophy for reasons of pure intellectual satisfaction that are still not entirely clear to me. In particular, I was overwhelmed by a book called *Evil in Modern Thought*, a revisionist history of modern philosophy by Kant scholar Susan Neiman (who has since become a friend). Nothing challenges one's making sense of the world like the great questions of evil, but much of what she had to say about the role of reason (particularly Kant's view) in doing it resonated with me about making sense of things in general. It was a life-changing book. I turned to her far more technical book, *The Unity of Reason: Rereading Kant*, where she details the view of reason that filters through all of her work. And because I'm built that way, I followed her citations back to the original text in translation.

To be clear, I don't claim to be a Kant scholar like Susan or Christine Korsgaard or Onora O'Neill. I doubt anyone studies Kant's writing without significant assistance from interpreters, any more than one picks up and reads the Talmud, and I don't purport to have studied all or even most of his vast body of work. That Kant may have been obtuse or inconsistent or contradictory makes no difference to me. Nor does it matter to me if other Kant scholars were to have disagreed with Susan's interpretations (if they did), which I have adopted throughout the discussion. Rather, I care about the insights into my own personal and professional life that some of his thinking and her interpretation triggered. I wish I were smart enough to have originated them myself, but I have to give credit where it's due. And if that means you have to read "Kantian" as "Neimanian" or even "Lipshavian," so be it.

---

1 Roberta Romano, *The Sarbanes-Oxley Act and the Making of Quack Corporate Governance*, 114 YALE L. J. 1521 (2005).

In any event, it wasn't long before the two threads—corporate and business law, on one hand, and Kant's view of reason, on the other—combined. The result was the realization that the "thinking like a lawyer" of our collective law school training and indoctrination is only one particular (and often limited) way of making sense of the world, particularly when one's career as a lawyer moves outside of the litigation arena. That theme has been at the core of almost every scholarly piece I've written over the last ten years. It is the subject of this book.

For the last ten years, I have engaged in the doctrinal and theoretical stuff of an academic career, but my long gestation as a generalist in the real world is relevant to this project. I have previously written about the particular skill it takes to be a disciplined interdisciplinarian, as a general counsel of any business must be. You might not be an expert in pension or patent or German law, but the chief executive officer and the board of directors are relying on you, a non-expert in those areas, to tell them whether they should rely on the experts. So you have to learn enough about the area to have a sense of whether to believe the answer you are getting from the person who knows far more than you about the subject. If that sounds paradoxical, trust me, it is. I wrote an article about it several years ago, some of which I've incorporated in later chapters, in which I coined the term "metadisciplinarian." I described it later in a faculty workshop at the Boston College Law School as expertise in the very deep art of being strategically shallow.

And the need for non-expert interdisciplinary judgment about expertise in business doesn't end with you, the general counsel. The chief executive officer is processing not only your legal input, but those of the profit and loss leaders and the leaders of the other support functions like human resources and marketing. Unless you happen to be dealing in an area in which the law as applied to the facts is black and white ("no, you may not meet with your competitors to divvy up customers"), you may well get a response like another general counsel once described to me. I think the issue involved the nebulous rules governing when a company may repurchase its own shares on the open market.[2] The chief executive officer wanted to be aggressive about extending the time of share repurchases, and the general counsel sounded a note of caution. The chief executive officer asked, "Are you telling me it's illegal?" The general counsel responded, "Well, no, it's just riskier." To which the chief executive officer concluded, "Then we are buying back shares." In other words, the CEO, who wasn't an expert in the law, was also making an interdisciplinary judgment about law and investment strategy.

2 In a nutshell, the closer in time to a release of quarterly or annual financial statements the company buys its shares, the less likely there will be any undisclosed, material inside information about which the Securities and Exchange Commission or public sellers could later complain. The rationale of public company share repurchases is that it reduces the supply of shares, raising their value for all the remaining shareholders. Companies justify it by saying that management is so confident in the strength of the company that the best use of the company's cash at the moment is effectively to invest in itself. The counter-argument is that it may not be a good sign that the company is so short of good projects for the investment of capital that share repurchases are attractive.

In the business world, significant interplay between the disciplines is normal, even if occasionally dysfunctional. (Sales always hates credit, and engineering is famous for not talking to manufacturing.) In academia, however, as Louis Menand correctly portrayed in his book *The Marketplace of Ideas*,[3] finding a space across and between academic disciplines can be tricky. You get your certificate, your Ph.D., by means of acceptance in the community of scholars in that discipline. Leveraging ideas from one discipline to another can be wonderfully creative, but the interdisciplinary theoretician needs to be careful not to be perceived as a dilettante or simple-minded regarding the "borrowed knowledge."

I read a wonderful story about the risk and reward of overstepping disciplinary bounds in academia. At some point, I happened upon the work of Thomas Haskell, an eminent historian, whose work on the rise of professional disciplines was relevant to my own intuitions about the artificiality of their boundaries. Back in 1974, when Haskell was getting his Ph.D. and I was still a serious undergraduate history student thinking about getting a Ph.D., economists Robert Fogel and Stanley Engerman wrote a controversial history of slavery entitled *Time on the Cross*.[4] The thesis was that slave labor was more productive than free labor, based on an economic measure called the "index of total factor productivity." I vividly remember the substantive stir it caused as well as the methodological issue among historians. The goal was to make the discipline more of a science, where historians would no longer be narrativists but "cliometricians." Haskell described his reaction to the thesis upon reading the book:

> By the time I was halfway through it I suspected the authors had committed a blunder. Untrained in economics and having received my Ph.D. in history only a year earlier, I knew it would seem absurdly presumptuous of me to accuse two of the nation's most distinguished economic historians of misusing a tool of their trade . . . .[5]

Haskell succeeded in getting the *New York Review of Books* to publish his review, the first paragraph of which contained the following sentence: "I am not an econometric historian or a specialist in the history of slavery, but I am a reasonable man and, as such, entitled to judge the plausibility of the author's argument."[6]

I found that inspiring, and it is how I feel about my own inter- or metadisciplinarity. I was: (a) never coopted or socialized as a graduate student into any particular discipline, and (b) energized by learning enough about a subject area

---

3 LOUIS MENAND, THE MARKETPLACE OF IDEAS: REFORM AND RESISTANCE IN THE AMERICAN UNIVERSITY (2010).
4 ROBERT FOGEL & STANLEY ENGERMAN, TIME ON THE CROSS: THE ECONOMICS OF AMERICAN NEGRO SLAVERY (1974).
5 THOMAS L. HASKELL, OBJECTIVITY IS NOT NEUTRALITY: EXPLANATORY SCHEMES IN HISTORY 25 (1998).
6 *Id.* at 31.

to borrow from it. I know I am a reasonable man. Sometimes crossing the boundary works and sometimes it doesn't. You only hope that when it doesn't, you figure it out before publishing it in a non-peer reviewed law journal where the editors don't know any more about the subject than you do. I got on a kick a number of years ago about Gödel's Incompleteness Theorem. I came to the conclusion, after trying my hand at a piece that fortunately ended up on the cutting room floor, that there are only limited metaphors for the law that you can draw from that particular insight about formal and complex logical systems.

But there's no doubt that most of my articles have been significantly longer than they needed to be. I was being defensive. I wanted to establish that I understood the underlying discipline, even if all that understanding wasn't strictly necessary for the point I happened to be making. Doing so here would not only cause me to exceed the length of the book Routledge is willing to publish, but it would be like reading the unabridged *Les Misérables* or *Moby Dick*. Parisian sewers and stripping off whale blubber are necessary parts of the stories, but you don't really need to know as much as Hugo and Melville wrote about them to get the point. Whether or not I succeeded in curbing my desire to understand and explain everything in mind-numbing detail, please be assured that I tried.

As to my subject matter, the critique of pure lawyering, what could I be adding after more than 100 years of scholarly discussion of what it means to think like a lawyer?[7] It may be helpful to compare the most recent significant contribution to the literature, Fred Schauer's aptly titled and excellent *Thinking Like a Lawyer*.[8] My approach differs in at least three ways. First, Professor Schauer's grist is primarily the litigation process and the application of public law. I want to explore the pluses and minuses of thinking like a lawyer in the broader context of all the things lawyers do, not just arguing cases. Second, if Professor Schauer has metaphorically drawn a circle around the lawyering discipline, I want to explore edges of the boundary and beyond, something (understandably, given the nature of his project) Professor Schauer largely leaves behind in Chapter 1. Third, he identifies but largely leaves to psychology the mental leap from the articulation of a rule itself to its application in a particular circumstance.[9] He doesn't assess what it means to *follow* a rule, whether in law or otherwise.[10] Whether or not I have answers about that leap, I do ask questions about it.

I am not original in focusing on lawyering beyond the litigation arena. There are invaluable texts and articles for lawyers who do not aim to be sublimated

---

7 On September 4, 2015, I did a search for "think! like a lawyer" in the Westlaw Next "Law Reviews & Journals" database. The search returned 2,605 documents, not all of which I have read (nor will I).
8 FREDERICK SCHAUER, THINKING LIKE A LAWYER: A NEW INTRODUCTION TO LEGAL REASONING (2009).
9 *Id.* at 3.
10 *Id.* at 98–100.

warriors.[11] This will be different. It is an effort to think about the thinking itself. Legal reasoning is merely one way of creating meaning out of circumstances in the real world. In its pure form, it does nothing more than convert a real-world narrative to a set of legal conclusions that have no necessary connection either to truth or morality.

My critique of pure lawyering is the product of someone who has had the inner and outer experience through his career of: (a) first practicing the art of pure lawyering, (b) then acting as an intermediary between lawyers who practice the art and business people who don't, and (c) then finally subjecting that experience to his own sense-making exercise. I suspect it will be helpful even for those who want to do nothing more than hone their pure lawyering skills. For those lawyers, however, who want to counsel, create, engineer, plan, or make policy, it is a guide for getting beyond legal reasoning.

---

11 *See, e.g.,* DAVID HOWARTH, LAW AS ENGINEERING: THINKING ABOUT WHAT LAWYERS DO (2013); DAVID A. BINDER, PAUL BERGMAN, PAUL R. TREMBLAY, & IAN S. WEINSTEIN, LAWYERS AS COUNSELORS: A CLIENT-CENTERED APPROACH (3d ed. 2012); PAUL BREST & LINDA HAMILTON KRUGER, PROBLEM SOLVING, DECISION MAKING, AND PROFESSIONAL JUDGMENT: A GUIDE FOR LAWYERS AND POLICYMAKERS (2010); ANDREW S. WATSON, THE LAWYER IN THE INTERVIEWING AND COUNSELLING PROCESS (1976); Paul Brest, *Skeptical Thoughts: Integrating Problem-Solving into Legal Curriculum Faces Uphill Climb*, 6 DISP. RESOL. MAG. 20 (2000); Dina Schlossberg, *An Examination of Transaction Law Clinics and Interdisciplinary Education*, 11 WASH. U. J. L. & POL'Y 195 (2003); Carrie Menkel-Meadow, *The Lawyer as Problem Solver and Third Party Neutral: Creativity and Non-Partisanship in Lawyering*, 72 TEMP. L. REV. 785 (1999); Paul A. Brest, *The Responsibility of Law Schools: Educating Lawyers as Counselors and Problem-Solvers*, 58 L. & CONTEMP. PROBS. 5 (1995); Thomas L. Shaffer, *Lawyers, Counselors, and Counselors at Law*, 61 A.B.A.J. 854 (1975); Harrop A. Freeman, *The Role of Lawyers as Counselors*, 7 WM. & MARY L. REV. 203 (1966).

1 Why a Critique?

[T]here is a natural and unavoidable dialectic of pure reason, not one in which a bungler might be entangled through lack of acquaintance, or one that some sophist has artfully invented to confuse rational people, but one that irremediably attaches to human reason, so that even after we have exposed the mirage it will still not cease to lead our reason with false hopes, continually propelling it into momentary aberrations that always need to be removed.[1]

This book is a critique, not a criticism, of the rigorous mode of rationality that has come to be known as "thinking like a lawyer." For reasons that will become clearer over the course of this book, I refer to it as "pure lawyering."

Our approach to teaching the lawyerly thinking process hasn't changed all that much since C.C. Langdell assembled his first contracts casebook in 1871.[2] Little more than a hundred years later, my professors still used similar casebooks and only seldom moved away from the podium to scrawl something on the blackboard. PowerPoint, YouTube, Blackboard, clickers, and other marvels of classroom technology had not yet arrived. Nevertheless, I doubt I would get serious resistance to the claim that, even while the techniques have changed, the substance of what we do (and usually very well!) is to inculcate the reasoning abilities captured in some iconic books.[3] Those worthy works address the technical proficiencies of legal reasoning: how to derive the applicable rules and holdings from cases and apply those rules to new situations. There isn't much wrong with either the substance or the pedagogy of that subject. My focus is rather the kind of thinking

---

1 IMMANUEL KANT, CRITIQUE OF PURE REASON 386–87 (Paul Guyer & Allen W. Wood, trans. 1998) (1781).
2 ROBERT STEVENS, LAW SCHOOL: LEGAL EDUCATION IN AMERICA FROM THE 1850S TO THE 1980S 35–72 (1983).
3 *See, e.g.,* KARL N. LLEWELLYN, THE BRAMBLE BUSH (Quid Pro Books 2012) (1960); EDWARD H. LEVI, AN INTRODUCTION TO LEGAL REASONING (1949); NEIL MACCORMICK, LEGAL REASONING AND LEGAL THEORY (1994); FREDERICK SCHAUER, THINKING LIKE A LAWYER: A NEW INTRODUCTION TO LEGAL REASONING (2012).

that non-litigating lawyers need to undertake over the course of a career. It is therefore a consideration of what it takes to get *beyond* legal reasoning.

My perspective as teacher, scholar, and practitioner is relatively unusual. I have been a law professor for over ten years. But I brought to the party something relatively rare among law professors—over a quarter century in a wide variety of legal roles. During the first ten years of my career, as a traditional litigator in a big Midwestern firm doing big cases (i.e. antitrust, securities, and complex commercial litigation), I never questioned what seemed to have been a natural segue from my legal education to my practice. Nor do I question it now. So much of my later practice career, however, took place outside the courtroom. It was unusual, but I quit being a litigator cold turkey over the course of a traumatic weekend, and spent the next sixteen years as a transactional lawyer within the firm, then as a company general counsel and business executive.

In the business world, my primary function was to be the liaison between the lawyers and law with its unique language and structures, on one hand, and non-lawyer decision-makers, on the other. I still needed to be fluent in the language and forms in which lawyers spoke to each other. What I learned over the course of a long career, however, is that legal reasoning is merely one form of making sense of things. Its application in non-legal settings requires the effective lawyer to hear it as non-lawyers might hear and respond to it, for better but often for worse.

Just as I felt myself a bridge from the legal profession to our business executives, I now want to bridge from the rigor of legal reasoning to the other kinds of nuanced judgments good lawyers have to make. I spent too long as a litigator myself and, as a general counsel, hired too many great litigators to denigrate the subtleties of judgment in litigation and trial practice. But as many of my academic colleagues now recognize, lawyering "before the fact" in transactions is quite different from "after the fact" dispute resolution. Despite some efforts to make it otherwise, the primary means of teaching the most transactional of the first-year subjects, contracts and property, is still by way of analyzing litigated appellate cases. Our methods of teaching the "deal" part of those subjects are still in their infancy. And the law-business judgments in the deal context can be quite different as well.

Nevertheless, this is not a rehash of most of the current criticisms of legal education. In many respects, what I will say here runs counter to the clamor for reform in legal education that has arisen since the MacCrate Report of 1992[4] and the Carnegie Foundation's 2007 assessment of legal education, *Educating*

---

4 AMERICAN BAR ASSOCIATION, SECTION OF LEGAL EDUCATION AND ADMISSIONS TO THE BAR, LEGAL EDUCATION AND PROFESSIONAL DEVELOPMENT—AN EDUCATIONAL CONTINUUM, REPORT OF THE TASK FORCE ON LAW SCHOOLS AND THE PROFESSION: NARROWING THE GAP ("MACCRATE REPORT") (1992).

Lawyers.[5] After the Financial Crisis of 2008–09, the legal profession and law schools experienced the Great Contraction. The number of Law School Admission Test (LSAT) takers and law school applicants tumbled. The war of words between the establishment of legal education and its critics achieved new levels of venom. The American Bar Association (ABA), state bar regulators,[6] and our students have come to demand professors teach skills, not just Langdellian-style doctrine, and certainly not abstract theory.

Nor is it a practical guide to restructuring the so-called skills curriculum. I offer a course in entrepreneurship and venture capital to our upper level students. Teaching them the mechanics of documenting a venture capital investment is relatively easy. The far harder task is conveying to my bright law students the extent to which their entrepreneurial clients don't think like them. In our simulation, I play the client on both sides when the lawyers need to consult about a business decision. I'm sure I am one of their first experiences in dealing with a client who views lawyers as an impediment to the real goal, whatever it is.

To the contrary, if anything I want us as educators and lawyers to think even harder, and apply *more* theory if necessary, to what it means to think like a lawyer in the 21st century. What we teach so well, particularly in the first-year courses, is an enchanting way of thinking rationally and methodically. Legal reasoning is a method for converting narrative from the real world into a particular model, one that spits out legal consequences. That works perfectly in the purest form of pure lawyering, advocacy. Reason is a weapon. In transactional and other lawyering work beyond litigation, however, weapons may not be appropriate.

Thinking and, whether students want to hear it or not, the ability to theorize are the seedbed that underlies all the other lawyering skills. I want to understand where the traditional forms of lawyerly thinking fit the bill. But I also want to consider, particularly for those of our students who won't be litigators, where they might not. The theme is deliberately *beyond* legal reasoning and not *instead* of it. The last thing I want to do is dull the sharp edges of the steel trap analytic minds I'm teaching in first-year contracts. Rather, at some point in their careers (perhaps even before they finish law school), they ought to consider the kinds of judgments for which the classical conceptions of thinking like a lawyer either do not provide satisfactory answers, or provide the kinds of judgments in which a naked rationality can lead to error.

One of the stereotypes of legal rationality is its relative amorality. It evokes a crafty cleverness, whether it is Portia's examination of Shylock in *The Merchant*

---

5 WILLIAM M. SULLIVAN, ET AL., EDUCATING LAWYERS: PREPARATION FOR THE PROFESSION OF LAW (2007). In addition, the authors prepared a summary of the report, available on the Carnegie Foundation's website at http://archive.carnegiefoundation.org/pdfs/elibrary/elibrary_pdf_632.pdf (hereinafter "Carnegie Summary").

6 *See, e.g.,* Press Release, New York State Unified Court System, *Rules for New York Bar Admission Amended to Include New Experiential Training Component* (Dec. 16, 2015), http://www.nycourts.gov/press/ PDFs/PR15_20.pdf.

of Venice, or Don Corleone's advice in *The Godfather* that Tom Hagen go to law school "because a lawyer with his briefcase can steal more than twenty men with guns." Another stereotype is "CYA" caution where, as my simulation students learn, business people perceive lawyers as the corporate wet blanket, spinning out the downside legal risk of every good idea in their capacities as "Vice Presidents of 'No.'"[7]

There's a reason for the stereotypes. Almost two decades ago, UCLA law professor Gary Blasi offered an encyclopedic assessment of how lawyers go about solving problems. He noted at the outset the prototypical lawyer in cultural context was

> a litigator, very likely a trial lawyer, knowledgeable about both legal doctrine and procedure, and able to put that knowledge to use on behalf of an individual client, generally in a fairly simple dispute with another party, in order to achieve a desired result.[8]

Pure lawyering is how that happens. It is a mode of converting real-world narratives into a logical progression of rules and facts. Deepak, a typical client, tells his lawyer a story of tripping on his neighbor's rake or of a seller confirming a bargain price for a coffee maker and then reneging on the deal. His lawyer recasts the story into a series of if-then propositions, the effect of which is to turn out a conclusion that somebody is liable to Deepak for his injury or his disappointment. The heart of legal training is learning how to argue persuasively that the situation in dispute bears the greatest analogical resemblance to a case precedent in which the if-then rule just happens to generate a result favorable to that lawyer's client. The arguments may involve the rule's meaning, applicability, legitimacy, universality, or fairness. These are subjects of classroom debate.[9] But once the process of lawyerly argumentation resolves the applicable rule, the legal consequence follows syllogistically. That, in a nutshell, is the core of pure lawyering: to force the resolution of the dispute into an otherwise amoral syllogism the result of which is binary: I'm right and you're wrong.

It is difficult to talk about thinking like a lawyer without connecting it to the historical happenstance in which it developed. Law school introduces students to what Professor Elizabeth Mertz described as "a closed linguistic system that is capable of devouring all manner of social detail, but without budging in its

---

7 Mike France, *A Compelling Case for Lawyer-CEOs*, BUS. WEEK (Dec. 13, 2004), at 88. ("Business attorneys are often considered the 'vice-presidents of No,' says Jeffrey A. Sonnenfeld, Associate Dean of Executive Programs at Yale School of Management.")
8 Gary L. Blasi, *What Lawyers Know: Lawyering Expertise, Cognitive Science, and the Functions of Theory*, 45 J. LEGAL EDUC. 313, 325 (1995).
9 *See* Susan Haack, *On Logic in the Law: "Something, But Not All,"* 20 RATIO JURIS 1, 21–25 (2007).

core assumptions."[10] That is another way of expressing what legal sociologist Gunther Teubner called law's "epistemic trap." Law as a social institution develops its own models and constructs of reality. Its "cognitive operations . . . construct idiosyncratic images of reality and move them away from the world constructions of everyday life and from those of scientific discourse."[11] Those are some of the hallmarks of the professional identity described in *Educating Lawyers*.[12]

Modern conceptions of law in the United States began with Langdell's formalist vision of law. It didn't take long for others to object to that view. Holmes's dictum was that law's life comes from experience, not logic. But the nature of the closed system didn't change.[13] Even the legal realism of the first half of the 20th century, the first significant intellectual objection to Langdellian formalism, was still *legal*. It was a vision from within the community of lawyers about how its closed linguistic system should best reflect the outside world.

The closed community of the profession has social as well as intellectual attributes. In the real world, we still congregate in firms and law departments. When I left the law firm to become the young general counsel of a large multi-product business, I wanted all the lawyers to congregate in the home office like a miniature firm. The CEO overruled me, demanding that they be physically dispersed to the businesses they represented. He viewed the chief lawyer for each business as no different from the chief financial officer, the chief technologist, or the chief human resources executive. I wanted to keep the system closed. Not only did the CEO want it opened to the constructions of everyday business life, he thought my view was parochial. When I left the business and returned to the law firm, I remember the overwhelming sense at the first large meeting that it was viscerally diverse. Just a bit deeper, however, everybody looked alike.

Apart from the structure of lawyer communities, anticipating and conducting litigation is the quintessential version of that theoretical closed system in action. Lawyers own the turf. Business and lay people are generally uncomfortable participants in the game. Ordinary people see parsing the meaning of "is" (so famously demonstrated by Bill Clinton's deposition) as an example of pure lawyering. That view of lawyers is not generally one that carries high esteem, even though parsing the meaning of words is precisely what lawyers do.

Transactional lawyers who see their jobs as anticipating all the possible bases for litigation can create the same impression. The big-city lawyer for a client building a vacation home in rural Michigan sends the small town contractor a twenty-five-page single-spaced construction agreement, full of if-then sentences that create legal structures, define duties, and allocate risks and liabilities. The internal

---

10 Elizabeth Mertz, *Inside the Law School Classroom: Toward a New Legal Realist Pedagogy*, 60 VAND. L. REV. 483, 504 (2007).
11 Gunther Teubner, *How the Law Thinks: Toward a Constructivist Epistemology of Law*, 23 LAW & SOC'Y REV. 727, 742 (1989).
12 SULLIVAN, *supra* note 5, at 3–4, 31.
13 For a nice summary, *see* Haack, *supra* note 9, at 3–9.

meaning of the draft document, as an expression of pure lawyering, is commonplace and uncontroversial among lawyers, even if it requires negotiation before it becomes final. To the contractor, however, it has an external meaning, wholly apart from the thrust of its sentences. It says something, and not very positively, about relationships, trust, and the form of discourse between the owner and the contractor going forward. It is no surprise when the contractor declines to do the work under such a contract because his customer has provided a tangible demonstration of how the relationship is going to proceed. Life is too short. Over-lawyering, being oblivious to implicit meanings beyond the rational import of the words, is one transactional consequence of pure lawyering.

My purpose here is to share what it took much of a reflective practice and academic career to figure out. The "thinking like a lawyer" or "pure lawyering" that a law student learns in most of the first year of law school and for much of the next two years (despite the pressure for curriculum change) turns out to be just part of the kind of thinking a *good* transactional lawyer actually does. Successfully getting beyond legal reasoning means finding a way to avoid both the cynicism of crafty cleverness and the self-deceptions and illusions of mistaking your own advocacy for truth or moral rectitude. Many (or most) good lawyers figure that out without too much (or any) reflection, perhaps because they are too busy just practicing law to spend a lot of time down the rabbit hole of thinking about how they think.

The underlying themes of the book

The critique of pure lawyering

The primary objective of the book is a critique of the legal reasoning process. There are three fundamental themes about the process that wend their way through the book. First, traditional legal reasoning, as a subset of reason generally, is "content-neutral" in that the process of reasoning itself doesn't tell you whether the outcome is true or right. Second, the process can be the means of rationally persuading oneself (or one's clients) not only that "we're right and you're wrong," but that "what we believe is true and what you believe is false." If your only job as a lawyer is to litigate to victory, you needn't worry about the implications of that too much. On the other hand, if your job as a lawyer is to resolve something by contract, compromise, or cooperation, thinking like a lawyer can be a problem. Third, the process is amoral and can be used for wholly instrumental ends. If you can sell even an immoral, opportunistic, or daft argument to some judge who is willing to buy it, that's what the system is all about.

Let's address each of those themes in a little more detail.

Legal reasoning as a subset of reason

My allusion in the subtitle to Kant's *Critique of Pure Reason* is deliberate, because the problems of pure reason he identified apply to legal reasoning as well. To be clear, I want a practical payoff: a more nuanced view of what we are doing when we think and argue like lawyers. In view of Chief Justice Roberts's example of references to Kant as the prototype of obscurity in legal academia, however,[14] I want to reassure you that I will not be providing a lengthy exegesis on Kantian philosophy. But my continuing joke is that I am one of the world's leading scholars, if not the only one, on the intersection of venture capital and Kant. There is one, and it won't be too hard to explain.

Kant thought that the process of human reason was fundamental to expanding what we could know, as in science. His critique, however, was that reason was also capable of creating *illusions* of knowledge. That is, when not applying the reasoning process to matters of experience or possible experience, the rational mind could come to equate that which is empirically knowable with things that really were matters of faith. For example, the benign power of reason in science allows us to imagine beyond what we presently know and conjure up something like the Standard Model of particle physics. For good or sometimes for ill, however, the power of reason can also let us posit a deity whose existence we can never prove or disprove other than by the reasoning process itself. Kant's great contribution, as far as I'm concerned, had to do with having confidence in asserting what you can *know* empirically, being humble in asserting what you merely believe by faith (i.e. the non-empirical fruits of your reason), and having the wisdom to distinguish between the two.

Reason's capability of conjuring up non-empirical gods and demons applies in spades to the rigorous but amoral rationality that lawyers employ as their primary stock in trade. I've seen even good lawyers (and I include myself), armed with the tools of reasoned advocacy they honed in law school, confuse that which *is* true or false, that which *ought to be* true or false, and that which *they want to be* true or false. So I believe it's worth examining once more how lawyers think.

As to the point that the form of legal reasoning is neither moral nor immoral, but simply a means of converting narrative to a legal implication, Garry Trudeau aptly caricatured the stereotype in four panels of a *Doonesbury* strip many years ago. His character Joanie Caucus is a first-year Berkeley law student. She is sitting in the student café with Woodrow, Trudeau's bow-tied caricature of the over-enthusiastic "gunner" who sits in the front row with his hand in the air, demanding the professor call on him. In the first panel, Joanie says, "Torts? . . . No, I don't want to talk about torts! We just spent all morning talking about torts!" In the second panel, she continues, "Woodrow, what you've got to realize is that the world doesn't begin and end with casebooks! There are many other equally acceptable ways of looking at life." There is a pause in the third panel as Woodrow stares out at us and utters, "Hmm." And then in the fourth panel, he turns back to Joanie and says, "Yeah, I suppose you could make a case for that."[15]

---

14 Orin S. Kerr, *The Influence of Immanuel Kant on Evidentiary Approaches in 18th-Century Bulgaria*, 18 GREEN BAG 2d 251 (2015).
15 G.B. TRUDEAU, THE DOONESBURY CHRONICLES (1975).

What Trudeau understood is that thinking like a lawyer will not in itself provide a compass for moral, ethical, business, and personal decisions. For example, the Supreme Court upheld the constitutionality of the individual mandate in the Affordable Care Act.[16] Supporters of Obamacare were thrilled and opponents outraged. Nobody can deny, however, that Chief Justice Roberts's opinion characterizing the penalty as a tax was a thorough, if debatable, justification of a legal outcome by way of rule-application, the very prototype of pure lawyering.[17] The same pure lawyering is at the heart of something as noble as the desegregation of Topeka schools, as unseemly as patent trolling, and everything in between. Pure lawyering is agnostic as to the non-legal acceptability of outcomes. It is the source of the comment in *Educating Lawyers* that "[a]t a deep, largely uncritical level, the students come to understand the law as a formal and rational system, however much its doctrines and rules may diverge from the common sense understandings of the lay person."[18] Or, at least, I can make a case for that.

The best of us teach our law students a powerful thinking tool. When I teach first-year contracts, I am not particularly concerned with making sure that we've covered every aspect of the law. My goal instead is to teach students how to listen to a client's narrative and turn it into a legal theory that is consistent with the desired outcome. Chapters 2 and 3 contain my views on how best to instill that kind of thinking rigor.

But the intensity of that training comes with baggage. Within the cocoon of our professional socialization, we naturally give a special privilege to the particular way we think and talk. We "disassemble the world around us into a vocabulary of abstract symbols, which we can arrange in our minds to produce notions of alternative worlds."[19] To take a common issue in agency law, for example, am I accountable to my neighbor, Deepak, when he trips over a rake that my landscaper negligently left on the sidewalk? A trial of this case might well have little to do with Deepak's injury, and much to do with resolving the factual issues about whether the landscaper status qualifies as my "employee." That is because I will only be responsible if the landscaper was my employee-agent rather than an independent contractor-agent. What the judge or jury will hear about is the extent to which I controlled or had the right to control not just the outcome but the way in which the landscaper did his job. In short, the litigation process is one of culling out the irrelevant legal aspects of the narrative, and reducing the entire dispute to the particular "if-then" rules that will resolve the case. We will explore that reduction closely in Chapters 2 and 3.

---

16 Nat'l Fed. of Ind. Bus. v. Sebelius, 567 U.S. ___, 132 S. Ct. 2566 (2012).
17 *See* Randy Barnett, *Chief Justice Roberts was principled but wrong in his ObamaCare decision*, VOLOKH CONSPIRACY (May 6, 2016), https://www.washingtonpost.com/news/volokhconspiracy/wp/2016/05/06/chief-justice-roberts-was-principled-but-wrong-in-his-obamacare-decision.
18 Carnegie Summary, *supra* note 5, at 5.
19 Ian Tattersall, *Evolution by Other Means*, AM. SCHOLAR 18 (Winter 2016).

Pure lawyering and truth

The second theme in the critique of legal reasoning has to do with whether the reductive process leads to true or correct conclusions.

Academics often say that law is a normative exercise. They mean that rules of law are about what ought to be. We use them to correct things in the real world that are *not* as they ought to be. A personal injury lawyer inclined to lofty justifications of her craft could well think of herself as an agent of Aristotelian corrective justice. She is repairing an injury that ought not to have occurred if the world had operated as it should have in the first instance. What the lawyer uses to achieve that normative result—compensation to Deepak for his bruised shin or his commercial disappointment—are legal rules: "if-then" statements that constitute the major premises in the logic of legal reasoning. If the lawyer establishes the antecedent conditions, the "if" of the rule, the "then" must follow. In undertaking this normative process, it seems reasonable we would *believe* that our side is *right* and the other side is *wrong*.

My concern is the easy move from mere belief to a sense that we have access to moral facts and truth. Coming to think like a lawyer entails adopting a vivid disciplinary ontology, one in which the law comes to be real. In other words, pure lawyering is also capable of persuading us that what our side believes is *true* and what the other side believes is *false*. As one legal philosopher asked, when we think about law, what can we say is "the fact of the matter?"[20]

There certainly is a real and objective aspect to law: the complex web of cases, treatises, statutes, and commentary that make up the sources of the legal rules that lawyers use in the process of pure lawyering. Among practitioners and law professors alike, the law takes on thingness sufficient to support the idea, even if metaphoric, that the law embodied in those texts is an animate subject, as in "the law requires or demands that we do X." Moreover, because it can appear to be real and objective, the law ought then also to be the object of *science*. My thesis is that the conflation occurs because there is, on one hand, a family resemblance between the normative arguments that pure lawyering uses to achieve what clients consider to be justice and, on the other, the kind of descriptive theory-making in which scientists engage. Thinking like a lawyer thus becomes a powerful way for one to make sense of the world, not only as to what is *just* but additionally as to what is *true*.

I am hardly the first person to assess whether lawyerly thinking leads to either justice *or* truth.[21] When you move, as I have, from a law firm litigation practice to a corporate environment, the lawyers are merely another support function. CEOs don't simply accept what you say because you're a lawyer. You begin to

---

20 Ralf Poscher, *Why We Argue About the Law: An Agonistic Account of Legal Disagreement*, in METAPHILOSOPHY OF LAW (Tomasz Gizbert-Studnicki, Adam Dyrda, & Pawel Banas, eds.) (2016), http://papers. ssrn.com/sol3/papers.cfm?abstract_id=2734689, at 15–16.
21 *See, e.g.,* DENNIS PATTERSON, LAW & TRUTH (1996).

appreciate one academic observation that the paradigm of legal language is the argument from authority, and it is more akin to religious thinking or the assertion of brute power than to reasoned problem-solving. Within the limited confines of a law firm litigation practice, that's not a problem. The argument from authority underlies our idealized metaphor for lawyers; they *are* the zealous warriors on behalf of the client when the goal isn't to come to an agreement, but to win. The essence of the metaphor lies in the image of upholding truth and righteousness, vanquishing one's opponents, and doing so by using tools of intellectual rather than physical brutality.

That metaphor for lawyering doesn't work so well when you are trying to oversee all of the legal affairs of a business. One of my mantras when assessing our legal positions in a business context, was that being right or knowing what was true was not all it was cracked up to be. That is because we were rarely dealing in legal issues that invoked the kind of moral righteousness and outrage that the great social cause lawyers might muster. At best, one might invoke the sanctity of keeping one's promises in a contract dispute, but invariably the situation was more nuanced, the real issue being what the promise, if any, really was.

My skepticism when I was in practice about the ability of legal thinking to find truth or moral certainties in mundane circumstances would likely have put me uncomfortably in the company of academic post-modernist skeptics about the existence of *any* truth or moral certainty. Now, from my academic perch, I am not a post-modernist or much of a fan of most of what I see from the Critical Legal Studies movement. Even so, Robert Cover's assessment of the brutality of legal thinking in *Nomos and Narrative*[22] resonates with me as a former business person, as does Pierre Schlag's take-down of lawyerly enchantment with the power of reason.[23] The weapon, thinking like a lawyer, manages to mask that brutishness with an appeal to reason and reasonableness—if the law is real, if it's a thing, then it ought to be coherent, consistent, and produce determinate answers even when the moral absolutes are few and far between.

In fact, I am not a skeptic about either truth or morality, but when it comes to the vast majority of mundane issues, I treat them gingerly. I am cautious about attempts to use legal argument to *reason* the path to truth, particularly normative or moral truths. Our cooptation into the professional discipline of lawyering has the effect of privileging the legal way of getting to an answer. The overwhelming majority of people in the world who are not lawyers (business clients chief among them) are not so coopted into the powerful social and linguistic system of the law. They may well not feel compelled in the first instance to turn to law rather than all the other possible norms that inform relationships. That is, the reasoning we happen to do as lawyers is not particularly privileged in the broader world, notwithstanding its standing as a professional discipline.

22 *See* Robert M. Cover, *Foreword: Nomos and Narrative*, 97 HARV. L. REV. 4 (1983).
23 *See* PIERRE SCHLAG, THE ENCHANTMENT OF REASON (1998).

I believe lawyers and their professors employ their powers of reason to conflate knowledge and belief (or what they want to believe) all the time. Just as thinking like a lawyer (i.e. reasoning like a pure lawyer) is agnostic as to outcomes, it does not produce truth. Kant wanted to "deny" that reason necessarily led to real empirical knowledge in order to make room for reasonable faith, that is, the things we know we can't prove but believe nevertheless.[24] In a similar way, I want to deny the law, at least for the business lawyer, is something we know. Rather it is an activity, one particular mode or process of thinking by which one argues for the primacy of a belief in the process of adjudicating a dispute.

To believe the law is real and knowable in any objective way, that it speaks or authorizes, that it is or that it is obliged to be coherent, consistent, or determinate, is to be caught up in an illusion. I can understand the illusion: it is the easiest way to resolve the cognitive dissonance between the professional demand that lawyers act like the law, on one hand, is a real and animate thing and, on the other, knowing that it is an abstraction. I am not giving up on truth. Rather, I seek to make room for other modes of thinking that take account not only of law, but also of morality, principle, compromise, civility, and pragmatism.

Pure lawyering and instrumentality

The third theme of the critique of legal reasoning process is its potential for instrumental use. Instrumental pure lawyering can give authoritative color to policy or counseling outcomes, traveling the logician's or sophist's route from reasonable assumptions to outrageous (or at least debatable) legal conclusions that really need to be assessed morally. I have in mind Dan Kahan's 2006 commencement speech at the Yale Law School, in which he contrasts reflective and intuitive professional practice of any kind with the pure lawyering logic of John Yoo's infamous memo on the permissibility of torture.[25] In the business world, are you willing to file a lawsuit on grounds that barely survive the Federal Rule of Civil Procedure's Rule 11 test for colorability of a claim, not because you really think you can win, but for intimidation or leverage value? There's no reason not to do so under the bare logic of pure lawyering.

Instrumental use of the law, however, is as much a tool for purported angels as purported devils. There is a strong family resemblance between natural causation and moral blame. The reasoning that takes operative facts and infers legal conclusions is capable as well of conflating the advocate's normative authority-based blame with the scientist's observations of causation in the physical world. The goal in the blaming game is not necessarily a deal or a better world, but retribution and recompense. I have in mind the frustration felt in many quarters

---

24 KANT, *supra* note 1, at 117.
25 Dan M. Kahan, *Yale Law School Commencement Remarks (Revised)*, May 25, 2006, http://digitalcommons.law.yale.edu/cgi/viewcontent.cgi?article=1007&context=ylsca.

that too few Wall Street executives have been prosecuted for whatever role they played in the sub-prime mortgage crisis. The likely answer is that the causes of the crisis were too complex to lay at the feet of the bankers, regardless of their motives, and even ambitious prosecutors couldn't come up with colorable criminal charges. The critique of pure lawyering is that assigning blame often ought *not* be the object of a lawyer's work. When the goal is not to litigate to a conclusion, but to counsel, create, plan, engineer, or make policy, the cure of assigning blame can be worse than the disease.

Making judgments

In addition to undertaking a critique of the mechanics of the legal reasoning process itself, the book attempts to situate lawyerly thinking within the broader sphere of making judgments. I focus on business judgments because those are the ones with which I am most familiar. They are an example of non-litigation decisions lawyers often have to make. I don't, however, minimize or denigrate the decision-making litigating lawyers have to make. My assessments of judgment occur from the "inside-out" rather than the "outside-in." That means that I am less of a behaviorist or observer of others than someone engaged in the examined life.[26] In my case, it is the examined life of someone who spent an entire career as a lawyer dealing both with big issues and with the detailed nuts and bolts of little ones. I spend inordinate amounts of time considering my own inner experience of coming to terms with difficult issues—what it is like to have the experience of making a decision.

In short, this is the problem business people sometimes mock as the "two-handed lawyer." The stereotypical reaction of business people is that their lawyers are far more adept at analysis than decision. Explained one corporate counsel with regard to his outside counsel, "The thing I hate most is a 'two-handed' lawyer, one who says 'you could do this, but on the other hand . . . .' I want a lawyer who understands what I need and has a point of view that helps me come to a conclusion. I'm not looking for more problems."[27] Decision-making is not

---

26 To be clear, I do not subscribe to the Socratic dictum about the worth or worthlessness of an unexamined life. I know and love many people who either dislike introspection or find it tiresome to talk about.

27 Tom Phillips, *Talking Shop: Leon Shelley, Westfield Shoppingtowns,* THE LAWYER (Mar. 16, 2009, 10:33AM), http://www.thelawyer.com/ talking-shop-leon-shelley-westfield-shoppingtowns/137153.article. For a sampling of other references to the "two-handed lawyer," *see also* D. Michael Risinger & Lesley G. Risinger, *Innocence is Different: Taking Innocence into Account in Reforming Criminal Procedure,* 56 N.Y. L. SCH. L. REV. 869, 891 n.66 (2012); Craighton Goeppele, *Second This! A Look Back at My Secondment,* 17 BUS. L. TODAY 31, 32 (2008); Ronald W. Davis, *Antitrust Analysis of Mergers, Acquisitions, and Joint Ventures in the 1980s: A Pragmatic Guide to Evaluation of Legal Risks,* 11 DEL. J. CORP. L. 25, 51 (1986); David Walk, *Choice of Law, Punitive Damages, and Harry Truman,* DRUG & DEVICE LAW (Feb. 17, 2010), http://druganddevicelaw.blogspot.com/2010/02/choice-

quite like thinking and it's not quite like acting, but my conclusion is that it's a lot more like choosing and doing than reasoning and drawing conclusions. There are aspects of philosophies with less favorable assessments of the power of reason—existential thought and the Critical Legal Studies movement among them—that have spoken to me. That may be surprising coming from a person who unapologetically spent most of his professional life in commerce.

It's probably the case that all of my thinking is merely a footnote to Karl Llewellyn's description of the undefinable, irreducible aspect of judgment he called situation sense. The punchline, when we get to the end, is that I do not believe there are teachable or learnable rational analytics that will substitute for the experience of having to choose or decide, rather than merely thinking about the choice or the decision beforehand or rationalizing it afterward. Nor will rationality incline someone to look for compromise rather than total victory. I don't discount the value of the analytics I used in decision-making. Whether the issue was law, human resources, engineering, marketing, or any other area of professional expertise, they contributed to making more informed choices. But coming to terms with rationality in choosing and acting is categorically an altogether different matter. One *reflects on* or *practices* solutions, but the underlying inclination to do so is a matter of heart rather than mind. It's why I don't worry too much about a robot replacing me.

To think about the inner experience of situation sense, in essence to have situation sense *about* your situation sense, invites precisely the endless and circular (and possibly pointless) speculation that causes people to throw up their hands and reject philosophical introspection altogether. But that's the point. There is no executive summary, no pithy set of bullet points, no easily absorbed list of "how tos" when talking about the sublime judgments that litigation lawyers as well as transactional lawyers have to make. There are very few answers, but that doesn't mean there are none; what I will suggest in Chapter 7 are emotional or affective modes of thinking that temper the crisp rationality of thinking like a lawyer. Whether our students end up as lawyers for great causes, plaintiff's personal injury lawyers, corporate in-house counsel, or lawyers for patent trolls, I want them to have reflected at some point in their careers about how they use pure lawyering as a tool for justifying outcomes on behalf of their clients, and whether that tool—agnostic to outcomes—has affected their view of the outcomes.

Beyond legal reasoning

Is it possible to get beyond legal reasoning? Can one maintain an ability to think like a lawyer while at the same time understanding lawyerly rationality may not be what the situation demands, either because war isn't the answer or because we

of-law-punitive-damages-and.html (attributing the "one-handed/two-handed" distinction to a comment Harry Truman made about economists).

need to get off the fence and decide? F. Scott Fitzgerald said famously, "The test of a first-rate intelligence is the ability to hold two opposed ideas in the mind at the same time, and still retain the ability to function."[28] That is what I hope my students eventually learn to do. For now, as first-year students, they are learning the ability to disassemble the world and rearrange it with the abstract symbols that constitute legal language. If there is to be a "getting beyond" pure lawyering, it will take place at a meta-level of the kind to which Fitzgerald alluded.

I want them to understand, even as they are crackerjack pure lawyers, that what they are using is only one of a myriad alternative languages available for ascribing meaning to circumstances their professional worlds will present. The moral of the story is that not understanding is to increase the odds that they will fall victim to the dark side of legal reasoning: the conflation of what we can know to be true or real with what we can argue to be true or real, instrumental lawyering, loss of ethical perspective, rationalization, cynicism, blame, and poor judgment.

The plan for the book

What follows then is my assessment of: (a) what it means (and how) to think like a lawyer in the traditional metaphors of pure lawyering, (b) the implications of that mode of thinking when removed from situations that call for it, and (c) how one might go about, having been thoroughly inculcated as a lawyer, understanding when and how to employ it and other modes of thinking.

Chapter 2 unpacks what the mechanics of thinking like a lawyer really are. First, the core of all pure lawyering is modus ponens logic by which we use legal rules to derive consequences from sets of antecedent conditions. Second, the real mystery and difficulty in learning to think like a lawyer has to do with the process by which lawyers and judges choose the applicable rule. I will argue that the source of the difficulty is the irreducible process by which we leap mentally from a morass of facts and events to an explanatory theory, whether normative or descriptive. Within the way we reason to coherent connections of real-world events is a paradoxical lawlessness or "rulelessness" that is the "aha" moment of intuition, creativity, and judgment.

Chapter 3 explores the significance of theory-making in pure lawyering. What does it mean to develop a legal theory in pure lawyering? Scientists use theory as a means of seeking truth in the physical world, and lawyers think in legal theories. There is a family resemblance between the two, as both are mental exercises using deductive, inductive, and other forms of reasoning, to draw conclusions. But scientific theories about what is—i.e. descriptive—and the legal theories of pure lawyering are about what ought to be—i.e. normative. The social sciences struggle with the gray areas in which the descriptive and normative overlap.

---

28 F. SCOTT FITZGERALD, THE CRACK-UP 69 (Edmund Wilson, ed. New Directions Books 1993).

Nowadays nobody would be surprised at the idea of feminist jurisprudence, for example, but the idea of feminist quantum mechanics is incongruous. The fact we are dealing in legal theories of explanation—albeit normative—makes it difficult to avoid thinking of law as a thing, even an animate thing, like a God or a sovereign, when learning to think like a lawyer. The science of the law—the theory-making of pure lawyering—drives us to posit a meaningful abstract positive law of the subject under consideration. That abstraction is an ideally coherent doctrine existing somewhere "out there," removed from its application to real-world experience. I suggest that the key to the conundrum is that moment of rulelessness in theory-making when we leap from what we know to a previously unconsidered conclusion. I propose an alternative way of thinking about rule-application, based in metaphor theory, that allows us to think like lawyers in what usually passes as pure lawyering, without all the baggage that goes along with ascribing truth and thingness to the law.

In Chapter 4, I offer a thesis about two possible consequences—one cynical and one naïve—of thinking like a lawyer. I then propose a mental game as a way of stepping away from pure lawyering and considering the context in which lawyers are practicing it. The mental game involves another set of metaphors about reality and its representations—namely, games and models. Is law one or the other? The challenge to lawyers "thinking like lawyers" is in the family resemblance and the possibility of inappropriately treating a model like a game or vice versa.

Chapter 5 is an assessment of one possible consequence of thinking like a lawyer: the conflation of the concept of causation with concepts of responsibility and blame. It derives from the conception of law as a thing knowable (rather than merely believable) that has developed over more than a century of professional and scholarly aspiration to a normative science of the law in which thinking like a lawyer is the primary means of inquiry. Pure lawyering transforms causation into an assessment of blame, an unhelpful conflation when the role for the lawyer is something other than justifying one's own side's behavior and vanquishing the other.

Chapter 6 deals with some of the consequences of the rationality of legal thinking. One consequence is the mental gridlock of the colloquial "two-handed lawyer": because we can think our way to almost any conclusion, deciding or choosing is a different kind of activity than merely thinking like a lawyer. There is simply a limit to how far thinking can take us. A second consequence is the problem of the argument from authority. One way of resolving the problem of the limit of rationality is to work your way back to some authority whose reason is "Because I say so." The third consequence is justification, and from there rationalization and self-deception. That is, once we've made a decision or acted, we can rationalize or deceive ourselves into believing just about anything, and the thinking that characterizes pure lawyering is a handy tool for rationalization and self-deception. At the core of all of these problems is the fact that rationality really is something different than judgment, and to move from mere thinking to action involves traversing a lawless and rule-less domain of choice that is far more akin to acting than to thinking. And the story has, at best, a mixed conclusion. Judgment is a lonely process, and there's no alternative. Nevertheless, it may be what makes us uniquely human and is probably not replaceable by artificial intelligence.

Chapter 7 considers some of the ways we might appropriately temper pure lawyering. If anything here resembles a practical toolkit, this is it. I challenge the idea that thoughtfulness and even theory are restricted to the kind of thinking that purports to be the coin of the realm for advancement in legal academia. My goal is, ironically, to theorize about the bridge between academic and practical thinking, and to give academic cover to alternative professional self-conceptions. Legal relationships, the ones lawyers get trained to see, do not exist in a vacuum. The challenge for lawyers getting beyond legal reasoning is not just to understand legal conditions and consequences, but also to understand the meaning created by the law and the work lawyers do.

I am skeptical whether one can think one's way to this more modest professional self-conception. The means to such insight is not rational but affective. At the risk (and self-aggrandizement) of doing no more than providing the ipse dixit of what passes for accumulated wisdom, the book concludes with thoughts about getting beyond legal reasoning: how to reflect and reconsider what you are sure you know by way of your reason; understanding that there is another "I" and not merely an "It" on the other side of the negotiating table; mediating between epistemic courage (sticking by what you know) and epistemic humility (acknowledging that which is merely belief); and taking responsibility for decisions.

2 The Logic of Pure Lawyering

The purpose of the chapter

There is probably no phrase more used, overused, misused, abused, and mocked within and without the legal profession than "think like a lawyer." It reached its apotheosis in popular culture when the fictional Professor Kingsfield told his students, "You come in here with a skull full of mush; you leave thinking like a lawyer."[1]

I begin with the proposition that, despite its triteness, the phrase means something. I won't try to replicate what so many law professors have already done so well in teaching the processes of thinking like a lawyer. My primary purpose in this chapter is to lay the foundation for challenging in Chapter 3 the idea that theory-making in pure lawyering is an avenue to truth or moral certainty, at least in any issue capable of a colorable difference of opinion. If, however, this chapter helps explain what it means classically to think like a lawyer, all the better. So we will begin by picking apart the core logic of pure lawyering—the mental tools lawyers use to translate a real-world narrative into a legal one with the intention of getting a result for a client.

The thesis of the two chapters taken together is that the law is a model of events in the real world but distinct from the reality of those events. In an analogous way, the Google Maps app on my iPhone provides me with a model of Boston distinct from the reality of the actual city. Each model provides a useful and meaningful function but with fewer bytes of information than comprise the subject of the model. The legal model takes selected inputs from the real world, uses them in "if-then" algorithms, and spits out a result. Unlike the map, however, we don't use the legal model to churn out a *true* result. Instead it produces a legal conclusion, for example, the attribution of blame, the award of damages, a finding of innocence or guilt, or the prospective allocation of risk. In advocacy, the point is to find such an algorithm that, when used, also just happens to

---

1 THE PAPER CHASE (20th Century Fox 1973). For what it's worth, at the same time as my Westlaw search for "thinking like a lawyer," the one I performed for "skull full of mush" turned up forty-two documents.

produce a legal conclusion that is advantageous to the advocate's interests. To repeat, pure lawyering is a process that is agnostic as to truth and moral value outcomes. Or, to put it another way, a legal conclusion can be the result of the exercise of impeccable legal logic but still, as *Educating Lawyers* noted, diverge from the common sense understandings of the layperson.[2] That isn't wrong; it is simply how the system works.

I deliberately have used the word "lawyering" rather than the word "law." Law is a creation of mind, something we as humans impose on the world, not a natural thing unto itself. Not everyone believes that, but I do.[3] Accordingly, I prefer not to treat law as a knowable *thing* that is the object of study. A contract or a statute is of itself a relatively trivial thing or an artifact. Law as it matters meaningfully instead is a *practice*, an activity by which people apply certain rules to events in the world for the purpose of allocating consequences. My concern is that even unabashed legal positivists, those who accept that law and morality are separate concepts,[4] still give an unwarranted "thingness" to law. Understanding theory-making in pure lawyering allows us to see why we might think of law as an abstract yet very real thing, even when we don't believe law in action has a mind-independent objective reality.

To be clear, I do not know if law is a thing any more than I know whether there is a God. My concerns are the consequences that follow if you attribute thingness to law. If law is a thing and real, well, real things ought to be true. I very much believe there are things that are true, but my confidence in their truthfulness varies when considering things like the existence of the computer on which I am typing this (very sure), things like the Higgs boson (relying on other people who seem to be sure), or a deity (highly skeptical but still open-minded). I retain a healthy skepticism that anything is true, including a legal conclusion, merely because it results from the process of pure lawyering.

This chapter begins the analysis with a close look at the role of logic that is at the heart of pure lawyering. There are deductive and inductive aspects to it. But the art of issue-spotting so central to our students' success on exams is a product of neither deduction nor induction. It is instead a distinct creative or intuitive thinking process in which a lawyer looks at a mess of facts and thinks something like, "Aha, we could make claims in contract or tort, but the best avenue is to assert a private right of action under the Anti-Mopery Act of 1843."[5]

---

2 WILLIAM M. SULLIVAN, ET AL., SUMMARY OF EDUCATING LAWYERS: PREPARATION FOR THE PROFESSION OF LAW 5 (2007), http://archive.carnegiefoundation.org/pdfs/elibrary/elibrary_pdf_632.pdf.

3 *See* David O. Brink, *Legal Interpretation, Objectivity, and Morality*, in OBJECTIVITY IN LAW AND MORALS 54–57 (Brian Leiter ed., 2001).

4 *Id.* at 54.

5 Mopery was what my criminal law professor, the late and inimitable John Kaplan, used as an imaginary crime. *See* Janet C. Hoeffel, *A Student Remembers*, 42 STAN. L. REV. 852 (1990).

To capture the nature of issue-spotting on an exam, I might tell a student the following: "Imagine that, on the left side of the page, you see the narrative of the problem to be solved. On the right side is a list of legal rules and theories. Do you see some of them but not others as relevant (or arguably relevant) to the problem?" It is far harder to *explain* than simply to *do* the particular aspect of the reasoning process that prioritizes the theories. Through experience, we have an intuitive sense that some of the theories clearly apply. Some of the theories so clearly don't apply that it's not worth discussion. Some are in between. They need to be explored in detail, even if we ultimately reject them as helpful. Guiding students toward these issue-spotting judgments is among the most important steps we take in teaching them how to think like lawyers.

Having worked our way through the logic of pure lawyering, we will turn in Chapter 3 to how we use that logic to develop legal theories of explanation.

The context

Sometime in the first few months after starting law school, students receive their most powerful introduction to thinking like a lawyer. Each student sits in a room with others, yet is truly alone with nothing other than a mind, a pen, and a bluebook (or their computer equivalent). If the examination is open book, the student has a stack of texts, notes, supplements, and outlines. The proctor distributes the exam packet, the student opens it, and confronts a bewildering olio of facts and events in the typical "issue-spotting" law school examination question.

On a tort law examination, for example, this might be the narrative. Andrea, a motorcyclist, runs a stop sign and collides with a car whose driver, Bernard, was texting at the time, and whose brother-in-law, Charles, loaned him the car knowing Bernard had the bad habit of texting while driving. Andrea is wearing a helmet manufactured by the Denver Helmet Corporation and sold at retail by Edward's Bike Shop. The helmet must comply with certain regulatory standards and it did not. An ambulance owned by Franklin Emergency Services, Inc., and driven by its employee, George, picks up Andrea, but Hannah, one of the EMTs, also a Franklin employee, neglects to fasten the straps to the stretcher. Another car driven by Isabel runs a red light and hits the ambulance, causing the stretcher with the motorcyclist to bounce around the inside of the ambulance. Finally, when the ambulance reaches the Jackson General Hospital, Dr. Kahn, a neurosurgeon, performs a risky operation that is unsuccessful, leaving Andrea in a persistent vegetative state.

The law student's job is to assess the legal obligations to Andrea of all of the people and organizations identified. Those of us who test this way ought not to be defensive about it. Perhaps real-life situations are not as cartoonish as this example or other exam questions tend to be, but there is a sound pedagogical reason for using this form of assessment. Clients do not walk into a lawyer's office, sit down, and announce that they have a contract, or torts, or civil procedure problem. Rather they tell a story that has not yet ended and express a desired outcome. Successful law students and lawyers will convert the narrative into a legal theory. The theory is an integrated set of rules applied to the situation to generate a legal outcome.

Let's therefore turn to the reasoning process by which we apply rules.

Deduction and beyond in pure lawyering

Normative rules

If we are going to unpack rule application, we first need to talk about rules. My *American Heritage College Dictionary* gives one definition as "[a]n authoritative prescribed direction for conduct."[6] That is a *normative* rule. In their seminal book *How to Do Things with Rules*, William Twining and David Miers agree this is the kind of rule with which the law is most often concerned: "A typical rule in this sense prescribes that in circumstances X, behaviour of type Y ought, or ought not to be, or may be, engaged in by persons of class Z."[7] One set of rules applicable to the tort law examination might be that an individual is under a duty to exercise due care when operating an automobile and is liable for monetary damages to someone injured as a proximate result of the failure to do so (i.e. is negligent). As Twining and Miers correctly observe, there are four key aspects:

- It is normative or prescriptive, being concerned with what one ought or ought not do, rather than being concerned with factual descriptions of behavior.
- It is general in that it characterizes types of behavior in types of situations rather than dealing with unique events. (A parent's admonition to a child not to play near the stove is not a rule; a rule would be the statement that children are not to play near stoves.)
- It serves as a guide and standard for behavior.
- It provides one kind of justifying reason for decisions or action.[8]

The deductive core

Even if it can be difficult in execution, in concept the core logic of pure lawyering is pretty simple. We use normative rules, like those Twining and Miers describe, to impute deductively a legal consequence arising as a result of particular antecedent circumstances. The prototypical example of deduction is a syllogism, consisting of a major premise, a minor premise, and a conclusion. In deductive reasoning, what makes the conclusion true is nothing more than the truth of the required

---

6 AMERICAN HERITAGE COLLEGE DICTIONARY 1214 (4th ed. 2002).
7 WILLIAM TWINING & DAVID MIERS, HOW TO DO THINGS WITH RULES 80 (5th ed. 2010).
8 *Id.* at 81.

premises. If we assume the premises are true, then the rule of inference dictates conclusion must also be true.

Perhaps the most famous example of a syllogism is this:

(1) All men are mortal.
(2) Socrates is a man.
(3) Therefore, Socrates is mortal.

The major premise (1) attributes a characteristic to the set of "all men." The minor premise (2) holds as true that Socrates is a man. The rule of inference here is called "universal instantiation." If we accept as true the premises in proposition (1) that men as a set of individuals are mortal and in proposition (2) that Socrates is member of that class, it is valid (and true) *logically* in (3) Socrates has the characteristic of being mortal. We could change each premise to something factually untrue like the following:

(4) All mice come from Mars.
(5) Socrates is a mouse.
(6) Therefore, Socrates comes from Mars.

While "thinking like a lawyer" in real life ultimately involves several forms of reasoning, the overarching form by which lawyers use rules to create legal theories is syllogistic, although in a different form of syllogism.[9] The rule of inference is called modus ponens. It is a counterpart to, and performs the same logical role as, the rule of "universal instantiation" in the Socrates syllogism. Modus ponens works in "if-then" sequences like this:

(7) If p, then q.
(8) p.
(9) Therefore q.[10]

(The logical notation for the phrase "if p, then q" is $(p \supset q)$.) We could restate the Socrates syllogism in modus ponens form: if Socrates is a man, then he is mortal. Assuming we are able to conclude it's true he is a man, the conclusion that he is mortal must be valid.

In other words, the major premise of the modus ponens syllogism in law (expression (7)) comes from the kind of normative rules Twining and Miers describe. We are not saying that the legal rule itself is somehow true or false in the same way that something can be true or false in the physical world. Rather, we

---

9 Richard Posner appears to agree. In his treatment of the relationship of legal outcomes to truth—that what judges do is the exercise of practical reason and not deductive logic—he nevertheless acknowledges that "most legal questions are resolved syllogistically." RICHARD A. POSNER, THE PROBLEMS OF JURISPRUDENCE 42 (1990).
10 NEIL MACCORMICK, LEGAL REASONING AND LEGAL THEORY 24 (1979).

use the legal rule to establish the "if-then" major premise between antecedent real-world circumstances (i.e. the facts of the situation) to the consequent legal conclusions. If we accept the "if-then" rule as valid, and establish that the "if" occurred, then the legal conclusion *must* follow.

Deduction is certainly not all there is to thinking like a lawyer, but I agree with the esteemed legal philosopher Neil MacCormick that it is the "relatively simple and straight-forward" deductive core of legal reasoning:

> [A]ll legal rules however formulated in statutes or precedents can without alteration be recast in the form that if certain facts and circumstances obtain, a certain legal consequence is to follow. The requisite facts and circumstances we may call the 'operative facts' of the rule. Then, with regard to our canonical form, if p then q (p $\supset$ q), the symbol p stands for a proposition stipulating a set of operative facts, q for the legal consequence which is to follow.[11]

As Louis Wolcher observed,

> An expression taking the form of the modus ponens typically characterizes the end-moment of legal justification regardless of what went before—that is, regardless of how elaborate, messy, and/or confused the actual process of judicial decision making may have been.[12]

Here is a simple example. My street has a twenty-five miles per hour speed limit. We could restate the rule in logical form:

(10) If you drive more than twenty-five miles per hour, then you are guilty of speeding.

To complete the modus ponens inference, we would start with proposition (10), the major premise, which is the rule that if the fact of driving in excess of twenty-five miles per hour (p) has occurred, then the driver is guilty of speeding. The minor premise in the deductive form is that driving in excess of twenty-five miles per hour has occurred:

(11) You drove in excess of twenty-five miles per hour.

Because the minor premise is true, the consequence q must necessarily follow:

(12) You are guilty of speeding.

---

11 *Id.* at 45.

12 LOUIS WOLCHER, LAW'S TASK: THE TRAGIC CIRCLE OF LAW, JUSTICE, AND HUMAN SUFFERING 93 (2008); *see also* Giovanni Tuzet, *Legal Abduction*, 6 COGNITIO 265, 269 (2005).

You may or may not be going forty miles per hour down my street, but if you are, then by virtue of modus ponens inference, you must be guilty of speeding.

Here is a further example of modus ponens logic in an area of contract law generally taught in the first semester of law. Many professors use the Restatement (Second) of Contracts as a handy reference for the rules and principles used to decide contract law disputes. Section 1 of the Second Restatement defines a contract as a promise or set of promises for the breach of which the law provides a remedy.[13] One way that courts have distinguished enforceable contracts from gratuities is to determine that there has been both a promise and "consideration," that is, a quid pro quo for the promise.[14] Thus, it is a valid inference that a contract (and not a mere gratuity) exists if the antecedent premises of promise and consideration are true.

The deductive rule just expressed is a compound proposition of the form:

(13) If p and r, then q.

In other words, the consequence q entails if and only if both p and r are true.[15] In our example, p is the operative fact that there was a promise, and r is the operative fact that there was consideration. If both p and q are true, then it must be the case that there is an enforceable contract. And the lawyer's job is to demonstrate the existence of promise and consideration from which the conclusion must flow.

But the simplicity of the overarching modus ponens structure is deceiving. Our law students' travails in learning how to think like lawyers are just beginning. In this particular example, the operative facts of "promise" and "consideration" are themselves legal conclusions that need to be established by way of modus ponens inference. As MacCormick puts it, "rules may be interrelated by reason of the very fact that a proposition stating the 'legal consequence' of one rule may in turn state the operative fact of another."[16] As to the first element in the form of inference for the existence of a contract, was there a promise? Section 2 of the Second Restatement supplies a rule by which we can formulate the major premise for the existence of a "promise": it is a manifestation of an intention to act in a specified way so made as to justify a promisee in understanding that a commitment has been made.[17] As to the second element, was there consideration? Section 71(1) of the Second Restatement supplies a rule from which we can formulate the major premise: "To constitute consideration, a performance or a return promise must be bargained for."[18]

---

13 RESTATEMENT (SECOND) OF CONTRACTS [hereinafter "SECOND RESTATEMENT"] § 1 (1981).
14 SECOND RESTATEMENT §§ 17, 71.
15 MACCORMICK, *supra* note 10, at 27–28.
16 *Id.* at 45.
17 SECOND RESTATEMENT § 2.
18 *Id.* § 71(1).

Let's focus first on the promise element. Suppose Uncle said out loud something like "Nephew, I promise to pay you $5,000 if you behave as I have directed."[19] Given the clarity of that statement, Uncle would have a hard time arguing that he had not satisfied the antecedent conditions for the modus ponens inference of a promise. There would be no reasonable way to dispute that Uncle manifested an intention to pay money in a way that justified Nephew in thinking there really had been a commitment. The operative facts of the "if" clause are established, and the conclusion must follow that there was a promise.

When the statement doesn't so obviously satisfy the definition of a promise, the task of thinking like a lawyer continues. To recap, we started by analyzing the operative facts of the "if" clause for establishing the legal conclusion of "contract." Those operative facts were "promise" and "consideration." Now "promise" becomes the legal conclusion for which we need to find the operative facts. That means drilling down another level into the operative facts that make up the Restatement's definition of a promise. Those facts are: (1) a "manifestation" of (2) a "commitment" that (3) has allowed the promisee justifiably to understand a commitment has been made.

To make the point in a silly way, let's assume Nephew contends Uncle made a promise by a series of eye blinks in Morse Code. To get to the issue on which the outcome may hinge, we now have had to drill down through three levels of legal conclusions. The analysis has become a regress from legal conclusion to operative fact that is in turn a legal conclusion that in turn is an operative fact, and so on.[20] At each level, however, the relationship of the operative facts and the legal conclusion is modus ponens. If the "if" conditions are satisfied, we have logically established the legal conclusion that becomes the operative fact for the higher level "if" clause. All of this work is directed to the issue that began the logical sequence: do the circumstances lead to a legal conclusion there was a contract?

Does eye blinking constitute a "manifestation" of a "commitment" "justifiably so understood by another"? If yes, it becomes an operative fact for the deduction of the existence of a promise; if no, it does not. Let's just focus on "manifestation." It turns out we have hit the limit of the Restatement's ability to give us a rule; it doesn't define "manifestation." We could do case law research to find an instance where a court has adopted one. But for our purposes here of outlining the logic, let's simply take the dictionary definition that something is manifest when it is "clearly apparent to the sight or understanding."[21] Modus ponens logic works as follows. If there was a physical movement in the eye blinking clearly apparent to the sight or understanding (A), then it is a manifestation (B). There was such a physical movement (A). Therefore, it is a manifestation.

---

19 This was effectively the operative promise in Hamer v. Sidway, 27 N.E. 256 (N.Y. 1891).

20 For an argument that the regress is infinite, *see* Andrew Morrison Stumpff, *The Law is a Fractal: The Attempt to Anticipate Everything*, 44 LOYOLA U. CHI. L. J. 649 (2013).

21 AMERICAN HERITAGE COLLEGE DICTIONARY 841 (4th ed. 2002).

This is the essence of identifying the rule and its modus ponens application in pure lawyering. Lawyers pick apart smaller and smaller bits of the rule to find bases for arguing about its application. But no matter where the regress ends, the rule application will be a modus ponens inference, which then allows the lawyer to move back up the chain of logic to the ultimate conclusion he wants.

This deductive aspect of pure lawyering is wholly consistent with arguments in the alternative. Assume Nephew established to a court's satisfaction that he and Uncle had communicated in the past by way of eye blinking in Morse Code, and thus it satisfied the modus ponens application of the manifestation rule. The rule of promise still has a second element requiring that the promisee justifiably understand a commitment has been made. Uncle might still be able to establish that the requisite antecedents for justified understanding (whatever they might be) have not been satisfied (e.g., a rule like the following "one is not justified in understanding manifestations by way of eye blinking to be commitments when the circumstances do not suggest a need for secrecy or coded communication").

Up until now, we have only been drilling down on the "promise" element of the compound proposition necessary to establish deductively the existence of a contract. Thinking like a lawyer may also require drilling down on the consideration element. Assuming Uncle made a promise to pay $5,000, it was related to Nephew's refraining from undertaking certain acts. Was Nephew's restraint consideration? Section 71(1), restated in logical form, provides:

(14) If a performance or return promise is bargained for, it constitutes consideration.

The operative fact is the existence of a bargain related to Nephew's performance. But it turns out, once again, that "bargain" itself is a legal consequence arising deductively from the existence of other operative facts. Section 71(2) of the Second Restatement provides a rule: "A performance or return promise is bargained for if it is sought by the promisor in exchange for his promise and is given by the promisee in exchange for that promise."[22] In logical form, this is another compound proposition requiring two operative facts, the result of which leads to the legal consequence of a bargain.

(15) If (a) the promisor sought a return promise or performance in exchange for his promise, and (b) the promisee gave the performance or return promise in exchange for the promisor's promise, then (c) the return promise or performance was bargained for.

What lawyers do—the core of pure lawyering—is to fit messy experience into precisely these kinds of logical models, some of which are more complex than

---

22 SECOND RESTATEMENT § 71(2).

others. It is not easy, and takes significant mental discipline. As MacCormick observes of a judge's opinion in a particular case, "the entire argument . . . can be restated in the most ruthlessly deductive form; and that each step of the argument, and the argument as a whole, are logically valid."[23]

Recall, however, the comment from *Educating Lawyers* about how legal conclusions can vary from common sense understandings. It happens for the same reason that Socrates as a Martian mouse can be valid logically but factually nonsensical. One of the most famous examples of this comes from *Oliver Twist*. Oliver escapes from the orphanage workhouse run by Mr. Bumble only to fall in with Fagin and the pickpockets. At the end of the story, Mr. Brownlow, Oliver's kind protector, confronts Mr. Bumble with his having stolen a locket that is conclusive evidence of Oliver's parentage. Mr. Bumble is now worried about losing his job. He blames the whole thing on Mrs. Bumble. Mr. Brownlow articulates the law's syllogistic (and gendered) result. If ($p1$) Mr. Bumble was present on the occasion of the destruction of the trinkets, and ($p2$) Mrs. Bumble was his wife, then (q) Mr. Bumble is guilty because the law infers that she acted under his direction. To which Mr. Bumble famously replied about *that* rule and its modus ponens operation (foreshadowing Holmes's famous dictum about law and logic):

> If the law supposes that, the law is an ass—an idiot. If that's the eye of the law, the law is a bachelor; and the worst I wish the law is, that his eye may be opened by experience—by experience.[24]

A more recent example of the law being an ass (at least to some) occurred in the 1980s. Congress passed the Racketeering Influenced Corrupt Organizations Act ("RICO")[25] to outlaw the practice of using legitimate businesses as repositories for profits gained through racketeering. The act contained a provision for civil actions as a result of which plaintiffs could obtain treble damages and attorneys' fees. The problem lay in the algorithm used to define a pattern of racketeering. All a plaintiff needed to allege were two "acts of racketeering activity," which included mail and wire fraud. Suppose, then, that a McDonald's franchisee's business turned out to be unsuccessful. The claim in a hypothetical RICO lawsuit might have been that McDonald's executives, on several separate occasions, used the telephone to make materially misleading statements about the franchise's prospects. Under the modus ponens logic of the statute, that was arguably sufficient to craft a claim that there had been a pattern of racketeering, and that McDonald's was the legitimate business funded by it. Not surprisingly, the majority of civil cases under RICO had nothing to do with organized crime.

23 MACCORMICK, *supra* note 10, at 29.
24 CHARLES DICKENS, OLIVER TWIST (1846).
25 18 U.S.C. § 1961 *et seq.* (2012).

Rather, lawyers could turbocharge an ordinary securities fraud, commercial fraud, wrongful discharge, or divorce case into far a more lucrative racketeering claim.[26] And despite outrage about a statute in which business executives could be labeled "racketeers" in garden-variety lawsuits, the Supreme Court upheld that usage of the statute under its literal and logical modus ponens operation.[27]

Whether or not you are sympathetic to using RICO to go after non-Mafioso business executives, this is truly what we mean by thinking like a lawyer. It can occur after the fact to resolve a tort or criminal claim where the rules come from statutes and cases. It can occur in after-the-fact contract disputes where the parties may have had something to do with the creation of the contract rule that determines an outcome.

The complexity arises not just from the logical drilling down we've just explored, but also from the vagueness of the rules or from factual disputes about whether the operative facts have occurred. In the 1980s, I was involved in a series of trials in which we represented coal producers against public utilities who wanted to establish they had legal excuses for not taking as much coal as the contracts provided. In one such case, the coal companies contended that the utility's invocation of a particular environmental clause was a pretext for the real reason: the utility had built a nuclear facility and just didn't need the coal it had contracted to buy. The core of the utility's position, however, worked by way of a modus ponens inference under which its motivation was irrelevant. If the circumstances fit the "if" clause of the environmental provision, then it was entitled to reduce its purchase obligation by fifteen million tons of coal with a value in the billions of dollars over ten years. We won because the jury found that the conditions necessary for the right to exercise the provision did not exist.[28] That is, in the sequence of "if p, then q; p; therefore q," the jury found there was no p.

The logic of pure lawyering also lies at the heart of transactional practice. Contract drafters implicitly pour the messy facts of reality into a deductive rule-application mold. If I am writing a contract on behalf of the acquiring party in a corporate acquisition, for example, I will want it to include a provision requiring indemnification upon a breach of the contractual representations and warranties. The modus ponens logic of pure lawyering applies. We agree the model will work as follows: "If there is a breach of warranty, then Seller shall indemnify Buyer (If A, then B). There was a breach of warranty (A). Therefore, Seller shall indemnify (B)."

It is important to remember that mere deduction does not tell us whether a rule is good or fair. But Twining and Miers suggest a way to think about the quality of a legal rule in the deductive context, namely by assessing the relationship

---

26 Steven Greenhouse, *Business and the Law; The Argument Against RICO,* N.Y. TIMES (Oct. 15, 1985), http://www.nytimes.com/1985/10/ 15/business/business-and-the-law-the-argument-against-rico.html.

27 Sedima S.P.R.L. v. Imrex Co., 473 U.S. 479 (1985).

28 Big Horn Coal Co. v. Commonwealth Edison Co., 852 F.2d 1259 (10th Cir. 1988).

of the operative facts (i.e. the required premises) to the conclusion. Twining and Miers refer to what MacCormick calls the operative facts as the protasis of the rule, and what MacCormick calls the legal consequence, they call the apodosis. They agree, however, that any rule of this type can be restated in the "if p, then q" form. They do not discuss, as MacCormick does, the deductive necessity of the apodosis in light of the truth of the protasis, but that necessity is implicit in their view that *"all ingredients that have a bearing on the scope of the rule should be included in the protasis."* In other words, because the deductive logic of the law requires the conclusion to follow from the premises, any good rule will make sure that it includes as antecedent premises all of the necessary elements of the legal claim.[29]

We could use almost any legal claim as the basis for an example of this relationship between deduction and fairness, but I will take one from my early years as a civil antitrust lawyer. Section 2 of the Sherman Antitrust Act[30] deals with monopolies, but merely being a monopolist is not a violation of Section 2. The policy underlying the law recognizes that it is possible to acquire a monopoly simply by being better than everyone else, and does not seek to prohibit merely being very good. Rather the major premise (the operative facts or protasis) of a monopolization claim is as follows:

(16) If the defendant (a) possesses monopoly power, and (b) willfully acquires or maintains such power through exclusionary conduct, then (c) the defendant must pay treble damages to anyone proximately injured as a result.

The case law distinguishes the exclusionary conduct of operative fact (b) from "growth or development as a consequence of a superior product, business acumen, or historical accident."[31] It is conceivable that any monopoly could violate Section 2, and in that case, operative fact (b) would not be part of the protasis. The deductive logic as between the protasis and apodosis would remain the same, but most of us would agree that it is no longer a good rule, because the absence of the "willful acquisition" element would make firms liable for otherwise exemplary conduct.

Induction and beyond

To be sure, the complexities of legal reasoning (and the legal process) go beyond this core of deductive logic. As we have seen, deductive conclusions can be valid in the context of the syllogism, even if the syllogism is nonsensical in relation to the way the world really works. The complexity of lawyering, as MacCormick

---

29 TWINING & MIERS, *supra* note 7, at 90–91 (emphasis in original).
30 15 U.S.C. § 2 (2012).
31 United States v. Grinnell Corp., 384 U.S. 563, 570–71 (1966).

acknowledges, is in the variety of ways litigants contest, by way of non-deductive elements of legal argumentation, at least the following: (a) whether the operative facts have occurred, (b) whether the parties have correctly stated a legal rule, (c) whether the legal rule is in itself appropriate, or (d) whether a different rule ought to apply in light of the operative facts. As in our coal supply contract case, those non-deductive elements are the ones that are "exciting, difficult, and highly subtle."[32]

Inductive reasoning about why things happen in the real world is not the same logical process as modus ponens. It can be confusing, however, because it still involves the concept of a "rule." In induction, however, what we mean is that something happens "as a rule." Here the word "rule" has a descriptive rather than normative implication; it is "[a] generalized statement that describes what is true in most or all cases."[33] We derive these rules through the process of inferring the general from the particular. This is the basis of scientific explanations. Hypotheses, theories, and scientific laws are all inductively reasoned rules or algorithms built on combinations of rules about the way things work, based on the observation of past regularities.

Unlike in deductive reasoning, conclusions in inductive reasoning are not true merely because the premises are true. The premises are based on observations of events, and the conclusion is a generalization we infer from the particular events. One's conclusion that the sun rises in the east is inductive. We have observed the repeated rising of the sun in the east, and our generalized conclusion—the rule—is that the sun always rises in the east. Our dog Tia has a distinctive bark for which the inductive rule is "if you let me outside to pee, I won't do it in the house any time soon." The truth of the premise does not guarantee the conclusion. She had an accident recently even though I had just let her out. (This provoked the use of another inductive thought: if she pees in the house, she doesn't feel good.) The difference in the inductive conclusion between the sun rising in the east, on one hand, and Tia not having accidents in the house, on the other, merely reflects the level of confidence I have in the likelihood my conclusion is correct based on the evidence that constitutes the inductive premises.

There is a significant aspect of inductive reasoning in what lawyers do, particularly in counseling clients about possible outcomes. They learn the arguments that have worked in the past in particular circumstances, and use that knowledge to make a prediction about what will work in the future. That is one of Oliver Wendell Holmes, Jr.'s most famous statements about the nature of the law: it is nothing more than a prediction that if certain events have occurred one may be required to pay the consequences.[34] As I write this, two large industrial companies, Honeywell and United Technologies, are at odds over a possible merger of the

---

32 MacCormick, *supra* note 10, at ix.
33 American Heritage College Dictionary 1214 (4th ed. 2002).
34 Oliver Wendell Holmes, *The Path of the Law*, 10 Harv. L. Rev. 457 (1897), *reprinted*, 110 Harv. L. Rev. 991, 992 (1997).

two companies. At least as reported in the business press, the primary source of the disagreement is about the value of the merged business in light of divestitures the government might require under the antitrust laws (Section 7 of the Clayton Act) to avoid the merged company having monopoly power in some product lines. Honeywell's lawyers appear to be predicting that the regulators will only require tolerable divestitures; United Technologies lawyers appear to disagree.[35] In either case, it is an argument supported by inductive reasoning—in so many words, "This is what has happened in the past in similar mergers with similar levels of concentration, and we can expect the same pattern to hold in this case."

Moreover, a lawyer cannot know the rules themselves—the myriad assortment of "if p, then q" statements of the vast body of legal doctrine—merely by deduction. As MacCormick observed:

> In large measure . . . it is knowledge of legal rules which enables the relevant—and unquestionably highly partial and selective—choice to be made from the bewildering and infinitely complex continuum of facts and events with which we are presented. That inevitably puts a large premium on the possession of legal knowledge, or on the capacity to pay, and indeed to capture the effective attention of, those legal professionals who have it.[36]

A nice (and perhaps more accessible) example of the complexity of non-litigation lawyering beyond mere deduction took place in Episode 6 of the first season of *The West Wing* (a show significantly populated by fictional but not wholly unrealistic lawyers). The Democratic President and his staff supported the passage of a banking bill. Some Republicans attached a rider to the bill that would permit strip-mining on federal lands in Montana. The staff was divided on whether to compromise their environmental principles to get the banking bill passed. Josh, the Deputy Chief of Staff (and a Harvard-educated lawyer), hears his assistant, Donna, complain about "antiquated" computer files, and has an inspiration: the "Antiquities Act" allows the President, by executive order, to designate any federal land a national park (in reality a "national monument," but the script takes a bit of literary license), and therefore immune to mining. The magic, as it were, of this lawyering is a combination of empirical knowledge (the existence of the rule), deduction (that the logical consequences of the application of the rule will kill the efficacy of the strip-mining bill), induction (a prediction that the application of the rule would cause a particular result), and something we will discuss later, the "aha" moment of inspiration in which Josh realizes that the rule is available to be applied in this instance.[37]

---

35 Ted Mann & Jon Ostrower, *Honeywell, United Technologies Diverge Over Prospects of Tie-Up,* WALL ST. J., Feb. 24, 2016, at B3.

36 *Id.* at 47.

37 *Enemies,* THE WEST WING WIKI, http://westwing.wikia.com/wiki/ Enemies.

Nevertheless, if you are going to turn to law as a means of getting something done, then lawyering, as in the case of Josh's work on *The West Wing*, means applying this central *deductive* logic of rule application:

> the private complainer or public rule-enforcer must bring forward some assertions about the state of facts in the world, and attempt to show how that state of facts would call for intervention on the ground of some rule that applies to the asserted facts.[38]

That sounds simple. But the execution is not. That is the subject to which we now turn.

The leap

More context

We have now seen the "ruthless" process of deduction that Professor Kingsfield from *The Paper Chase* would likely view as the opposite of a mind full of mush. We have touched on the role of induction in predicting legal outcomes. But we still have not addressed the most difficult aspect of what it is like to encounter a morass of complex facts and to come out on the other side with a legal theory.

Assuming we know a bunch of rules, or know how to research to find them, and can make inductive predictions about outcomes if we apply them, how do we come to choose the rules that are the basis of the translation of the narrative into a deductively sound legal consequence? If two rules might apply but dictate disparate outcomes, how do judges decide between them? Take, for example, one of the first cases often studied in the contract law class, *Hamer v. Sidway*.[39] A rich uncle promises his nephew that, if the latter refrains from drinking and gambling until he is twenty-one years old, uncle will give him $5,000. Is it an enforceable contract? Or is it merely a gift? How does a lawyer go about connecting the compendium of possibly applicable rules to the situation at hand?

Let's look at three situations, the first two of which are hypothetical, and the third is a real case that appears in many contract law texts.

The bad deal. Adrienne is considering the purchase of a condominium Ben owns in an older development. The development has 150 units with identical floor plans. Five units have been sold in the last six months for an average of $170,000. Ben's unit, however, is a disaster. It will need significant work to bring it up to the standard of the rest of the community. Adrienne estimates this will cost $25,000. Adrienne and Ben execute a contract under which Adrienne buys the unit for $145,000. As it turns out, it costs $50,000 to refurbish the unit.

---

38 MacCormick, *supra* note 10, at x.
39 27 N.E. 256 (N.Y. 1891).

In *Adrienne v. Ben*, Adrienne sues Ben for $25,000 on the theory that the purchase price was too high by $25,000—i.e. the contract price should have been $120,000, reflecting the actual value of the unit. Ben's defense is based on an application of the following rule: "If the requirement of consideration is met, there is no additional requirement of . . . equivalence in the values exchanged."[40] This is an example of the operative fact being the legal consequence from the application of another rule. We can be about as certain as anything in the law that the application of the consideration rule (Second Restatement § 71, discussed above) here means that, as between Adrienne and Ben, the requirement of consideration was met. Hence, in the next logical step, "if *p*, then *q*," if the requirement of consideration was met, the fact that Adrienne gave $145,000 for a condominium only worth $120,000, that is, there was no equivalence in the values exchanged, is simply irrelevant. Adrienne has no legal recourse for making a bad deal.

Unconscionable exploitation. Sam, an adult, has significant mental disabilities. Mary, a real estate broker, knowing this, nevertheless persuades Sam to pay $5,000 for an acre of Florida swampland that has a true value of $500. In *Sam v. Mary*, Sam's guardian sues Mary to rescind the deal, arguing the application of the common standard of unconscionability: "if a purported contract was such as no person in one's senses and not under delusion would make on the one hand, and as no honest and fair person would accept on the other, then the contract is unconscionable."[41] Once again, we can feel about as certain as anything in the law that this would be a prime candidate for the application of the unconscionability rule, and that Mary would lose.

Alleged profiteering. This involves a deal made in Greece during World War II. Batsakis advanced Demotsis 500,000 drachmas in exchange for the latter's commitment to pay $2,000 plus eight percent interest when the war was over. After the war, now in the United States, Batsakis sued Demotsis, and the latter defended on the basis that the former was profiteering—at the time the 500,000 drachmas were only worth $25. If you had been the lawyer representing Batsakis, you would have argued that operative facts in this case were like those in *Adrienne v. Ben*, and the rule of decision in that case ought to apply here. There was consideration, and the law provides no additional requirement that the exchanged values must be equivalent. Demotsis made a bad deal. If you had been the lawyer representing Demotsis, you would have argued the operative facts were like those in *Sam v. Mary*, and that the law will not permit the enforcement of contracts made under unconscionable circumstances. Batsakis was greedy and victimized Demotsis.

---

40 SECOND RESTATEMENT § 79.

41 I have paraphrased the rule from Hume v. United States, 132 U.S. 406 (1889) (quoting Earl of Chesterfield v. Janssen, 2 Ves. Sen. 125, 155, 28 Eng.Rep. 82, 100 (Ch.1750)), which appears in Comment 2 to RESTATEMENT (SECOND) OF CONTRACTS § 208, dealing with unconscionable contracts.

Traditional explanations

The foregoing is a typical example of pure lawyering. Lawyers listen to the narrative and figure out what the client wants as the outcome. They search a mental or physical catalog of arguably relevant rules that, when used as the major premise of the modus ponens algorithm, churn out the result the client wants. The facts of the war profiteering case were not precisely the same as either those in *Adrienne v. Ben* or *Sam v. Mary*. Which case (or more precisely, the rule of law announced in it) should apply?

Most of the traditional academic commentary about thinking like a lawyer concerns this issue.[42] For example, in his iconic *Introduction to Legal Reasoning*, Edward Levi characterized legal reasoning as the process of: (a) identifying a case in the reporter that bore some similarity to the matter at hand, (b) articulating the rule from the reported case, and (c) applying the articulated rule to the matter at hand.[43] What made the common law reasoning uniquely legal, and not merely an assessment of rule following, was step (b). That is, each exercise of legal reasoning was an occasion for potential re-articulation of the rule. Hence, the constituent rules of the common law evolved from case to case to case, allowing for or reflecting changes in social norms and attitudes.[44] In Levi's conception, the particularly *legal* part of the reasoning process in the application of the unconscionability rule in *Sam v. Mary* to war profiteering would be the willingness of courts to abandon a norm that accepts rational (if desperate) deal calculations as a normal occurrence during war in favor of a norm that sees such victims as acting as though they were of unsound mind or under delusion.

In his recent *Thinking Like a Lawyer: A New Introduction to Legal Reasoning*, Frederick Schauer contends the inferential processes of legal reasoning are not unique. He argues instead that what marks legal reasoning in particular is using precedent to come to conclusions that may not constitute the "best" result in individual cases, but which nevertheless affirm the generalization (a rule- rather than case-utilitarianism) that the rule was meant to embody.[45] Similarly, Neil MacCormick explained the process of legal rule application as involving something more than merely reaching a result:

> [T]he notion of formal justice requires that the justification of decisions in individual cases be always on the basis of universal propositions to which the judge is prepared to adhere as a basis for determining other like cases and deciding them in like manner to the present case.[46]

---

42 As does a good part of the jurisprudential debates about whether the legal conclusion arises from a formal body of rules, some requirement of natural law, or the proclivities of the judge doing the deciding. See *generally* Brink, *supra* note 3.

43 EDWARD H. LEVI, AN INTRODUCTION TO LEGAL REASONING 2 (1949).

44 *Id*. at 3–4.

45 FREDERICK SCHAUER, THINKING LIKE A LAWYER: A NEW INTRODUCTION TO LEGAL REASONING 8 (2012).

46 MACCORMICK, *supra* note 10, at 99.

In these conceptions of legal reasoning, what is important is not so much the result in the individual case (like *Demotsis*), but the rule itself continues to make sense as a generalization after its application to those facts.

The missing link—abductive reasoning

What all of this admirable analysis still fails to address is the missing link—the mental leap from situation to applicable rule. We have seen that simply understanding the deductive core of rule application is not enough to explain thinking like a lawyer. A lawyer also needs a mental warehouse of rules or the ability to find one through research. Assuming you have a warehouse of rules from which to select, either because you already know them or because you have done the research to find them, what is the source of the mental spark that lets you connect the rule to the situation, to know which is the correct tool to take from the correct shelf? We now turn to that difficult topic. It turns out that there is a kind of lawlessness, or unpredictability, or absence of "rule" at the core of thinking like a lawyer (or making sense of things generally) that is the source of some of the most fundamental disputes about how we think about the law.

Looking at the alleged profiteering case, we can see that neither deductive nor inductive reasoning adequately describes the process by which a lawyer looks at a jumble of facts and arrives at a legal theory. There is an element of deduction but it operates only after we have a rule to apply and the operative facts that fit the rule. We cannot determine merely by deduction whether the rule to be applied ought to be the "equivalence of consideration not necessary" rule or the "unconscionability" rule.

Nor is it merely a matter of induction. Inductive reasoning would work as follows. The facts of the case bear a resemblance to past cases in which the unconscionability rule has applied. The generalized inductive rule would be something like: "we have observed that where there is a gross inequity of bargaining power and exigent circumstances, courts do not enforce contracts." Based on that inductive inference, we might predict that a court would not enforce the contract in the profiteering case. But why see this as an "inequity" case versus a "bargain" case in the first place?

One respected commentator, Cass Sunstein, has argued that reasoning by analogy is "inductive analogy."[47] What he is suggesting is that we ought to be able to identify a pattern of cases involving fact situations from which we can make predictive conjectures about future outcomes in cases yet to be decided.[48] In fairness, Sunstein recognizes the problem with induction, which is that the lawyer making the argument by analogy has to develop the hypothesis for the prediction,

---

47 Cass R. Sunstein, *On Analogical Reasoning*, 106 HARV. L. REV. 741 (1993).
48 *Id.* at 743 n. 7, 744–49.

and in induction, a correct conclusion does not flow inevitably from the truth of the premises.[49]

In fact, the conceptual problem of viewing argument by analogy as inductive is more difficult than Sunstein acknowledges. Even in the physical sciences, where we can test and falsify hypotheses empirically, inductive reasoning involves a significant riddle or paradox, most famously exposed by the philosopher Nelson Goodman.[50] Assume you want to state a hypothesis about the color of emeralds. The fact is that you have never seen an emerald that is other than green. So it would be reasonable to assert the hypothesis "all emeralds are green." But what about an alternative hypothesis that "all emeralds are green until time t (which we haven't reached yet) at which point all emeralds will be blue"? Hence, the hypothesis is that "all emeralds are grue;" grue being the condition that emeralds seen before t are green and those seen after t are blue. The evidence so far is as consistent with the "grue" hypothesis as the "green" hypothesis. Why do we jump to the intuitive conclusion that the "green" hypothesis is valid but the "grue" hypothesis is not? Rather than try to resolve the paradox, Goodman proposed rules of thumb for how we actually go about favoring certain hypotheses over others that depend on our past experience with similar hypotheses.[51]

Sunstein's solution is similar to Goodman's. He too proposes rules of thumb (what he calls "defining characteristics") for deciding whether a particular pattern of past cases justifies its application to a new case.[52] What is clear is that he is no more able to identify the missing link from particulars to hypothesis than Goodman.What is the source of the hypothesis that leads one to think that particular analogy works in the present case? Induction does not tell us either: (a) how we came to perceive the similarity of patterns in the cases we now think are relevant to the prediction of outcome, or (b) why, if we could make a similar inductive inference and prediction from the "equivalence of consideration not necessary" cases, one rule should prevail over the other. Moreover, the riddle of induction (even if by analogy) is even more difficult in law where, as Sunstein acknowledges, the projections are normative and not empirical as in science.[53]

We have now arrived at the thing about thinking like a lawyer that is both hardest to do and hardest to explain. In my view, this particular ability goes to the

---

49 *Id.* at 745, nn. 18–19.
50 Daniel Cohnitz & Marcus Rossberg, *Nelson Goodman,* STAN. ENCYC. OF PHIL. (Spring 2016), Edward N. Zalta (ed.), http://plato.stanford.edu/archives/ spr2016/entries/ goodman.
51 *Id.* ("Goodman observes that predicates like 'green' are favored over predicates like 'grue', because the former are much better entrenched, i.e., in the past we projected many more hypotheses featuring 'green' or predicates co-extensional with 'green than hypothesis featuring the predicate 'grue.'")
52 These are "principled consistency; a focus on particulars; incompletely theorized judgments; and principles operating at a low or intermediate level of abstraction." Sunstein, *supra* note 47, at 746.
53 *Id.* at 745, n. 18.

heart of some of the most significant debates in legal philosophy and perhaps to how our minds work. Susan Haack described the literature on this aspect of legal argument as "luxuriant, to say the least—a steamy, tangled jungle in which it would be easy to get hopelessly lost."[54] Karl Llewellyn famously described the process as "situation-sense:"

> the sizing up of "the case" into some pattern is of the essence of getting to the case at all, and the shape it starts to take calls up familiar, more general patterns to fit it into or to piece it out or to set it against for comparison.[55]

Llewellyn himself rejected the idea that one could reason one's way to the application of situation sense, seeing it instead as a kind of professional know-how or intuition: "It is quite independent . . . of any philosophy as to the proper sources of 'Right Reason' which may be held by any 'Natural Law' philosopher . . . . It answers instead to current life, and it answers to the craft."[56] Harvard professor Scott Brewer classified (and Professor Haack re-summarized) several other approaches including (a) "mysticism," that is, a rational force that is either ineffable (e.g., Cass Sunstein)[57] or finds its source in "spiritual acts" (e.g., Theodor Heller),[58] (b) "trained, disciplined intuition" (e.g., Charles Fried),[59] (c) "skepticism" (e.g., Richard Posner),[60] and (d) Brewer's own thesis of an inferential structure he called "Modest-Proposal Rationalism."[61]

The late Donald Schön was an MIT scholar who studied the processes of professional thinking generally. He had a view similar to Llewellyn's. Schön described something called "knowing-in-action," a kind of knowing that is inherent in the action itself, and which the actor cannot explain because it is action and not thinking.[62] When the professional actor thinks about her actions, it is instead a subjective contemplation Schön called "reflection-in-action."

> [S]omething falls outside the range of ordinary expectations . . . . [T]he practitioner allows himself to experience surprise, puzzlement, or confusion in a situation he finds uncertain or unique . . . . He carries out an experiment

---

54 Susan Haack, *On Logic in the Law: "Something, But Not All,"* 20 RATIO JURIS 1, 21 (2007).
55 KARL N. LLEWELLYN, THE COMMON LAW TRADITION: DECIDING APPEALS 268 (1961).
56 *Id.* at 422–23.
57 Scott Brewer, *Exemplary Reasoning: Semantics, Pragmatics, and the Rational Force of Legal Argument by Analogy,* 109 HARV. L. REV. 923, 952–53 (1996).
58 Haack, *supra* note 54, at 22.
59 Brewer, *supra* note 57, at 952–53.
60 *Id.* at 953–54.
61 *Id.* at 954–55.
62 DONALD SCHÖN, THE REFLECTIVE PRACTITIONER: HOW PROFESSIONALS THINK IN ACTION 49–69 (1985).

which serves to generate both a new understanding of the phenomena and a change in the situation.[63]

This is the aspect of thinking like a lawyer we need to explore. We have in front of us a complex set of facts, and need to sort them out. Like Josh in *The West Wing*, we want to find, if not the silver bullet rule that indisputably resolves the matter, at least the basis for a good argument. (Note that law professors deliberately craft their exams so that there is no silver bullet and more than one rule could apply.) In Professor Brewer's taxonomy of this aspect of legal rationality, I am an unrepentant mystic. It's because I see no way around the magic or mystery in it. The leap from problem to avenue of solution we are talking about here could also be characterized by words like "inspiration," "imagination," or "creativity." What is going on is the application of professional *judgment*.

If a student had just spent a year in my contracts class and was preparing for the final, she would undoubtedly create an outline of what we had covered in the class. I might tell her that the detailed outline will be less helpful during the pressure of the exam than an index card or two that simply list the possible issues and a set of rules that might be applied. She could read the hypothetical situation on the exam, and then check down her list of issues and rules, asking for each, "Might this apply here?" That would be a good start, but it still doesn't address the "aha" moment when she needs to connect the list of rules with the situation. It is not enough to see the rules and see the facts; something in her brain has to perceive the connection and only then begin to work with it in answering the question.

What makes explanation here so difficult is that we can give practical tips like these for helping with the leap of judgment, but we cannot state a rule for it. Nelson Goodman couldn't for judgments underlying scientific hypotheses, Cass Sunstein couldn't do it for analogical judgments in law, nor, as Professor Haack observed, could Professor Brewer, even with all the 20th-century developments beyond Aristotelian logic.[64] Another way to put it is that there is no rule for the application of a rule. In order to apply a rule (or an algorithm or a model) to a particular situation, we have to choose the rule. If you try to determine what circumstances fit within a rule, setting another rule merely leads to another rule to another rule to another rule, all the way down. In short, there is no final answer for selection of the rule; it is an infinite regress.

Philosophers, at least since Aristotle, have been pondering this dilemma of rule choice. Aristotle himself referred to the ability to choose well as *phronesis*, or "practical wisdom," and described it as a natural attribute that includes, among other things, the ability to deliberate well, to deal with universal principles as well as particular actions, to assess which actions are conducive to ends, to employ sympathetic understanding in the effort to determine what is fair, and

---

63 *Id.* at 68.
64 Haack, *supra* note 54, at 22–24.

to distinguish and abjure mere cleverness in the pursuit of a bad end.[65] In the *Critique of Pure Reason*, Kant simply punted on the essence of judgment, concluding that someone could learn it even if it could not be defined.[66] Professor Haack says it's a mistake to call it "mysticism": "it is plain good sense."[67]

The philosopher Charles Sanders Peirce coined the term "abductive reasoning" for the cognitive process that creates hypotheses; in other words, the intuition that there is something common to the data from which we might predict the next instance according to the rule of the hypothesis.[68] It is the intuitional moment in which we decide that a particular result ought to obtain even before we state the propositions that take us to that conclusion. How do we explain moments of inspiration in science? The philosopher Carl Hempel noted the relationship between the judgment leading to the hypothesis and its later confirmation by way of induction:

> There are . . . no generally applicable "rules of induction," by which hypotheses or theories can be mechanically derived or inferred from empirical data. The transition from data to theory requires creative imagination. Scientific hypotheses and theories are not *derived* from observed facts, but *invented* in order to account for them. They constitute guesses at the connections that might obtain between the phenomena under study, at uniformities and patterns that might underlie their occurrence.[69]

The chemist Kekulé was inspired to hypothesize the ring structure of benzene when staring into a fire; Kepler's theory of planetary motion arose from "his interest in a mystical doctrine about numbers and a passion to demonstrate the music of the spheres."[70] There are no mechanical rules one applies to the mass of antecedent data in order to draw scientific conclusions. "Induction rules of the kind here envisaged would therefore have to provide a mechanical routine for constructing, on the basis of the given data, a hypothesis or theory stated in terms of some quite novel concepts, which are nowhere used in the description of the data themselves."[71] Rather, the physical or social science theorist proceeds "by inventing hypotheses as tentative answers to a problem under study, and then subjecting these to empirical test."[72] Just under the surface of routine and methodical advancements in physical and social science is some process of creativity

---

65 ARISTOTLE, NICOMACHEAN ETHICS 152–73 (Martin Ostwald trans., 1962).
66 IMMANUEL KANT, CRITIQUE OF PURE REASON 268–69 (Paul Guyer & Allen W. Wood, trans. 1999) (1787).
67 Haack, *supra* note 54, at 24.
68 CHARLES S. PEIRCE, PHILOSOPHICAL WRITINGS OF PEIRCE 150–56 (Justus Buchler, ed. 1955).
69 CARL G. HEMPEL, PHILOSOPHY OF NATURAL SCIENCE 15 (1966) (emphasis in original).
70 *Id*. at 16.
71 *Id*. at 14.
72 *Id*. at 17.

or inspiration that is not mere observation of experience, and is not the process of confirming or disproving the hypotheses by further observation or experiment. The development of the most mundane hypothesis to explain data has some element of intuition that cannot be the product of the data itself.

The same abductive process that serves as the source of scientific hypotheses is the source of legal theories. It is, as Richard Posner, has observed, like Peirce's abduction in science, "a mysterious process, distinct from logic and scientific observation."[73] Professor Brewer's analysis of the role of abduction in legal reasoning captures the idea that something rational is going on, but which is not deductive or inductive.[74] I do not want to repeat that work here, except to take a stand on two particular issues. First, as we'll explore in the next chapter, and as Professor Haack observed, abduction in the development of explanatory scientific theories is significantly different than its application to normative legal theorizing.[75] Unlike deduction, which always produces a true conclusion if the premises are true, or induction, which makes a testable prediction, abduction is not only "law-less" or "rule-less," but notoriously unreliable. Even in the physical sciences, all abduction gives one is the basis for a hypothesis that in turn leads to an inductive inference. In other words, one tests the inductive hypothesis, not the process of abduction itself. When the abductive process leads to normative theory, nothing about it is testable.

Second, abduction is sometimes referred to as "inference to the best explanation," but that is not only incorrect but sells the mystery a little short. Once one has come up with a set of potential hypotheses to explain a phenomenon, it may well be that what one is doing is selecting the best one to fit the facts observed. That is "inference to the best explanation." But what is the source of the panoply of proposed explanatory hypotheses in the first place? Professor Brewer notes that this is the subject of considerable debate. One side believes that there is logical or rational structure or constraint on this "aha" moment of discovery; the other argues "that the processes of scientific discovery are not themselves subject to rational discipline, neither in the way deduction is, nor even in the way that induction is."[76]

The philosopher of science Karl Popper stated that "[t]he initial stage, the act of conceiving or inventing a theory, seems to me neither to call for logical analysis nor to be susceptible of it." What was important to Popper was that these moments of pure conjecture or discovery in fact occurred, and thereafter became the subject of testing.[77] Professor Brewer aligns himself with the former group, believing "that discovery, in both science and other realms of reasoning, is itself

---

73 POSNER, *supra* note 9, at 105.
74 Brewer, *supra* note 57, at 945–49; *see also* Tuzet, *supra* note 12.
75 Haack, *supra* note 54, at 22–24.
76 *Id.* at 946.
77 KARL R. POPPER, THE LOGIC OF SCIENTIFIC DISCOVERY 31 (1959).

a disciplined inferential process."[78] I am inclined to think it is not, and the reason is the infinite regress at the core of any attempt at rule application.

To return to the profiteering case, it is clear in retrospect that there is rational force in either the argument that the "equivalence of consideration" rule applies, or that the "unconscionability" rule applies. Taking the application of either rule to the case as a hypothesis, there is an aspect of "inference to the best fit," and the debate in court or in class will involve advocates claiming that one rule or the other is the best fit. But is here a right or true answer to the question? Let's turn to that in Chapter 3.

---

78 Brewer, *supra* note 57, at 946–47. The closest I can come to something like this conclusion would be an intuition supported by the logic of the theory. Something like that happens in science frequently. When Mendeleev developed the periodic table of the elements, there was a space unfilled where germanium now sits. Quantum physicists have theorized that particles ought to exist long before they get discovered in the lab. Sometimes their own theories seem so wacky that they themselves are skeptical of them. I have no doubt that thousands of legal research assignment have begun, as many of mine did, with a senior partner wanting there to be a rule on a particular issue, and hypothesizing as follows, "There has to be a case on that somewhere."

3 Assessing Theory-Making in Pure Lawyering

Recapping the bidding

In the previous chapter, we explored the logical nuts and bolts of the legal reasoning process. In the modus ponens logic of the law, legal rules are the "if-then" statements of the major premise. The purest form of pure lawyering is advocacy, in which lawyers construct a series of "if p, then q" statements, the desired effect of which is for the client to prevail. The legal consequence in each step of the argument is q, and the lawyer's job is to demonstrate all of the elements of p are satisfied. When lawyers practice, the integrated sets of these "if p, then q" statements constitute their theories of the case. The theories and their constituent rules are the means by which they impart legal meaning to real-world events. They provide value to clients when that meaning happens to coincide with the outcome the client wants.

That is the essence of pure lawyering. In this chapter we turn to the critique. As the book's subtitle promises, it will echo Kant's critique of pure reason. This is not as intimidating or highfalutin as it sounds. Legal reasoning is a subset of reasoning generally. It is a thinking process by which we make sense and understand, whether the objects of the thinking are things around us in the physical world or ideas about how people ought to act. The former is *descriptive*, and reflects itself in matters as sophisticated as quantum mechanics or as mundane as figuring out why the car won't start. The latter is *normative*, and reflects itself in matters as impenetrable as religious salvation or as ordinary as deciding whether to let one's child stay home from school.

The first relevant aspect of Kant's critique of reason is that its exercise is benign and productive when applied empirically for purpose of knowledge. That is, reason is the source of theoretical (or, in my example, mundane) *knowledge* if applied to experience and possible experience. There is a second relevant aspect to the critique. When reason gets applied to matters other than experience of the physical world, that is, in the moral or normative sphere rather than in physical, it might well be benign and helpful in getting to correct answers for practical questions of what we ought to do.

But there is a third aspect as well. The answers that reason gives us in the moral or normative sphere are something distinct from knowledge. They are certainly ideas in which we can *believe* rationally. But conflating knowledge and belief, both of which can be the products of reason, can lead to illusions of knowledge. In Kant's estimation, the worst of these conflations of belief and knowledge occurred when people were certain rather than humble in their assessments of their own moral conclusions. In the extreme, the moral advocate persuades himself so thoroughly of his own virtue and rectitude as to become a moral dogmatist or fanatic.[1]

The appearance of moral certainty (and even a little fanaticism) is an asset to a trial lawyer who is constructing the logical chain that would lead to a favorable result. Professor Lawrence Solan has argued persuasively that lawyers have a professional license to be insincere (within limits) in a way that would ordinarily violate social norms, and this is at least some of the basis for the less-than-admiring public perception of lawyers.[2] That makes perfect sense. There is a permissible double-think going on, in which everyone knows that the lawyer is a hired gun, earning a living by employing the methods of pure lawyering to fit the facts into legal theories that just happen to benefit the advocate's client. The most effective rhetoric style in front of a judge or jury is to encourage the willing suspension of disbelief, as in all fiction. We are transported from the real world in which the desired outcome is merely one that *ought* to occur to a hypothetical world in which the outcome *must* occur because the deductive logic of the law *requires* it. That is what the lawyers for the utility in the coal contract case described in the last chapter wanted. As Professor Solan suggests, "the best lawyers are so convincing that they are able to cause their audience to let down their guard and forget they are dealing with an advocate."[3]

What I want to explore in this chapter is how this powerful thinking tool is capable of creating the same illusions, with similar implications, as Kant described for reason generally. Does this exercise of legal reasoning lead to objectively true answers as in science? Or does it lead to answers that, despite their normativity, are capable of being objectively right or wrong? If everyone, including the most heinous actors, is entitled to zealous representation, and we accept the idea of "insincere advocacy," it must mean that the *process* of legal theory-making—i.e. pure lawyering—is somehow different from the outcome of the reasoning. That outcome is *either* the objective knowledge or the normative belief that the legal theory-maker seeks to instill in the listener. Pure lawyering is merely a process of using reason to advocate an outcome. The process itself is agnostic as to the truth and moral values of the outcome. But to what extent might we, as lawyers, even as we understand this distinction between process and outcome, allow ourselves to believe what we are advocating is objectively true and knowable?

---

1   Susan Neiman, The Unity of Reason: Rereading Kant 125–29 (1994).
2   Lawrence M. Solan, *Lawyers as Insincere (But Truthful) Actors*, 36 J. Leg. Prof. 487, 488 (2012).
3   *Id.* at 489.

The punchline will be that results we get purely from legal theorizing don't provide objective knowledge in the way that theories about the objects of physical science do. Nor is a conclusion right or wrong in a moral sense, merely because it results from a process of legal reasoning. This is not pie-in-the-sky philosophy. I am not interested in rehashing jurisprudential debates about the separability thesis or formalism versus realism. My interest, rather, is in the amoral activity that constitutes the process of lawyering as it ordinarily occurs in the everyday world. I believe law is a formal system but that it gets used realistically and opportunistically. One might think the process of legal theorizing, or what it generates as a result, as carrying with it truth, justice, or goodness. But to do so is to stand a good chance of conflating what one can *know* is true, on one hand, with what one can only *believe* is true or morally correct, on the other.

What I will contend here and in the following chapters is that there are potentially untoward consequences when one's growth as a lawyer gets stunted at the pure lawyering stage. The unreflective lawyer may well conflate what one can *know* by way of legal theorizing, and what one merely *believes*. My goal in this chapter is simply to show that the conflation of knowledge and belief can occur and offer an explanation why.[4]

My answer has to do with the conception of the discipline we have developed over the last 150 years or so, from Langdell forward. The substance and form of the theory and practice of law have been to approach it, though normative, as though it can be understood as science.[5] But at least prototypically, scientific theorizing focuses on objects that exist empirically, independently of our minds. Science is descriptive in that it tries to explain how and why those objects *are*. In contrast, the legal exercise is prototypically normative, in that the lawyer tries to demonstrate what the outcomes, given the antecedent facts, *ought to be*. Yet, despite these prototypes, because law occurs within social institutions that exist empirically and independent of our minds, there is a gray area between the objectivity of scientific reasoning and the normativity of legal reasoning that is amenable to conflation of the two.

Moreover, when considering the stuff of the law itself, rather than merely the institutions that generate it, the urge to conflate the descriptive and empirical, on one hand, with the normative, on the other, is understandable. As Oliver Wendell Holmes described (and underestimated) it more than a century ago in a metaphor

---

4 One of the best available assessments of the relationship of truth to legal propositions is Dennis Patterson's *Law and Truth* (1996). Professor Patterson undertook there a thorough assessment of the competing jurisprudential approaches to law and truth. If it isn't already clear, I wholly agree with Professor Patterson's conclusion that trying to find the "fact of the matter" in legal propositions (in what I call "pure lawyering") is a misdirected exercise. Another volume of essays, authored by distinguished legal philosophers, devoted to the issue of objectivity of legal propositions is OBJECTIVITY IN LAW AND MORALS (Brian Leiter, ed. 2001).

5 *See* Thomas C. Grey, *Langdell's Orthodoxy*, 45 U. PITT. L. REV. 1 (1983); Susan Haack, *On Logic in the Law: "Something, But Not All,"* 20 RATIO JURIS 1, 21–25 (2007); Phoebe C. Ellsworth, *Legal Reasoning and Scientific Reasoning*, 63 ALA. L. REV. 895 (2012).

of sibylline growth, the stuff of law is "a body of reports, of treatises, and of statutes, in this country and in England, extending back for six hundred years, and now increasing annually by hundreds."[6] It is so easy to think of something with an ancient, albeit metaphoric, corpus as being real and *knowable*, even mind-independent and discoverable, and capable of truth. My claim, however, is that what can actually be *known* about what the law *is*, in the sense of being true or false, is relatively trivial. There are statutes or contracts, for example, with sentences that purport to establish rules. But in any matter in which people turn to lawyering as a means of resolving a dispute, the law is inherently normative, and the meanings established by the argumentation of pure lawyering are invariably matters of belief rather than objective knowledge.

To be clear, not for a minute would I suggest that just because someone is capable of thinking like a lawyer means she is somehow blinded to truth or morality in making decisions about what to do in law, lawyering, business, or life. What I am distinguishing is the form of the theorizing from its content. It is entirely possible, but not necessary, that legal outcomes can be consistent with truth and/or good morals. In his masterful article on normative methods for lawyers, Joseph Singer posits the case of a church deciding the way to honor God is to ring its steeple bell all night. Does the "freedom of religion" or the "nuisance" rule apply? Legal theorizing does not supply the values themselves—they have to come from somewhere else. Singer provides a thorough typology of the arguments that might persuade a court to take the leap of rule application one way or the other.[7] But once the court has adopted a theory and its component rules, for example, that nuisance rules trump freedom of religion in this instance, the logic of pure lawyering dictates the result.

Nor does legal argument validate any truth or moral value as something mind-independently objective or knowable in the same way we think of a quantum particle as real even though we can never see one. All legal argument does is provide a reasoned and formal basis for justifying one's belief in the correctness of the outcome. Hence, in the last part of this chapter, I will propose a way of framing hard cases that allows us to separate the truth, moral, or instrumental value of possible outcomes in those cases from the amoral process by which pure lawyering reasons to the outcomes.

Theories and truth in science and law

Science and descriptive theories

To get to a thoughtful conclusion about pure lawyering and the truth of outcomes when we engage in it, we ought to start with what it means to theorize in science.

---

6 Oliver Wendell Holmes, *The Path of the Law*, 10 HARV. L. REV. 457 (1897), *reprinted in* 110 HARV. L. REV. 991, 991 (1997).
7 Joseph William Singer, *Normative Methods for Lawyers*, 56 UCLA L. REV. 899 (2009).

Karl Popper, who thought the "aha" moment of discovery was not a matter of logic or reason, nevertheless articulated one of the most widely accepted formulas for deciding whether a hypothesis or theory was capable of being scientific. If the proposition is capable of being falsified by empirical evidence, then it is scientific; otherwise it is not. Popper's particular bugaboos were Freudian psychology and Marxism, both of whose adherents made claims to science. In an oversimplified nutshell, Popper's thesis was that no evidence would ever be able to show either theory was false. Therefore, belief in the theory was more akin to believing in God than empirical truth. To know something by way of scientific theory, therefore, we have to be able to test the theory against empirical evidence. Popper's philosophy came to be known as "fallibilism." That is, it is not that we prove the theories to be true. Instead, we know they are fallible but take them as an approximation of truth the longer they stand without having been falsified.[8]

Let's take two extremes to demonstrate the differences among: (a) knowledge that is merely sense perception, (b) mere belief, and (c) knowledge that arises because of theory. As to (a), I know that there is a MacBook Pro sitting on my desk at this moment, because I am typing this sentence on it. I don't have to spend much time pondering whether I believe the computer is here. This is about as clear an empirical observation of fact as I am ever going to have. It is simply a sense perception. As to (b), my neighbor across the street, on the other hand, is quite sure that a person named Jesus living in Judea about 2,000 years ago was the Son of God, that he died, and was resurrected. Whether Jesus lived is an empirical claim and capable of knowledge. The belief that Jesus was resurrected is not. It is a matter of faith, not proof.

Knowledge as in (c) might be something like Einstein's theory of curved space, or the Standard Model of particle physics. The knowledge provided by those theories involves more than mere sense perception. Even though their respective proponents would likely acknowledge they will be shown some day to be inadequate as currently articulated, I am willing to accept them as "true," descriptive of something mind-independently real, and not merely a matter of belief. They are not as easily classified as knowledge as my sense perception of my computer, and they require more in the way of belief, if in nothing else, than in the power of the theory. They are, however, still very much within the category of mental *stuff* I would call knowledge.[9]

So, some simple knowledge is just a matter of sense perception, but sophisticated, scientific knowledge (and even a lot of day to day knowledge) is theory-laden. Scientific theorizing is different from, but not unrelated to, the kind of sense making we do every day. It is a reality of the human condition that each of us makes sense of the world through our subjective frames and points of view. It may well be that we are evolutionarily disposed to do so, as those of our ancient

---

8 *See* KARL POPPER, CONJECTURES AND REFUTATIONS: THE GROWTH OF SCIENTIFIC KNOWLEDGE 43–54, 309–13 (2002).

9 *Id.* at 47–48.

ancestors who did see the world as ordered and predictable were more likely to survive.

Apart from naturalistic explanations, however, one of Kant's great insights was that the impulse to theory is simply a subset of an *a priori* need to see the world in an ordered and predictable way. Our minds are predisposed to find purpose and order in nature even though we have "absolutely no *a priori* reason for presuming"[10] such purpose or order. Experience itself, said Kant, cannot prove to us the actual existence of such order; "there must then have preceded a rationalizing subtlety which only sportively introduces the concept of purpose into the nature of things, but which does not derive it from Objects or from their empirical cognition."[11] The novelist Bruce Duffy captured this concept in his fictionalized account of Ludwig Wittgenstein's doctoral *viva voce* (the British term for the oral examination) before Bertrand Russell and G.E. Moore. Duffy's Wittgenstein expresses his disillusionment with his own attempt, in the *Tractatus Logico-Philosophicus*, to capture a universal truth about language. He explains,

> I was captive to the illusion that, because there is a prior order to the world, there must be an essence to language—that my inquiries would yield a unified and utterly simple solution of the purest crystal. Much of this problem, I think, can be traced to this . . . scientific craving, this craving for generality that seems to permeate our thinking.[12]

Even in the hard sciences, descriptive theories, or explanations of the "is," merge subtly with normative theories, or justifications of the "ought." The reason is that we all seem to start with the usually unexamined *subjective* presumption that the *objective* physical world, the "is," has a discoverable order to it and we *ought* to be able to discover what that order is. We will come back to this later, but it is a key point. Pure reason is *regulative* and not *constitutive*. It is a process of sense-making and not an end in itself. Reason drives us to seek an unreachable "unconditioned" proposition at the end of all the conditioned propositions that constitute a theoretical explanation. Reason's "role must be seen as a normative one: *if functioning properly*, theoretical reason does not provide us with knowledge of its ideas but directs us in the task of realizing them."[13]

One need not, however, accept Kant's view of metaphysics to come to a similar conclusion about assumptions of underlying order. W.V.O. Quine, the empiricist *par excellence*, would have said that such a conclusion was not *a priori* but simply an empirical observation about the most successful hypotheses. But even he thought there were five "virtues underlying hypotheses: conservatism, modesty,

---

10 IMMANUEL KANT, CRITIQUE OF JUDGMENT 153 (J.H. Bernard trans., 2005) (1790).
11 *Id.*
12 BRUCE DUFFY, THE WORLD AS I FOUND IT 466 (1987).
13 NEIMAN, *supra* note 1, at 127–28 (emphasis in original).

simplicity, generality, and refutability."[14] Thomas Kuhn made a similar point in connection with theory choice when the evidence confirming hypotheses is capable of supporting more than one: a good scientific theory should be accurate, consistent, broad in scope, simple, and fruitful of new research findings.[15] As Kuhn and others argued, there is more subjectivity and value judgment within scientific communities and scientists themselves, not so much about the observable data, but about the inferences that need to be made to link the data together as explanation.[16]

Because scientific knowledge is theory-laden, it means that discovering why something is happening involves that difficult-to-explain leap sometimes called abduction that we examined in the last chapter. One of my favorite examples of the application of somewhat scientific theory to solve everyday problems occurs on the National Public Radio program, *Car Talk* (regrettably, since even before Tom Magliozzi's death, playing only in archived versions). A caller describes a problem with a car, for example, it is making a grinding noise but only when accelerating and going uphill at the same time. In the midst of a lot of self-deprecating humor, Tom and his brother, Ray, will propose theories that explain the problem—more accurately, hypotheses that fit the facts presented. Some problems are easier than others, and making an inference to the best explanation is easy. Ray and Tom know that when a car exhibits *that* particular symptom, ninety-nine times out of a hundred, it's *this* particular cause. It is the inductive thinking process at work. But the abductive spark is not nearly as apparent as when the brothers get stumped and have to develop new theories. And as with all scientific theorizing, sometimes they are right and sometimes they are wrong, as demonstrated when they bring callers back in the feature "Stump the Chumps," their own gesture toward fallibilism.

Social, as opposed to physical, science poses knottier problems with respect to the presumption that there is a discoverable and knowable order to the world. Most of the modern social science disciplines are a relatively recent development, beginning in the late 1800s.[17] With the rapidly increasing complexity of human society, there arose a division of labor with respect to the assessment of systematicity in human affairs, all predicated on the belief those affairs were capable of being analyzed like physical science.[18] One of the more controversial ideas, put forward

14 W.V. Quine & J.S. Ullian, *Hypothesis*, in INTRODUCTORY READINGS IN THE PHILOSOPHY OF SCIENCE 404, 405 (E.D. Klemke, Robert Hollinger & David Wÿss Rudge eds., 3d ed. 1998).

15 Thomas S. Kuhn, *Objectivity, Value Judgment, and Theory Choice*, in INTRODUCTORY READINGS, *supra* note 14, at 435, 436.

16 *Id.* at 439.

17 THOMAS L. HASKELL, THE EMERGENCE OF PROFESSIONAL SOCIAL SCIENCE: THE AMERICAN SOCIAL SCIENCE AND THE NINETEENTH-CENTURY CRISIS OF AUTHORITY (2000).

18 THOMAS L. HASKELL, OBJECTIVITY IS NOT NEUTRALITY: EXPLANATORY SCHEMES IN HISTORY 12–24 (1998) [hereinafter "HASKELL, OBJECTIVITY"].

by philosopher of science Carl Hempel, was that history itself could be reduced to a series of universal and scientific "covering laws."[19] It was a reaction to a perception that history as written was little more than a subjective narrative about why historical events happened the way they did. Yet that way of making sense of human affairs—an external observation of human events as though one were observing rats in a maze—simply left out any room for assessment of human beings as subjective agents. The historian Thomas Haskell has noted that making sense of how human actors interact involves both an assessment of objective cause and effect *and* reasons in the sense of subjective motivations of those human actors. In short, a meaningful explanation of historical sequences needs to avoid what he called the "over-ardent embrace of the Hempelians and the scorn of the narrativists."[20]

Quine and Ullian said, with respect to all scientific hypotheses, "What we try to do . . . is to explain some otherwise unexplained happenings by inventing a plausible story, a plausible description or history of portions of the world."[21] We can see that the development of theories about why people acted the way they did requires the same abductive leap as theories about gravitational waves or sub-atomic particles. If a social scientist is not going to plumb individual motivations, he needs to make generalized assumptions about what motivations are. The example *par excellence* is neoclassical economics, in which the theories depend at least upon one critical assumption, namely that economic actors operate rationally to maximize their utility. As Richard Posner noted in his seminal text on economic analysis of law,

> The basic assumption, that human behavior is rational, seems contradicted by the experiences and observations of everyday life. The contradiction is less acute when one understands that the concept of rationality used by the economist is objective rather than subjective, so that it would not be a solecism to speak of a rational frog.[22]

But those assumptions of rationality are the product of one particular leap to the particular theories that those particular theorists believe best fits the evidence. There is no rule requiring that their assumptions or conclusions about best-fit theories are the rule. And not surprising, because of this issue of subjectivity in human affairs, one can justifiably be more skeptical about claims to truth arising from social, versus physical, science theory.

The skepticism arises not just from more difficult questions about whether the theories are falsifiable in Popper's sense. It arises as well from questions about how the theorist herself made the leap from observation to conclusion. When we

19 HASKELL, OBJECTIVITY, *supra* note 18, at 16.
20 *Id.* at 23.
21 Quine & Ullian, *supra* note 14, at 405.
22 RICHARD A. POSNER, ECONOMIC ANALYSIS OF LAW 17 (6th ed. 2003).

encounter a problem to be solved, we need to come up with an explanatory hypothesis and then test it. As we saw in Chapter 2, something very difficult to explain as a reasoned inferential process lies at the heart of our ability to develop the hypotheses we use as the bases of alternative explanations. As one of the great scholars of rationality, Robert Nozick, conceded, "There is no mechanical (algorithmic) procedure for generating the most promising alternative—none that we know of anyway."[23] If our desires, rather than rationality, affect the processing of information and the justification of a course of action that we tell ourselves are our reasons for acting, it is not surprising that we might have a reason to question our own rational conclusions.[24]

Again, one example of such skepticism comes from critics of the assumptions rational actor economists need to make. For example, the behavioral economics pioneered by Amos Tversky and Daniel Kahneman focuses on how heuristics and biases of individual actors cause them (in a predictable way) not to be classically rational.[25] The New Institutional Economics of Oliver Williamson and others focuses on how firms actually deal with transaction costs in the play of the economic game. But once we understand the assumptions underlying the hypotheses, there are reasons to be skeptical of the explanatory power even of these theories. Williamson, for example, made it clear that the only kind of interpersonal trust that fits into his economic model was a kind of calculation about the costs and benefits of fulfilling one's obligations, and not the kind of personal and moral commitments arising from customs, traditions, norms, and religion that we might otherwise associate with the term.[26] The very nature of theory in any discipline aspiring to science is to look for regularities and universals in the scatter of data. That necessarily means that some of the data is noise and gets left out. In any single social science discipline, it could mean that theory, to be useful, leaves things like custom, tradition, norms, and religion, out of the story.

To make matters more confusing, there is the subjective interest of the theorist himself. That was the point Thomas Kuhn made in his iconic work *The Structure of Scientific Revolutions*. Even in hard science, "revolutions" occur when new research overcomes the scientific community's older "conceptual boxes supplied by a professional education."[27] The standpoint of the theorist matters even more acutely when policy-makers and advocates use the "knowledge" produced by social science in pursuit of normative ends. Very few physicists, for example, have normative debates about quantum mechanics on the editorial pages of the

23 ROBERT NOZICK, THE NATURE OF RATIONALITY 172–73 (1994).

24 ALFRED MELE, SELF-DECEPTION UNMASKED 25–46 (2001).

25 *See* DANIEL KAHNEMAN, THINKING FAST AND SLOW (2011).

26 Oliver E. Williamson, *Calculativeness, Trust, and Economic Organization*, 36 J.L. & ECON. 453, 479 (1993); Oliver E. Williamson, *Transaction Cost Economics: How It Works; Where It Is Headed*, 146 DE ECONOMIST 23, 26 (1998).

27 THOMAS S. KUHN, THE STRUCTURE OF SCIENTIFIC REVOLUTIONS 5–6 (3d ed. 1996).

Wall Street Journal and the *New York Times*. Gregory Mankiw and Paul Krugman are both economists, one is known to be "conservative" and the other "liberal," and they ply their disciplines in support of their advocacy of vastly different outcomes. Can they both be correct? What does economic theory thus tell us about what is true?

Normative theories and the fragile science of law

How does this discussion of theory apply to correct answers in law? To put it differently, are there objectively "true" answers to legal problems? Ronald Dworkin is the modern legal philosopher most often identified with an affirmative answer to that question.[28] That runs counter to what I think are the more "realist" inclinations of most of us. But even in dealing with my less ethereal and far more pragmatic academic colleagues, my strong impression is that they might *tell* you they don't believe in a natural or formal mind-independent law of something like contracts or security interests. Nevertheless, when they are dealing with the complex web of legal doctrine, they *act* like there is one.

Dealing with that paradox means understanding something about theory itself in the practice and the academic study of law. "Theory" has two different usages. Their relationship is at the heart of the conflation of knowledge and belief in pure lawyering. In the subsequent chapters, we will talk about the consequences of this conflation, but the task here is to demonstrate that it occurs in the first place. Answers that are the product of legal reasoning (and argument) are *not* like scientific answers. We may *believe* them to be right, but we can't *know* they are right in the same way we can know things scientifically. But the reasoning in each case is so similar to that of science that it can be relatively easy to give mere normative belief the privileged status of objective knowledge.

Lawrence Solum, whose blog is one of the leading modern repositories of current work on legal theory and philosophy of law, has a continuing series called *Legal Theory Lexicon* that he aims "at law students (especially first years) with an interest in legal theory."[29] He provides a standard and reasonable distinction between positive or descriptive theory and normative theory within the community of legal scholars:

- <u>Positive</u> legal theory seeks to explain <u>what</u> the law is and <u>why</u> it is that way, and <u>how</u> laws affect the world, whereas
- <u>Normative</u> legal theories tell us what the law <u>ought</u> to be.[30]

---

28 David O. Brink, *Legal Interpretation, Objectivity, and Morality*, in OBJECTIVITY, *supra* note 4, at 19–20.

29 Lawrence Solum, *Legal Theory Lexicon: Positive and Normative Legal Theory*, LEGAL THEORY BLOG (Mar. 13, 2016), http://lsolum.typepad.com/legal_theory_lexicon/2003/12/legal_theory_le.html.

30 *Id.* (emphasis in original).

This is a helpful way of distinguishing between the various academic approaches to the *law*, whether as a social phenomenon or as a philosophical construct. It is less helpful when thinking about *lawyering*, particularly advocacy, as a practice. The reason is that, in any real-world dispute worth litigating, any argument about the application of law is not about what the law is, unless you make the circular assumption that law is something. For me, the only kind of meaningful positive theory, to use Solum's distinction, would be in an anthropological, psychological, economic, or sociological sense. I am willing to credit that as the subject of knowledge.

In any matter worth hiring a lawyer, on the other hand, law in practice is always what Solum would call a matter of normative theorizing. When two lawyers stand up to argue to a judge, each of the them has a different view of what the law *ought to be* when applied in *this* instance, even if they use rhetorical techniques suggesting there is only one true answer resolving the issue. In other words, if everybody agrees this is a case of first impression, there might well be explicit acknowledgment that the argument is about the result the court *ought* to impose. I am suggesting here that every case worth fighting over is one of first impression, even if one side or the other suggests rhetorically that the law "requires" or "demands" an outcome.[31]

Let's explore this in some more detail.

Theory-making when practicing law

While there may well be inductive or predictive empirical insights that support decision-making (e.g., doing jury research, arguing to mock juries, or assessing the political predilections of the judge), theory in the pure lawyering game is the process of reasoning to a normative conclusion about legal consequences in real-world situations. For a practitioner, a legal theory is nothing more than an integrated set of "if *p*, then *q*" statements designed to generate the intended legal outcome. As I learned from my civil procedure professor in my first few weeks of law school, lawyers think in theories when they draft complaints even though nothing requires them to do so. The Federal Rules of Civil Procedure, which serves as a model for many states as well, provide only that a pleading stating a claim for relief must contain "a short and plain statement of the claim showing that the pleader is entitled to relief," the relief being damages, an injunction, or some other form of remedy.[32] There is no requirement that the claims for relief be stated in the form of counts or types of legal actions.

Nevertheless, it is a routine and standard practice that lawyers will aggregate all of the factual allegations under one heading, and then delineate the claims as "counts" under a series of separate headings. For example, Able Computer

---

31 As to going about making those arguments effectively, *see* Singer, *supra* note 7.
32 FED. R. CIV. P. 8(a)(2).

Company sold Baker a computer that was supposed to be able to calculate pi to one hundred places, and it turns out that it cannot. The complaint may conclude with a series of headings such as "Count I—Breach of Contract," "Count II—Breach of Implied Warranty of Fitness for a Particular Purpose," and "Count III—Fraud in the Inducement." These counts are stating explicitly the q in the "if p, then q" major premise of the legal claim. The complaint drafter sets forth all of the necessary allegations constituting p in numbered paragraphs under a heading like "Factual Allegations," and then incorporates those allegations into the paragraphs of the count asserting the legal consequence of the allegations.

This theory-making is at the heart of pure lawyering. As the *Educating Lawyers* Summary observed, "law schools emphasize the priority of analytic thinking, in which students learn to categorize and discuss persons and events in highly generalized terms."[33] Students learn to abstract from the real-life situations those facts that are critical to the modus ponens rule application in the pursuit of a client's cause. In my own experience as a litigator, for example, after the long slog of discovery, I would write a trial brief that set forth our legal theories and the facts we expected to adduce at trial. As the *Educating Lawyers* Summary suggests, that would complete the task of "redefining messy situations of actual or potential conflict as opportunities for advancing a client's cause through legal argument before a judge or through negotiation."[34] These were legal skills *par excellence*: the slicing, dicing, and sorting of disputes into factual nuggets that satisfied the "if p" portion of the major premise of the rules which, taken together, would spit out a result in my clients' favor.

Theory-making when thinking academically about law

In legal academia, theory has a different connotation. The overlap with legal theories in practice is that, in both instances, theory-making is the attempt to use organizing principles reductively to express coherent meaning about a set of events in the real world. As Holmes noted,

> The process is one, from a lawyer's statement of the case, eliminating as it does all the dramatic elements with which his client's story has clothed it, and retaining only the facts of legal import, up to the final analyses and abstract universals of theoretic jurisprudence.[35]

---

33 WILLIAM M. SULLIVAN, ET AL., EDUCATING LAWYERS: PREPARATION FOR THE PROFESSION OF LAW (2007). This appears in a summary of the report available on the Carnegie Foundation's website at 5, http://archive.carnegiefoundation.org/pdfs/elibrary/elibrary_pdf_632.pdf.

34 *Id*. at 6.

35 Holmes, *supra* note 6, at 991.

The problem with either practical or academic legal theorizing is the same as with all social science theorizing outlined earlier. Theorizing about law means we are trying to explain human interaction. In that case, the objects of the study, unlike planets or electrons, really do have purposes. The scholar generally regarded as the 20th century's pre-eminent jurisprudential theorist on the nature of law, H.L.A. Hart, understood this. It is not enough merely to be objective observers of legal actors going about their business to understand the law. Theorizing in a complete way about law means that we also have to understand that law is meaningful to the actors in legal systems as justifications for action or inaction *subjectively*, or in Hart's famous coinage, from their internal point of view.[36]

In essence, Hart presaged Thomas Haskell's critique of Hempelian covering laws in the context of jurisprudence. Take, for example, two lawyers, Kim and Sasha, negotiating a contract. There is something that is reminiscent of seeking equilibrium in the process by which they reach an agreement. The discussion resembles the oscillations of a wave as Kim and Sasha stake out their positions, including all the "wanna haves" with the "gotta haves." As they give and take, the amplitude of the wave reduces, and the equilibrium state is agreement.

Compare that to the equilibrium-seeking nature of a toilet bowl float or an economic market. We don't try to justify conduct in those cases; we seek simply to understand what appear to be physical or social mechanisms so regular that we can propose descriptive and predictive theories or laws. The meaning we take when the toilet tank fills and the water stops running or the market establishes a price for winter wheat is far different from the meaning we take when the negotiating stops and the parties sign their contract. Moreover, there is no subjective meaning for the toilet, only the meaning taken by observers of the physical process. That is not true of either the parties or the lawyers to the contract. They all have internal points of view about the process.

Theorizing is reductive. It pares the matter under consideration down to the essential rules or principles, explaining the whole of the thing with fewer bits and bytes of information than the whole of the thing itself. In law practice, it is entirely possible for otherwise competent lawyers to reduce the problem to a set of legal algorithms and nevertheless miss non-legal subjective meanings attributable to the very reduction itself.

Here's an example from my transactional practice. Some years ago, one of my clients worked with another company to create a complex joint venture in Europe. The two parent companies had complementary businesses, and there were clear cost and growth synergies available if they were to combine the businesses. The industrial logic of the situation dictated that the venture be organized as a single company. But neither company was willing to sell its business to the other. So instead they agreed to form a joint venture in which each parent would contribute the relevant assets. The problem for one of the parents, however, was that the tax

36 H.L.A. HART, THE CONCEPT OF LAW 88–90 (2d ed. 1994).

law of many European countries did not recognize, as does United States tax law, the concept of a tax-free contribution to a newly formed venture to be owned by the contributing venturers. Because the assets of the parent had a low tax basis but substantial current market value, a number of the European countries would have recognized substantial capital gains on the transaction, creating a prohibitive tax liability even though there was no cash changing hands.

We dealt with this ingeniously (so we thought as lawyers) through an exercise of transaction pure lawyering. We created a "virtual organization" in which the parties never formed a new company, never contributed assets, but operated under a complex web of lease, management, and services agreements. In terms of the legal effect, there was simply no difference in consequence between what we created and forming the venture under the umbrella of a single company. At least that was the legal and tax theory!

Within a short time, it became clear that the venture did not work. The organizational logic, so clear to us as lawyers, was insufficiently transparent to the two business organizations. Being organized as a single company with a single chief executive officer had a meaning to the employees that transcended the legal logic. Divisional, functional, and regional turf battles, present in even the most tightly integrated businesses, were largely unresolvable. Even though both parents vested authority under their management contracts in a single managing director, it was clear that very few people saw the relationship as permanent, or believed that their primary loyalties needed to be directed to the venture rather than their parent companies. The form of organization we had chosen evoked meaning far removed from anything we had considered as legal or tax technicians.

Nevertheless, the great value of reductive theory, whether in law practice or in the extension of scientific knowledge, is how it allows the theorist to make sense and impose order. The theorist could be employing reason to describe the natural world, justify a moral decision, litigate a tort case, or structure a tax-efficient joint venture. Business schools have departments devoted to organizational science, and no doubt there is theory that explains why our joint venture did not succeed. The great aspiration of the modern legal academia is to avail itself similarly of the explanatory power of theory.

Unsurprisingly, the conception of law as science arose contemporaneously with the emergence of social science disciplines generally. As Langdell observed in the foreword to his revolutionary 1871 casebook on contracts:

> Law, considered as a science, consists of certain principles or doctrines. To have such a mastery of these as to be able to apply them with constant facility and certainty to the ever-tangled skein of human affairs, is what constitutes a true lawyer; and hence to acquire that mastery should be the business of every earnest student of law.[37]

---

37 C.C. LANGDELL, SELECTION OF CASES ON THE LAW OF CONTRACTS vi (1871).

In Langdell's conception, scientific understanding of law was a matter of classifying and arranging the "if-then" rules that lawyers use in their modus ponens inferences so as to reduce the number of truly fundamental ones. In contract law, in particular, Langdell saw it as "possible without exceeding comparatively moderate limits, to select, classify, and arrange all the cases which had contributed in any important degree to the growth, development, or establishment of any of its essential doctrines."[38] The grouping of rules into the now almost universal subject matter classification of the first law school curriculum—contracts, torts, civil procedure, criminal law—is a legacy of this conception.[39]

To at least one scholar, Langdell was the Plato to the Aristotle of legal theorists who followed. He "had a faith that the common law had an inner logic, one that rested on principles, as did the physical universe [and] had an independent existence that could be discovered through careful study."[40] For a law professor to suggest nowadays that he conceives of law in the Langdellian sense is akin to saying he also uses a buggy whip when driving. But even now, when thinking about the law as the subject we study and practice, it is hard to shake metaphors of physical or metaphysical vastness and complexity. In Jewish tradition, for example, the metaphor for the Talmud, the multi-volume compendium of criminal and civil law and commentary, is "an ocean, vast in extent, unfathomable in depth, with an ocean-like sense of immensity and movement about it."[41]

Almost two thousand years later, the great realist Oliver Wendell Holmes was still evoking similar images. In his iconic essay, *The Path of the Law*, he began with the observation that legal duties were nothing but predictions of the legal consequence of acts or omissions (and that the number of such predictions "when generalized and reduced to a system is not unmanageably large"),[42] but ended with a peroration about the majesty underlying the theory of the law, and the non-monetary rewards available to those willing to explore it:

> The remoter and more general aspects of the law are those which give it universal interest. It is through them that you not only become a great master in your calling, but connect your subject with the universe and catch an echo of the infinite, a glimpse of its unfathomable process, a hint of the universal law.[43]

38 *Id.* at vii.
39 Grey, *supra* note 5, at 49 n.178; Ellsworth, *supra* note 5, at 896–98.
40 Douglas G. Baird, *Reconstructing Contracts:* Hamer v. Sidway, in CONTRACTS STORIES 165 (Douglas G. Baird, ed. 2007).
41 J.H. HERTZ, FOREWORD TO THE SONCINO TALMUD (1938).
42 Holmes, *supra* note 6, at 992.
43 *Id.* at 1009.

Whether many or most law professors still believe this is an open question. The authors of a contracts casebook I have used observe that what jurisprudence (the domain of law professors) supplies in studying contract law is the difference between "merely mechanical acquisition of rote doctrine" and "truly understanding it as an integrated whole."[44] That is one piece of evidence in my casual and non-rigorous empiricism where the impulse survives, even if surreptitiously or unconsciously, to presume law's immanent and mind-independent structure.

A fine example of this shadow of immanence is the bane of most first-year law students—the complex set of rules comprising the doctrine of consideration. The history of the doctrine is a microcosm of the development of Anglo-American common law generally, with roots in the English writs of covenant and debt, the evolution of those writs into something called assumpsit, the attempts by Langdell and his colleagues at the Harvard Law School to generalize the rules, and the application of the rules in significant cases decided by influential judges (like Benjamin Cardozo) in the first decades of the 20th century.[45]

The rules of consideration have an easily understandable doctrinal raison d'être. When promisor doesn't fulfill a promise, and the promisee sues to enforce it, the promisor might well defend by saying something like "even assuming it was a promise, it was a family or social and not a business obligation, and enforcing it really gets the courts into the unseemly business of enforcing family social obligations." So the rules developed, not by way of a comprehensive and coherent exegesis on the nature of business versus social obligations, but case by case as judges were obliged to articulate, when the issue of "enforce" versus "don't enforce" was at the heart of the particular litigation, the "if-then" rules that distinguished one from the other. We would laugh at the idea of a guardian *ad litem* taking on the case of a ten-year-old suing Daddy for failure to take her to the Dairy Freeze on Saturday as promised. Okay, but what about the case filed by several parents against the tee ball coach who broke his promise to give all the children equal playing time? The art of pure lawyering provides a basis for constructing such a claim if the lawyers for the parents can find colorable evidence that the antecedent circumstances supporting the legal conclusion of consideration were present!

The reason the doctrine of consideration is so frustrating to students and teachers alike is that the subject defies precisely the kind of reductive generalization to which the Langdellians aspired. The issue in each situation boils down to "enforce" or "don't enforce" a putative commitment. The prototype of an enforceable promise is a commercial bargain. Well, should you enforce the commitment if it wasn't really a bargain but the promisee did something on account of the promise? Lawyers and judges later articulated rules for promissory estoppel that would have avoided the bargain issue entirely, but that doctrine

---

44 CARTER G. BISHOP & DANIEL D. BARNHIZER, CONTRACTS: CASES AND THEORY OF CONTRACTUAL OBLIGATION 2 (2d ed. 2015).

45 *Id.* at 50–53; Baird, *supra* note 40, at 161–65.

wasn't available when the New York Court of Appeals decided the famous case of *Hamer v. Sidway* in 1891.[46] There the court enforced an uncle's purported promise to give his nephew $5,000 if he refrained from the usual vices of youth until he was twenty-one, the court held that a mere "detriment" to the nephew—refraining from his legal right to debauchery—was consideration. Samuel Williston, Langdell's successor as the dean of the Harvard Law School, included the *Hamer* case in the first edition of his contracts casebook, and it has been part of the canon used to teach consideration, even though its facts demonstrate anything but a prototypical bargain.[47] Rather, it was an intermediate case, resting somewhere in the middle of the continuum between cases that are prototypical commercial exchanges and those that are prototypical social obligations.[48]

Casebooks now include cases in which courts have applied or adapted the consideration rules where the commitments similarly aren't quite like prototypical exchanges: (a) the performance of, or the promise merely to perform, a pre-existing duty, (b) a promise where the consideration is sham or nominal, (c) the promise is in consideration of past rather than present or future performance, or (d) the promised performance is illusory. One of the fine study aids for contract law that I have used as a text says the following: "It is not that the basic rules of consideration are difficult, arcane, or unfathomable. The real problem lies in rationalizing these rules . . . ."[49] With all due respect, I disagree. The problem lies in thinking that we are obliged to classify and reduce, à la Langdell, the myriad specific rules devised to adjudicate "enforce" versus "don't enforce" into fewer more general and more essential rules, all collected under the label "consideration," as though law professors were biologists creating a taxonomy of flora and fauna.

And what about metaphors going beyond mere immanence, à la Langdell, invoking not just thingness but some kind of consciousness in the law itself? As practitioners *and* academics, we have never given up metaphors of subjective willfulness as in "the law demands . . ." or "the law requires . . . ." Professor Steven D. Smith called this "law's quandary." Smith posits we all are now legal positivists and realists believing, in a Holmesian way, that the law is what the judge says it is, based on all the predilections, prejudices, mores, and standards prevalent at the time of the decision. If so, he asks, why do we continue to speak of the law, metaphorically or otherwise, as though it were something that is the product of some transcendent Author, existed before the onset of the present dispute, and which must, upon discovery through argument and application, inexorably apply

---

46 Hamer v. Sidway, 124 N.Y. 538, 27 N.E. 256 (1891). One of the earlier reported cases permitting estoppel arising out of a commitment in the future (hence promissory rather than merely equitable) was Ricketts v. Scothorn, 57 Neb. 51, 77 N.W. 365 (1898).
47 Baird, *supra* note 40, at 165.
48 *Id.* at 161.
49 BRIAN A. BLUM, EXAMPLES & EXPLANATIONS: CONTRACTS 177 (6th ed. 2013).

to the present matter?[50] And Smith notes Richard Posner's complaint on the hundredth anniversary of Holmes's essay: "The traditional conception of law is as orthodox today as it was a century ago."[51]

Nowadays, on the question whether theory leads to objective truth in law, even though there are schools of "natural law" theorists,[52] my observation is that the real intellectual divide in the legal academy largely parallels what Haskell described as the divide between the scientific Hempelians and the more skeptical narrativists. On one hand, to some (I think most) law professors, the presumption of order, and hence theoretical explanation, is the *sine qua non* of any conversation.[53] For them, the modern path to academic assessment of law and legal systems is to import theoretical insights from other social science disciplines like economics, sociology, or psychology. A discussion that seems "anti-theory" or unduly capacious must avoid the charge that it is simply "lazy thinking masquerading as theory" or, worse, mere brute ipse dixit of Dean Robert Scott's bête noire, the "wise man."[54] Indeed, the modern buzzword for an area of law not so treated is "under-theorized," a phrase that appears never to have been used in a law review before 1987, and 1,864 times since.[55] On the other hand, there are contending schools of jurisprudential thinkers who echo what Haskell called the "narrativists"—thinkers who are skeptical that either legal consequence or reasoned scientific theory have much to do with what it *means* to draw a legal conclusion from an antecedent set of conditions. The doctrinal science of Langdell and Williston provoked the Legal Realism movement; the modern reaction to scientific (albeit cross-disciplinary) approaches to law goes generally under the rubric "Critical Legal Studies."[56]

---

50 STEVEN D. SMITH, LAW'S QUANDARY 157–59 (2004).

51 *Id.* at 2, *quoting* Richard A. Posner, *The Path Away from the Law*, 110 HARV. L. REV. 1039, 1040 (1997).

52 Brink, *supra* note 28, at 54–57.

53 That compares to earlier generations of law professors, when the focus was on doctrinal explanation, but similar presumptions of order prevailed. For an assessment of this particular turn, *see* Mark L. Movsesian, *Formalism in American Contract Law: Classical and Contemporary*, 12 IUS GENTIUM 115 (2006); Mark L. Movsesian, *Rediscovering Williston*, 62 WASH. & LEE L. REV. 207 (2005).

54 Robert E. Scott, *Comments on "The Future of Contract Theory,"* http://itunes.apple.com/us/podcast/the-future-of-contract-theory/id388453580?i=94188629.

55 On March 8, 2016, I searched "undertheorized under-theorized" in WestlawNext Law Review and Journals. The search turned up 1,864 documents. When I filtered out all documents before Dec. 31,1990, the result was 1,862 documents. For Dec. 31, 2000, it was 1,759. For Dec. 31, 2010, it was 882. For Dec. 31, 2014, it was 161. At least in this database, the first appearance of "under theorized" with or without a space or dash in a law review was in 1987, from David Kettler in the *Law & Society Review* and Milner Ball in the *Northwestern University Law Journal*.

56 *Critical Legal Studies*, WEX, https://www.law.cornell.edu/wex/critical_legal_theory (last visited May 19, 2016).

In each case, however, it is the non-reductive, rule-less, lawless leap from observation to hypothesis, or vice versa, that is the source of the observer's perspective.
For the practitioner, it is the matching of either a known rule to a situation, on
one hand, or a known situation to a hypothesized rule, on the other. For the
academic legal scientist, the goal is to find the ur-rule that generates all the other
rules at the end of the infinite regress, and is responsible for all the coherent
order we are capable of perceiving in the legal universe. The drive for coherence
reflects the fact that scholars and students still aspire to the philosophers' aspira-
tional "view from nowhere," in which the objective observer studies cases in
which the parties are fighting after the fact over the consequences of their actions
in the before the fact setting.[57]

For the narrativist skeptic, it is patently clear there is no such ur-rule. Echoing
Hume's famous dictum, all legal reasoning is slave to one's passions, the pursuit
of power, and all the instrumental ends in between. The source of incoherence—
that is, the intuition of the realists and critical legal scholars that judges are making
up the law as they go along—is really just confirmation of the lawlessness of the
leap we take in proposing hypotheses. Rules (including the formal rules of classical
contract doctrine) will not dictate their own application to particular circumstances. Even an impartial judge must make a seemingly irreducible subjective
judgment in order to interpret the rules set forth in a contract and apply what
appear to be the parties' objective manifestations of agreement to the dispute
under adjudication. If this is true of the judge, then there really is no "view from
nowhere" that is the source of objective truth and objective justice.

The desire for coherence in legal doctrine and theory

At the outset of this section, I posed the question whether there are objectively
true answers in law. "Correspondence" is one philosophical approach to dealing
with truth. There what makes a proposition true is that it satisfies a relationship
to a state of the world. For example, what would make legal propositions true to
somebody who takes the natural law approach would be the correspondence of
legal propositions to valid moral propositions. As I have noted, that is a matter
of considerable debate.[58]

Another approach to truth is "coherence." That may be an even more powerful
influence in law. Truth under the coherence theory "consists in the coherence
among a certain body of beliefs."[59] I don't want to try to settle any debates about
whether coherence is a valid index of truth, but only to acknowledge that it is a
powerful influence in science and elsewhere. At least when it comes to the law of
contracts, the first-year subject I teach, there is no more common ground among

57 Thomas Nagel, *What Is It Like to Be a Bat?*, 83 PHIL. REV. 435 (1974).
58 Brink, *supra* note 28, at 54–57.
59 GERALD VISION, VERITAS: THE CORRESPONDENCE THEORY AND ITS CRITICS 4–5
   (2004).

professors and students than to find structure and coherence in the doctrine as a whole. In other words, first-year students want to know whether there is a meaningful and non-contradictory way to organize our understanding of the propositions of contract dispute adjudication so that like cases are treated alike, the propositions do not contradict each other either as stated or applied, and we have some basis for predicting how a dispute on a new set of facts might be decided. As the great Legal Realist, Karl Llewellyn, observed, it is inherent in our case law system that "we require [courts], or they have come to require themselves, not only to decide but to lay down a rule for all 'like' cases."[60]

This is not restricted to legal systems based on the classical formalism of Langdell and Williston. Regardless how you theorize academically about jurisprudential concepts, when we theorize in practice, we still largely do so in the old-fashioned way. We place the facts of the case within a category, infer the rule from other cases within that category by means of the general principles and concepts, and argue that is the correct rule to apply in the circumstances.[61] Even if there is no immanent structure to law, it doesn't strike me as a stretch to say that any system worth teaching ought to achieve "like and like" coherence for new cases as to which no existing rule indisputably applies.

The point of theory, like all conceptual ordering, is to provide coherent meaning to the experience, which itself means to see the experience as having significance in relation to something else. The desire to find meaning in experience is a precondition of reasoned theory; we theorize because we have already been hardwired to seek meaning, and reasoned theory is how we do it. Hence, it is natural to try to read all the rules that purport to be a system as constituting a coherent system. Again, to echo Llewellyn, "[J]ustice demands, wherever that concept is found, that like men be treated alike in like conditions. Why, I do not know; the fact is given. That calls for general rules and their even application."[62] What I am recommending here is a catharsis about the desire for coherence in conceiving of the law, and consideration of the likelihood that we ascribe truth to legal propositions merely on account of it.

Coming to terms with knowledge and belief

The constitutive and the regulative

We have explored in some detail the process by which we use reason to apply rules, the way we reason with rules to develop coherent theories of scientific and normative explanation, and our inclination to find coherence in the doctrine. I have argued that what we do in pure lawyering isn't the production of knowledge,

60   KARL N. LLEWELLYN, THE BRAMBLE BUSH 17 (Quid Pro Books 2012) (1960).
61   Grey, *supra* note 5, at 11.
62   LLEWELLYN, *supra* note 60, at 43.

but a normative process that at most can produce justification of belief. And as to belief, we are better off with a good modicum of humility.

What I want to discuss here is why it is so easy to confuse the things we can *know* by way of theory, and the things that are merely our reasoned and coherent *beliefs* about the way things ought to be. If I have already persuaded you, move on to the next section. Otherwise, we need to return to how we come to know something. One of the great insights of the Enlightenment philosophers was the rejection of theistic or metaphysical explanations of cause-and-effect in the real world. (I will return to this subject in Chapter 5 in connection with theistic or metaphysical conflation of natural world cause-and-effect with moral blameworthiness.) God doesn't make billiard balls carom in a particular way. David Hume rejected any metaphysics at all; we can develop laws of physics that predict the caroms, but those merely justify our long-standing observations that they always carom the same way under the same rules. There is no metaphysical reason why they have to carom that way next year.

Kant was not a rationalist like Leibniz, who believed one could obtain knowledge, for example of God, merely through reasoned thought. Hume's skepticism about rationalism interrupted Kant's "dogmatic slumbers" about metaphysical thinking untethered from experience.[63] On the first page of the *Critique of Pure Reason*, Kant, agreeing with Hume, began with the proposition that what we know comes first from experience.[64] But Kant did not agree with Hume's view that knowledge *only* comes from experience of the physical world. Rather, Kant disagreed with Hume because there are things we seem to know *apart* from experience, like the relationship of cause-and-effect itself. That is, if you didn't have a prior (i.e. *a priori*!) ability to perceive cause-and-effect, you couldn't even begin to ask questions about cause-and-effect![65] He called this kind of insight "transcendental" rather than transcendent, in that it provides the connection between metaphysics of *a priori* knowledge (things like cause-and-effect, unity, plurality, totality, etc.) and experience of the real world sufficient to allow you to make sense of things going on in the real world.[66]

The first major division of the *Critique of Pure Reason* is about how these *a priori* abilities allow us to integrate our sense impressions into basic cognition of the physical world. The second major part goes to the use and abuse of reason in uncovering either things in the world (as in science) or positing objects that are "knowable" not by way of cognition, but only because of the exercise of

---

63 IMMANUEL KANT, KANT'S PROLEGOMENA TO ANY FUTURE METAPHYSICS 7 (Paul Carus, ed. 1949) (1783).

64 IMMANUEL KANT, CRITIQUE OF PURE REASON 127 (Paul Guyer & Allen W. Wood, trans. 1998) (1781).

65 Kant's argument to this effect, known as the Transcendental Deduction, is famously difficult. An accessible summary can be found in Michael Steven Green, *Hans Kelsen and the Logic of Legal Systems*, 54 ALA. L. REV. 365, 389–95 (2003).

66 KANT, *supra* note 64, at 133.

reason itself. Let's return to the concepts of the *constitutive* and the *regulative* discussed in connection with reasoning our way to scientific conclusions. Let's call things that are empirically real and mind-independent "constitutive." That is, they are constituted of something that we can know because we experience them or have the possibility of doing so, even if it takes *a priori* faculties to do so.[67] Let's call reason "regulative." It is a process of using rules (or regulations in the broadest sense) to draw a conclusion. The issue is whether the regulative activity of the reasoning process, when applied to understanding anything other than experience or possible experience, could be constitutive. Kant thought not. It can be the *means* to constitutive knowledge, as in science, but it is not the *same* as constitutive knowledge.[68] As the Kant scholar Susan Neiman observed, "reason's major function is not one of obtaining knowledge but of providing regulative ideas that guide us in constructing science and sustaining a moral life."[69]

That is the key distinction. If you confuse either the reasoning itself or any conclusion to which you just happen to reason with the kind of constitutive reality your basic cognitive abilities can perceive, you can end up back with the kind of metaphysical and theistic explanations of empirical events to which both Hume and Kant objected. That is a problem.[70] All the regulative principle can legitimately do for you in terms of *knowledge* is to help you make sense of real-world experience.[71] If you don't apply your reason to experience (or possible experience), you are off into a world of belief (or even fantasy), not knowledge. If you reason your way into thinking that everything happens for a reason apart that which you know from experience, you are entirely capable of coming to the conclusion that an earthquake destroyed a city because its inhabitants were evil, or that the AIDS scourge is meant as a punishment.

Kant called this conflation of knowledge for belief "transcendental illusion."[72] In a way, it was a precursor of Popper's falsification principle: the only things we can *know* rather than merely *believe* by way of reason were matters of experience or possible experience. The transcendental ideas, like cause-and-effect, the products of pure reason, can have a benign use, so long as they are not taken for real things.[73] It is the regulative *use* of the idea that is important. Hideki Yukawa reasoned his way to mesons in particle physics, and Peter Higgs reasoned his way to the idea that a particular boson—the God particle—existed long before experiments confirmed it. But supposedly real things, like God (not the particle),

---

67   We will put aside mathematics and deductive logic because that discussion is complicated, and we don't need it.

68   *See, e.g.,* KANT, *supra* note 64, at 520.

69   NEIMAN, *supra* note 1, at 155–56.

70   *Id.* at 127.

71   KANT, *supra* note 64, at 345. Another accessible treatment of this portion of the *Critique of Pure Reason* is Roger Scruton, *Kant,* in GERMAN PHILOSOPHERS 47–64 (1997).

72   KANT, *supra* note 64, at 384–87.

73   *Id.* at 590–91.

cannot be the subject of constitutive knowledge merely because we reason things out to persuade ourselves that they exist.[74]

Moreover, while the products of reason when not applied to experience or possible experience are not themselves constitutive knowledge, reason's regulative nature is powerful. It will impel us to make things fit together systematically, whether descriptively or normatively, and whether or not there is empirically an underlying system.[75] When we classify legal doctrine as Langdell did, for example, the classification is a product of our inherent tendency to look for universals and commonalities among the particulars of our experience. That is the source of all hypotheses and theories: "the particular being certain while the universality of the rule for this consequent is still a problem."[76] Importantly, however, there is no reason to think that nature itself abides by the product of what our minds do to classify it: "Such concepts of reason are not created by nature, rather we question nature according to these ideas, and we take our cognition to be defective as long as it is not adequate to them."[77] It is our teleological impulse, our inclination to find the ur-rule, and one that we simply cannot prove or disprove.[78]

Moreover, the regulative processes of reason do not distinguish between empirical and moral issues. By the very nature of reason itself, there is always another question to ask, another particular to try to fit within the systematic whole, and our entire experience of seeking reasoned explanation operates asymptotically, as it were, finding more and more systematic unity, but without ever reaching the final unifying principle of everything.[79] Whether it is making a demand of order upon nature (an appropriate theoretical use) or seeking a correct answer to the practical question "what to do next" (an appropriate practical use), reason looks to subsume the manifold of experience in fewer and fewer rules.[80] *That* is the regulative nature of theory-making. It characterizes both Langdell's formalism and Dean Scott's rejection of the wise man's *ipse dixit*.

But reason in theory and reason in practice are directed at two different outcomes: in the former, nature, and in the latter, living morally.[81] In the Preface to the Second Edition of the *Critique of Pure Reason*, Kant famously wrote, "I had to deny *knowledge* to make room for *faith*."[82] I leave to others the detailed exposition of what he might have meant by faith,[83] but what resonates for my purposes is fairly simple. There is a difference between what you know empirically and what you believe morally. The words "true" and "false" don't

---

74 KANT, *supra* note 64, at 590; NEIMAN, *supra* note 1, at 127–28.
75 NEIMAN, *supra* note 1, at 128.
76 KANT, *supra* note 64, at 592.
77 *Id.*
78 *Id.* at 595; NEIMAN, *supra* note 1, at 128.
79 KANT, *supra* note 64, at 601–02.
80 NEIMAN, *supra* note 1, at 126.
81 *Id.*
82 KANT, *supra* note 64, at 117 (emphasis in original).
83 NEIMAN, *supra* note 1, at 157–64.

really fit when talking about morality. Rather, morality is about right and wrong. When you think your non-empirical moral reasoning leads to truth rather than belief, you are on your way to dogmatism or fanaticism. Susan Neiman put it this way: "For Kant, human virtue requires a stance that is demanding and complex: we must guide our actions by an idea of reason, yet any purported assurance that we have attained this ideal would be self-defeating."[84]

Kant's insights about reason still resonate. We human beings have a teleological hard wiring that causes us, as students, practitioners, judges, and professors, to *want* the normative rules we are applying to be a coherent and immanent structure, emanating from and justified by some accepted authority (whether God, Grundnorm, or Rule of Recognition). The end result of that hard wiring is a professional ontology of the law—something we as lawyers construct in our minds and take to be real and therefore important. It is no surprise that first-year students demand a coherent conceptual structure for the data thrown at them. They are, by definition, not yet trapped by the closed linguistic system of the professional community, but have enough experience with reason to expect a system.

I have no doubt, given how much our students demand a coherent structure, that in the absence of one proffered by their professors, they will, rightly or wrongly, come up with one themselves. For example, law students invariably prepare for examinations by creating an "outline" that aspires "to impose structure on what seem to be a jumble of case summaries, questions, their fellow students' attempts at answers, jokes and professional war stories."[85] Students will create a single coherent image of the subject they are learning, whether or not it corresponds to the reality of before-the-fact lawyering. Not surprisingly, the next step is to try to find single coherent answers in individual cases. As Llewellyn observed, "Man . . . finds more than one right answer hard to conceive of. And if decision is to be 'by rules,' the rules must be dealt with as presaging, nay, forcing, that single one 'right' answer."[86]

But pure lawyering, like the regulative process of pure reason that powers it, is agnostic as to the truth and moral value of outcomes. And to believe in the "thingness" of the law, rather than to see law as an activity, is to engage in a form of transcendental illusion. Though I never speak of it in those terms to my first-year contract law students, it is transcendental illusion about which I caution them almost from the first day of class. In the real world of working lawyers and business people, the end of the legal process in contract is something we can know because it is a document or a judgment or an order that has conventional meaning. The legal process itself, in the sense of contracts, pleadings, discovery, motions, trial, and appeals, is also empirically knowable. Why? Because they are constitutive of experience or possible experience, whether we know them as a matter of cognition or the exercise of theoretical reason. We *employ* the tools of

---

84 *Id.* at 131.
85 STEWART MACAULAY, ET AL., CONTRACTS: LAW IN ACTION 2–3 (3d ed. 2010).
86 K.N. Llewellyn, *The Constitution as an Institution*, 34 COLUM. L. REV. 1, 9 (1934).

the law in making legal judgments; that employment is the regulative exercise of reason. To mistake either the *a priori* regulative process of reason or the ends to which we can reason for constitutive knowledge of a thing-in-itself (like law) *is* to fall into the transcendental illusion.

An example of this is the complex web of consideration rules in contract law we explored earlier in the chapter. The contracts casebook I used for many years (co-authored by one of my faculty colleagues and a first-rate scholarly treatment of the subject) has a delightfully ambiguous allusion to the immanence of the topic. It introduces the subject of consideration with the following sentence: "Perplexing and long the bane of every law student, consideration is nonetheless the dominant and leading theory of contract obligation and the way by which most promises are made enforceable."[87]

The passive voice usage "are made enforceable" leaves the reader unclear who is doing the making. The authors are correct if the active voice subjects were lawyers and judges litigating cases that occurred after the fact of the promise in dispute, and thus seeking to make or making the promises enforceable. They would be the ones using consideration doctrine (and its constituent "if-then" propositions) to theorize the transaction was more akin to a bargain than a family or social commitment. The idea, on the other hand, suggested by the passive voice usage, that there is some law-like aspect of mind-independent reality, more akin to physics than morality, sounding like an empirical description of the way promises become contractual obligations, strikes me as an undue ascription of thingness to the law. Rather, the illusion of thingness is nothing more than a product of our ability to reason—at its extremes, transcendental illusion. No wonder students are baffled.

I return to the clarifying conception that law is less a constitutive thing to be known than pure lawyering is a regulative process or activity for theorizing how to get to an explanatory result. In my conception, knowing the rules for consideration under *Restatement (Second) of Contract* § 71 without knowing how a litigant is employing them in pursuit of an outcome is as arid as understanding the rules of inference in modus ponens logic without applying them to solve a problem.

Law as an animate thing

The ultimate illusion, it seems to me, is one I discussed earlier, namely, taking literally the metaphors for the law in which it appears to have an independent consciousness, and is capable of speaking, desiring, and demanding. Consider the central plot twist in the movie *Her*, which won an Oscar for best original screenplay.[88] A computer operating system, the complex set of algorithms encoded

---

87 BISHOP & BARNHIZER, *supra* note 44, at 49.
88 HER (Annapurna Pictures 2013).

in zeroes and ones, has Scarlett Johansson's voice and is sufficiently capable of appearing so conscious that Joaquin Phoenix's character falls in love with it. But is the operating system conscious in the way that you or I are? A computer could certainly understand the chemical composition of an avocado, or its particular viscosity, but can it experience the taste and feel of eating an avocado in the same way you or I can?

In philosophy of mind, this is known as the explanatory gap, the mind-body problem, or the hard question of consciousness.[89] Science has yet to come up with a widely-accepted explanation of how it is we have subjective inner lives and experiences as a result of our sense perceptions. Though the subject of some dispute, it seems to me a fact of the world that each of us individually has these inner experiences and known as qualia.[90] That we assume each other does is an example of inductive reasoning. There is no assurance from the premise that I have inner experiences, that everyone I have ever spoken to also claims to have them, that the person I see walking down the street also does. I infer she does in the same way I infer it will get dark this evening. It has always gotten dark in the evening.

Fiction, as in *Her*, allows us to posit the not completely unfathomable idea that we attribute consciousness or at least personhood to something that we can be pretty sure isn't a person. For much of another movie, *Cast Away*, Wilson, a volleyball, becomes Chuck's only friend, and you have to be pretty coldhearted not to feel a pang when Wilson falls off the raft and "drowns."[91] It certainly doesn't strain our willing suspension of disbelief that a young man could fall in love with a sympathetic iPhone speaking to him in Scarlett Johansson's voice. (Another example is Rod Serling's story "The Lonely" from the old *Twilight Zone* series, in which a convicted prisoner in solitary confinement on an asteroid receives a female robot as a companion, and comes to see it/her as a person.[92])

There is at least a plausible theory about consciousness that says it is merely on a continuum with, and not something irreducibly different from, what we would think of as artificial intelligence. (This is at the cutting edge of what we understand about consciousness. I say it is plausible, but my intuition is that it is wrong. Nevertheless, I'm open-minded about it.) Douglas Hofstadter popularized the concept in his iconic *Gödel, Escher, Bach*[93] and later in the autobiographical *I am*

---

89 *See generally* DAVID CHALMERS, THE CONSCIOUS MIND: IN SEARCH OF A FUNDAMENTAL THEORY (1997).

90 Michael Tye, *Qualia*, STANFORD ENCYCLOPEDIA OF PHILOSOPHY (Edward N. Zalta, ed. Fall 2015 ed.), http://plato.stanford.edu/entries/qualia. For a view that qualia don't exist, see Daniel Dennett, *Quining Qualia*, in MIND AND COGNITION 519–48 (W. Lycan, ed. 1990).

91 CAST AWAY (20th Century Fox 2000).

92 ROD SERLING, FROM THE TWILIGHT ZONE (1960). The episode aired in the first season of the series, 1959. Internet Movie Database, http://www.imdb.com/title/tt0734656.

93 DOUGLAS HOFSTADTER, GÖDEL, ESCHER, BACH: AN ETERNAL GOLDEN BRAID (1999).

a Strange Loop.[94] Consciousness occurs when the thinking machine, whether biological or mechanical, develops algorithms so complex they permit the subject to refer to itself and to consider its own thinking.

> In the world of living things, the magic threshold of representational universality is crossed whenever a system's repertoire of symbols becomes extensible without any obvious limit. This threshold was crossed . . . somewhere along the way from earlier primates to ourselves.[95]

The thesis (articulated by Hofstadter and others) is that algorithmic recursion is the key element that distinguishes the human mind and language from that of all other species, precisely because that kind of computational ability generates "an open-ended and limitless system of communication."[96]

My thesis is that, whether or not you accept the recursion idea for what makes us uniquely human, the logical, algorithmic aspects of law and lawyering, in all their complexity, give off the same aura of complex recursiveness. Law is not a closed logical system (like the arithmetic systems that were the subject of Gödel's incompleteness theorem), but it is rich and self-referent enough to give off the sense, as Professor Steven Smith pondered, of being the product of an Author.[97]

My intuition is that the issues of law's authorship in that sense are legitimately the matter of reasoned belief, but not the subject of empirical knowledge, and that to confuse the two is to fall victim to transcendental illusion. Merely thinking that something reasonably *ought* to exist doesn't entail necessarily that it *does* exist. To take a less metaphysical and more pathological example of this confusion, recall Humphrey Bogart's mentally unstable Captain Queeg in the World War II drama, *The Caine Mutiny.* Another crew sends the officers of the *Caine* a tub of frozen strawberries, some of which go missing. At the court-martial trial of the alleged mutineers, Queeg's downfall under cross-examination begins when he insists, despite having learned that the mess boys ate them, a thief had made a copy of a key to the icebox padlock and stolen them.

> "Ah, but the strawberries! That's, that's where I had them. They laughed at me and made jokes, but I proved beyond the shadow of a doubt, and with, with geometric logic, that, that a duplicate key to the wardroom icebox did exist. And I would have produced that key if they hadn't pulled the *Caine* out of action. I, I know now they were only trying to protect some fellow officer."[98]

---

94 DOUGLAS HOFSTADTER, I AM A STRANGE LOOP (2007).

95 *Id.* at 246.

96 Marc D. Hauser, Noam Chomsky, & W. Tecumseh Fitch, *The Faculty of Language: What Is It, Who Has It, and How Did It Evolve?* 298 SCIENCE 1569, 1578 (2002).

97 SMITH, *supra* note 50, at 52, 155, 172–79 (2004).

98 Tim Dirks, *Movie Review: The Caine Mutiny* (1954), AMC FILMSITE, http://www.filmsite. org/cain2.html.

Unlike Captain Queeg and his imagined thief, a belief flying in the face of the empirical reality, believing in a Transcendent Author of the law isn't crazy. It is simply a belief (or a theory) that cannot be proved or disproved.

A metaphoric approach to rule application in pure lawyering

Let me suggest another path to making peace with the kind of theorizing we undertake as practicing lawyers and legal scholars. I am as skeptical as the narrativists that there is any coherent structure to law other than that which we create in our individual and collective minds, and propagate within the closed social system of our professional education and practice. But I am as sympathetic as the scientist to the underlying impulse that there ought to be discernible order if we just look hard enough for it. Adopting my dualistic perspective is no easy task. It requires you simultaneously to theorize while being reflective and even skeptical about your own impulse to theory.

I want to propose here another way of thinking about pure lawyering that is more helpful than the futile exercise of solving the infinite regress under which there is no rule for the application of a rule. Hard cases are hard because legal propositions are the tail of the dog. The rest of legal reasoning only comes after our having made the "rule-less" or "lawless," sometimes called abductive, mental leap to a potentially helpful legal theory. That leap is the insight by which we recognize patterns in our Case C that are akin to patterns in Case A or Case B and which if one of the latter is applied in Case C is advantageous to our desired outcome. Only then do we begin our argument that the present matter, Case C, is more akin to one than the other. In other words, rationalization by way of normative argument (of the kind Joseph William Singer outlined)[99] only comes second. What comes first is the intuitive hypothesis that a rule from Case A or Case B might apply in the first place.

Conceptual metaphor theory

Conceptual metaphor theory (or at least what I find useful about it) provides two benefits in thinking about that intuitive leap to a possible legal theory. Theoretically (as to which I invite your skeptical critique), it is the best approximation of what is happening in the "aha" moment of hypothesis, whether it is a matter of scientific theory or legal argument. Practically, it gives us a way of visualizing the possibility of two different rules applying to the same situation and choosing between them.

Some background is necessary. What we are going to do is distinguish metaphoric thinking from the kind of rule-based propositional thinking we have been exploring for the last two chapters. Conceptual metaphor theory holds that

99 *See* Singer, *supra* note 7.

metaphor is "not simply an ornamental aspect of language, but a fundamental scheme by which people conceptualize the world and their own activities."[100] To be clear, metaphor theory is the subject of substantial debate among philosophers of mind and cognitive scientists. Some believe that metaphors carry no meaning beyond the literal statement. On this account, language divides into semantics, which is meaning, and pragmatics, which are the flourishes and filigrees by which speakers draw attention to their literal utterances. Thus, Romeo's statement "Juliet is the sun" does not really convey meaning about Juliet, but "is like using italics, or illustrations, or odd punctuation or formats."[101]

At the other extreme, two pioneers of metaphor theory, George Lakoff and Mark Johnson, proposed that metaphors arising out of the physical experience of embodied minds explain all of thinking, such that even propositional thinking (logic and mathematics, for example) is metaphoric. On this account, there are no transcendent or universal concepts, nor is there any truly abstract reasoning; instead, minds, reason, and thought are "shaped crucially by the peculiarities of our human bodies, by the remarkable details of the neural structure of our brains, and by the specifics of our everyday functioning in the world."[102]

Like Steven Pinker, who has also written on the subject, I am pragmatic about metaphor theory. One need not adopt either extreme to find the insights of metaphor theory helpful in thinking about our thinking.[103] It is true that some metaphors are dead, in the sense that we use them with absolutely no recognition of the fact that they are metaphors. (Pinker's example is the phrase "coming to a head" which alludes to the accumulation of pus in a pimple.)[104] But all metaphors were once new and fresh, and some continue to be. Moreover, metaphors are a fundamental source of learning and understanding: they are "tools of *inference* that can be carried over from the physical to the nonphysical realms, where they can do real work."[105] Metaphor in science is a "way of adapting language to reality, not the other way around, and . . . it can capture genuine laws in the world, not just project comfortable images onto it."[106]

Thinking about pure lawyering without the baggage of "thingness" means focusing on the way our minds go about imposing order on the world through

100 Raymond W. Gibbs, Jr., *Metaphor and Thought: The State of the Art*, in THE CAMBRIDGE HANDBOOK OF METAPHOR AND THOUGHT 3 (Raymond W. Gibbs, Jr., ed. 2008).

101 RICHARD RORTY, CONTINGENCY, IRONY, AND SOLIDARITY 18 (1989). *See also* Donald Davison, *What Metaphors Mean*, 5 CRITICAL INQUIRY 31 (1978). For a summary of the deflationary accounts of metaphor, and a response, *see* Mark Johnson, *Philosophy's Debt to Metaphor*, in GIBBS, *supra* note 100, at 39–52.

102 GEORGE LAKOFF & MARK JOHNSON, PHILOSOPHY IN THE FLESH: THE EMBODIED MIND AND ITS CHALLENGE TO WESTERN THOUGHT 3–5 (1999).

103 STEVEN PINKER, THE STUFF OF THOUGHT: LANGUAGE AS A WINDOW INTO HUMAN NATURE 235–78 (2007).

104 *Id.* at 238–41.

105 *Id.* at 252.

106 *Id.* at 259.

categories rather than logical propositions. The metaphor theorists contend that human brains evolved as result of our interactions with the physical world. Natural selection favored those minds that could recognize and generalize from recurring patterns, for example, that danger was present. The patterns themselves are capable of description as "image-schemas" by which we conceive of abstractions in physical terms. The critical aspect of this process is the "conduit" metaphor, "a systematic set of mappings from the source domain of physical objects to the target domain of mental operations."[107] As law professor Steven Winter describes it:

> In this conceptual mapping, a concept or idea is understood as an object subject to inspection, physical manipulation, and transportation; words are vehicles for conveying this ideational "content"; and the resulting cognitive operation is understood as an acquisition or "taking in" of that object.[108]

Such mappings are implicit in metaphors like "ideas are objects," "action is motion," "understanding is grasping," "categories are containers," "purposes are destinations," and "life is a journey."[109]

Central to metaphor theory is the concept of an "idealized cognitive model" or "ICM." ICMs are the basis on which human beings organize their experience by way of categories. Prototypical instantiations of the category sit at the core of the model, and with less prototypical examples radiating out from the core. Professor Winter applies this to legal reasoning in his critique of the conventional approaches to reasoning by analogy. "Most of what passes for reasoning by analogy is actually the process of radial categorization by means of [idealized cognitive models]. Reasoning by analogy, in other words, is an ordinary mode of category extension."[110] As another cognitive scientist put it, analogies and metaphors put pressure on category structures by "unmask[ing], captur[ing], or invent[ing] connections absent from or upstaged by one's category structures."[111]

Classifications and categories in law

The metaphor I want to use comes from Langdell's own powerful conception of classification. It is no great stretch to think of each category of legal propositions as a container or bucket. We have buckets for tort rules, buckets for criminal rules, and so on. Within each large bucket, we have smaller buckets. In contracts,

---

107 STEVEN L. WINTER, A CLEARING IN THE FOREST: LIFE, LAW, AND MIND 52 (2003).
    I can fairly say that Professor Winter's views of metaphor are in the Lakoff-Johnson school.
108 *Id.* at 53.
109 *Id.* at 15–16.
110 WINTER, *supra* note 107, at 223.
111 Mark Turner, *Categories and Analogies*, in ANALOGICAL REASONING 3 (David H. Helman, ed. 1988).

we have buckets for contract formation rules, buckets for remedies, and so on. Whatever the source of the cognitive inclination, something about certain bucket characterizations is more powerful than others, and we find ourselves responding to them. In my presentation of the *Batsakis* case, all the legal reasoning directs itself to whether the case should fall in the "bargain" bucket or the "exploitation" bucket.

But how do these categories and classifications relate to the logic of that pure lawyering? The answer is that they come first. They are pre-logical and pre-propositional. Philosophers as far back as Plato have recognized that propositions, whether scientific hypotheses or legal conclusions, often follow on a more basic pre-prepositional ability to perceive that non-identical things fall or do not fall within concepts, categories, and classifications. In Plato's *Protagoras and Meno*,[112] for example, Socrates demonstrated the problem of defining virtue. He proposed an *inductive* process in order to have Meno find "something in common" among all the examples of virtue, so as to distill its essence.[113] After the usual Socratic banter, Meno concluded as follows:

> But how will you look for something when you don't in the least know what it is? How on earth are you going to set up something you don't know as the object of your search? To put it another way, even if you come right up against it, how will you know that what you have found is the thing you didn't know?[114]

This is the Meno Paradox: that, in order to propose a good definition of virtue, you already have to know what virtue is so that you can judge whether your definition is appropriate!

Legal reasoning is no different. The conceptual metaphor in which classification or categories are "containers" is a means of getting closer to the intuition of analytic distinctions between cases that precedes lawyerly rationalization of the distinctions by way of legal propositions.[115] We classify by way of associative images *before* we justify the distinction with rational if-then propositions.

The usual tensions in hard contract law cases, for example—promises versus gifts, bargains versus exploitation, risk taking versus mistake—have cultural meanings that precede their significance in contract law. Thus, we can judge whether a particular circumstance fits within a classification even before we are able to express the propositional reasons for that judgment. This strikes me as the best way to think about the leap or the abduction in the theory-making of pure lawyering. We have metaphoric images of doctrinal buckets or frames. In easy cases, nobody disputes that the fact pattern falls into only one particular bucket. In hard

---

112 PLATO, PROTAGORAS AND MENO (W.K.C. Guthrie, trans. 1977).
113 *Id.* at 103.
114 *Id.* at 128.
115 WINTER, *supra* note 107, at 69–92.

cases, however, there is more than one bucket into which the pattern might fall. The first piece of the thinking process is not a legal proposition, but how strongly the prototypical image within that bucket or frame draws on the fact situation in dispute. In hard cases, we frame differently, and thus two of us can look at the same facts and apply differing framing metaphors, long before we ever get to the point of propositional analysis. *That* is what makes a hard case hard. *This* is the irreducible "aha" moment of intuitive freedom, when somebody faces a new situation, as in *Batsakis*, and there is no decision path that demands to be followed.

I give my students examples of the same prototypical cases supporting the conflicting propositions described in Chapter 2: (a) the condominium for which Adrienne turned out to have grossly overpaid Ben because of the need to do far more renovation work than she expected in order to make it habitable, and (b) the outrageous case of exploitation in which Mary sells Florida swampland to mentally disabled Sam. Which proposition ought to apply in *Batsakis*? The problem is that the analog, continuous world does not divide up into neat little boxes in which it is clear that Adrienne's condo purchase falls on one side of the line, in the box that is labeled "free market, you pay your money and you take your chances transaction," and that the Florida swampland contract falls on the other in the box labeled "exploitation." Into which category does the alleged profiteering in *Batsakis* fall? In the real world, there has to be an answer.

The Venn diagram

My teaching method is to provide a tool for visualizing the competing buckets and their potential applicability to the case at hand. In *Batsakis*, for example, we have idealized conceptual models of "bargain" on one hand and "exploitation" on the other, and these arise from physical events in the world for which we have clear and unambiguous prototypes. We make an initial intuitive judgment in each case about how close the salient aspects of the circumstances in question meet the prototype. The question is whether we even look to the proposition in that initial intuitive process. My suspicion is that we do not. Even when we have defined a bargain and exploitation in propositional terms ("exchange" and "shocks the conscience," respectively), we do not, in the first instance, turn to the proposition. Rather we associate the circumstance in question with prototypical examples of the category the proposition seeks to encapsulate. That is the "analogizing" in argument by analogy.

What makes a case hard is that it may fall in either category. The graphic device often used to assess situations of overlapping categories or set definitions is the Venn diagram. To teach *Batsakis*, I would use a Venn diagram like Figure 3.1.

The facts in the case sit in the overlap. I ask the students to use another metaphor, one in which there is a tug-of-war between the prototypes, in which the prototypes pull on the facts toward the application of one concept or the other. In litigation, winning is getting the adjudicator to believe that the matter in dispute is more like one prototype than another. In counseling, good advice

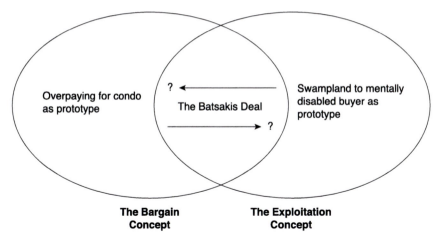

Figure 3.1 Competing metaphors of bargain and exploitation.

comes from recognizing where the fact situation rests on the horizontal axis that runs through the middle of the Venn diagram. Is it so much like the prototype of the category that no reasonable person would dispute that the proposition applicable to the category is the rule? If yes, it is an easy case. If no, the lawyer is going to have to call on inductive thinking to make a prediction about the inference others will make to the best fit as between the possible rules of decision.

Reasoning by analogy is simply one way of making the argument on one side or the other that the facts in the reported opinion resolving the condo case or the swamp cases, as the case may be, are more "analogous" to the transaction in dispute. Other normative arguments may be effective in pushing the judge to adopt one rule or the other.[116] Just as there is no algorithm for the abductive leap, there is no knock-down algorithm for deciding which analogy is better. (If there is such a program, it is going to depend on the parameters that the programmer determines are relevant for the quality of analogies, and that itself requires an abductive leap of theory, and so on down the infinite regress.)

Another example

"Is a corporation a person?" I submit there are only trivial answers to this question as a matter of knowledge. There are, however, a number of answers possible as a matter of pure lawyering, and some may or may not coincide with what you believe or want to believe about either corporations or persons. Let's use the Venn diagram to consider this. First, the word "person" has a number of meanings

---

116 *See* Singer, *supra* note 7.

in law, but it is reasonable to think that person first describes an idealized conceptual model, and the prototype of the model happens to coincide with the first definition of "person" in my *American Heritage College Dictionary:* "A living human."[117] That captures the idea that a person has a will, has consciousness, is entitled to rights, and is capable of assuming duties and obligations. A person is a subject, and has subjectivity. My son Matthew is a person. The opposite conception would be a "thing" or an "object." Despite the fact that my iPhone can talk to me and even answer simple questions, it is still a prototype of a thing or object (at least until I hear Scarlett Johansson speaking out of it).

There are things I can *know* regarding the "corporation as person" issue, but they and the deductive inferences from them are relatively trivial. For example, I know that a corporation exists if there is a certificate of incorporation filed in Delaware and the corporation has not been dissolved. I also know the Uniform Partnership Act in every state defines a partnership as an association of two or more persons to carry on as co-owners a business for profit.[118] Can a corporation be a partner? I *know* there is a definition of "person" in the act that expressly includes the word "corporation" as something that is a person.[119] I only need to apply the modus ponens syllogism to conclude that two corporations could form a partnership.

But there are circumstances in which the answer is not nearly so clear, and the tools of pure lawyering provide a means for arguing that a corporation ought to be considered either a person, on one hand, or a thing, on the other. We can visualize the problem once again as a Venn diagram as in Figure 3.2. In our particular case, is the corporation something more like my son Matthew or more like my iPhone? Which prototype pulls harder on the fact situation in dispute?

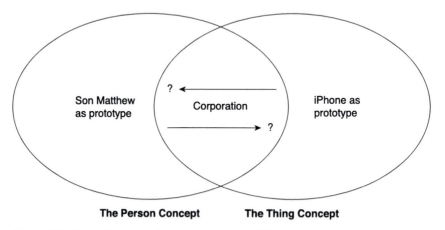

Figure 3.2 Competing metaphors of person and thing.

117 AMERICAN HERITAGE COLLEGE DICTIONARY 1038 (4th ed. 2002).
118 Uniform Partnership Act (1914) § 6(1); Uniform Partnership Act (1997) § 101(6).
119 Uniform Partnership Act (1914) § 2; Uniform Partnership Act (1997) § 101(10).

But we never care very much (at least I don't) about the philosophical or metaphysical question of whether the essence of a corporation is "person-ness" or "thing-ness." We do, however, care about it in context. Consider the following questions: (a) Does the attorney-client privilege extend to a dissolved corporation? (b) Is it constitutional to limit a corporation's ability to make contributions to political campaigns? (c) Can someone driving in a high-occupancy vehicle (HOV) lane claim to have two persons in the car because there is a certification of incorporation lying on the passenger seat?

As to question (a), the answer is not clear.[120] With respect to living human persons, the rule is that the privilege extends beyond death. Is a corporation like a person with dissolution being the analog to death? Or is it merely a thing that doesn't exist anymore? Pure lawyering is agnostic as to the outcome—if our abductive inference to the best fit is that the corporation is more akin to my son Matthew than to my iPhone, the privilege will not expire. As to question (b), the answer is *settled* as a matter of Supreme Court decision in *Citizens United*,[121] but hugely controversial and subject to reconsideration if the political balance of the Court were to change. The abductive leap in Justice Kennedy's opinion for the Court is that a corporation is more like my son Matthew than like my iPhone:

> "The identity of the speaker is not decisive in determining whether speech is protected. Corporations and other associations, like individuals, contribute to the discussion, debate, and the dissemination of information and ideas that the First Amendment seeks to foster" . . . The Court has thus rejected the argument that political speech of corporations or other associations should be treated differently under the First Amendment simply because such associations are not "natural persons."[122]

As to question (c), I am not making it up. A man named Jonathan Frieman traveled for ten years in a California HOV lane with the papers for one of his non-profit corporations on the seat. His defense to the ticket he received in Marin County from the California Highway Patrol was that the HOV regulation requires "two or more persons per vehicle" and that the corporation was a "person" under state law. Frieman's stunt meant to show that treating the corporation as akin to Matthew rather than my iPhone for purposes of an HOV lane was as absurd as doing so in political campaigns.[123]

120 Anne Klinefelter & Marc C. Laredo, *Is Confidentiality Really Forever: Even if the Client Dies or Ceases to Exist?*, 40 LITIGATION 47 (2014).

121 Citizens United v. Fed. Election Comm., 558 U.S. 310 (2010).

122 *Id.* at 342.

123 Justin Berton, *Corporation not person in carpool lanes*, SAN FRANCISCO CHRONICLE, http://www.sfgate.com/bayarea/article/Corporation-not-person-in-carpool-lanes-4173366.php (Jan. 8, 2013).

What Frieman demonstrated is the following: if you can pure lawyer your way to the conclusion that a corporation is like a living human for political contribution purposes, then you ought to be able to pure lawyer your way to the same conclusion for an HOV lane. In each of the three cases, and no matter which side you are on, pure lawyering is the same exercise—normative theory-making, applying rules to justify a legal consequence in light of antecedent conditions in a putatively coherent manner. The values underlying the pure lawyering come from somewhere else.

Conclusion

What we have explored in this chapter is the regulative nature of the process of pure lawyering. We have looked at the difference between knowledge and belief in physical science, social science, and the normative arguments lawyers make, not so much to resolve the difference, but to understand it. I have tried to make clear my view that we cannot know what the law is beyond very trivial aspects of it; the real game is in the theory-making that constitutes the pure lawyering process. For example, I might well believe that allowing corporations unlimited financial access to the political process undermines participatory democracy as I think it ought to operate, but that is a matter of normative belief, not objective, constitutive knowledge. My belief simply provides a source or a motivation for the normative outcome I desire, perhaps in the same way that your religious upbringing provides a motivation to use the pure lawyering process to seek justice—i.e. to make the world more like you believe it ought to be.

But does the activity of pure lawyering we undertake in advocacy or counseling justify us in believing the result of the thinking process, the "law," is either a constitutive moral truth or an abstract but coherent and knowable thing? You can believe that it does, but I will suggest in the following chapters that there are potential untoward consequences for doing so.

4   Games and Models

Someone says to me: "Shew the children a game." I teach them gaming with dice, and the other says "That sort of game isn't what I meant."[1]

A game for thinking about pure lawyering

We've explored the logic of lawyering, and how lawyers use theories to convert real life narratives into possible legal outcomes that favor their clients. In this chapter, I offer a thesis about two possible consequences of thinking like a lawyer, and then propose a mental game as a way of stepping away from pure lawyering and considering the context in which lawyers are doing it.

The consequences are, in a way, opposite sides of the same coin—how lawyers might come to think of the agglomeration of rules that make up the law. The first might be a cynical acceptance of the amorality of pure lawyering as an end in itself. As the ads in the airline magazines for Chester Karrass's seminars used to claim, "you don't get what you deserve; you get what you negotiate."[2] For lawyers who think like this, pure lawyering creates nothing but the result one wants. What is true or real is nothing more or less than the result one gets. I have a vivid recollection of when, as a young lawyer and father, I was having dinner at a Chinese restaurant with several of my wife's extended family, including a father and his sons, all of whom were solo practice lawyers. I don't recall the precise subject, but it was something like the merits of a lawsuit in which the plaintiff dove off a diving board into a partially filled swimming pool, and then sued the pool owner and manufacturer on a theory that they had negligently failed to warn. The gist of their attitude was something like, "Hey, if you can get a court and jury to buy it, it's fair game." I think I choked on my Mongolian beef sputtering how outrageous I thought that was. When you believe this, you make it sound like a

---

1 LUDWIG WITTGENSTEIN, PHILOSOPHICAL INVESTIGATIONS 28ᵉ (G.E.M. Anscombe, trans. 2001).
2 CHESTER L. KARRASS, "IN BUSINESS AS IN LIFE—YOU DON'T GET WHAT YOU DESERVE, YOU GET WHAT YOU NEGOTIATE" (1996).

game, and it's not. Yes, pure lawyering is itself amoral, but that doesn't mean you can't find standards somewhere! Be less cynical.

A second possible consequence of pure lawyering is at the opposite end of the cynicism continuum—an often unreflective and good-hearted willingness to accept that pure lawyering can lead to truth. Here, there is no distinguishing between empirical and normative theory-making, at least in terms of the truth value of what comes out of the regulative pure lawyering process. What I have in mind particularly are fellow law professors whose "scholarship" is really advocacy, and whose papers are legal briefs for an outcome that the author had in mind from the very beginning. We explored this in the last chapter: the very complexity of the law as a system of rules and theories gives it thingness, vastness, life, and often metaphoric subjective will, as in "the law requires" or "the law demands." Lawyers who think like this see the majesty or hear the voice of the law in the same way they open their eyes to the majesty and their ears to the voice of a deity. If that majesty and voice happen to line up with your moral inclinations, all the better.

This immanent morality has a way of showing up even in mundane disputes, particularly when the word "justice" appears in the rule. In the last chapter, we explored the consideration rule lawyers use to argue that a promise is binding as a contract because it is more like a bargain than anything else. In the early 20th century, cases arose in which the circumstances didn't look like a bargain, but the promisee significantly relied on the promise. The consideration rule, if adopted, would have been a coherent and logical extension of the law, but it didn't seem fair. Hence, lawyers argued for and judges adopted the rules that have come to be known as promissory estoppel.[3] The "if-then" logic of the modern expression of the rule is that the promisor has a legal obligation, not because there was a bargain, but because the promisee justifiably relied on the promise *and* "injustice can only be avoided by the enforcement of the promise."[4] In developing a theory based on promissory estoppel, a lawyer therefore has to establish operative facts that justify a legal conclusion about justice. Call me cynical, but if you really believe there is objective justice to be found when two parties are using the tools of pure lawyering (supplemented by Professor Singer's methods for normative argument)[5] to squabble over a broken promise, you credit the law with a reality and a moral sense I don't think it deserves. Be less naïve.

There is a middle ground in which the lesson is to understand the pure lawyering process for the amoral and non-constitutive thing it is, but not to accept that as the end of the story. I am as willing as the next person to cherish moral and ethical vastness, justice, and majesty. If there's justice and majesty, it's because of the just and majestic ends you seek with the lawyering, not arising from the lawyering itself. Thurgood Marshall's pure lawyering in *Brown v. Board of Education of*

---

3 *See* Allegheny College v. Nat'l Chautauqua County Bank, 159 N.E. 173 (N.Y. 1927).
4 RESTATEMENT OF CONTRACTS (SECOND) § 90(1).
5 Joseph William Singer, *Normative Methods for Lawyers*, 56 UCLA L. REV. 899 (2009).

Topeka[6] was the same as the lawyers who represented Lucy, Lady Duff-Gordon in her infamous attempt to weasel out of her marketing contract with Mr. Wood.[7]

The mental game in this chapter for stepping away from pure lawyering consists of thinking about law in terms of contrasting but related metaphors of games and models. Like the activity of pure lawyering, games and models are thick constructions of rules. Like pure lawyering, playing or using them is a matter of rule-application, either to win the games or to simplify the subjects being modeled. Are the following games or models? Football? Marginal revenue and cost curves? A jury trial? Financial statements prepared in accordance with generally accepted accounting principles? Business acquisition agreements? The game theory construct of the prisoner's dilemma?[8]

Is one's lawyering a matter of playing a game, making a model, both, or neither? If both, is one more *real* and does it have more *thingness* than the other? And what difference does it make in practice? The lesson from this chapter in getting beyond legal reasoning is to be able to identify when the matter at hand needs to be treated like a model not a game, or vice versa.

The family resemblance of games and models

In the last chapter, we borrowed from Kant the terms "constitutive" and "regulative." The former term is an adjective that describes the kinds of things about which we are capable of having empirical knowledge. The latter describes a *process* of reason, the end result of which *might* be sophisticated constitutive knowledge (like a scientific theory) or might be a belief that is incapable of proof one way or the other. In other words, we are equally capable of reasoning our way to scientific fact, to the existence of a deity, or transcendental illusion. But while I may respect our mutual beliefs in (most of) our (non-fanatical) respective conceptions of a deity, which each of us obtained by exercise of the regulative process of reason, it is not appropriate to consider the deities themselves as the subject of constitutive knowledge.

It turns out that philosophers of language and law have also used the adjectives "constitutive" and "regulative" to describe different kinds of legal rules. What they are doing is to distinguish levels of *realness* or *thingness* within the more general abstraction of the law.[9] While regulative rules "regulate antecedently or

---

6 347 U.S. 483 (1954).

7 Wood v. Lucy, Lady Duff-Gordon, 118 N.E. 214 (N.Y. 1917).

8 The prisoner's dilemma is the classic example in game theory of the paradoxical result occurring where the two players' dominant strategies result in each of them being worse off than if they stopped playing strategically and cooperated. DOUGLAS G. BAIRD, ROBERT H. GERTNER, & RANDAL C. PICKER, GAME THEORY AND THE LAW 33–35 (1994).

9 JOHN R. SEARLE, SPEECH ACTS: AN ESSAY IN THE PHILOSOPHY OF LANGUAGE 33–42 (1970). For other treatments of this distinction, *see* FREDERICK SCHAUER, PLAYING BY THE RULES: A PHILOSOPHICAL EXAMINATION OF RULE-BASED DECISION-MAKING IN LAW AND LIFE 6–7 (2002); H.L.A. Hart, *Definition and Theory in Jurisprudence*, in

independently existing forms of behavior," constitutive rules "do not merely regulate, they create or define new rules of behavior."[10] Classic examples of constitutive rules can be found in games like football or chess. The rule that crossing the goal line is a touchdown creates the concept of *touchdown*; the rule that we may not turn right on a red light merely regulates the antecedently created behavior of driving. New forms of activity created by constitutive rules may contain regulative rules. Fred Schauer used the example of clipping in American football. It is a constitutive rule to call blocking someone from behind *clipping*. It is a regulative rule to make it something that merits a penalty.[11]

A law professor friend of mine noted once that the law of property is distinctive because it has a "thingness" about it.[12] I think she meant it deals with real *stuff*, like land and buildings and inventions. It strikes me as being true in another way as well. The rules of property are more constitutive than most rules in other areas of the law where the rules merely regulate. Before we can play the game of estates in land, for example, and transfer Blackacre or create an easement across it, we have to build the game in which one has a fee simple absolute or other property interest capable of being violated. Constitutive rules in sports define the bounds of the playing field; regulative rules determine that there is a consequence for going out of bounds. Constitutive rules in property define the estate in land; regulative rules determine there is a consequence for trespass.

Both games and models are the product of constitutive and regulative rules. Practicing law can involve lawyers in some activities where the more appropriate metaphor is playing a game and some activities where the more appropriate metaphor is creating a model. Here I want to establish that there is a family resemblance between games and models in the law. In the next section, we will see how the process of pure lawyering might conflate them, and why that is a problem.

Let's first work with what a game is. Consider, merely for the range, the number of alternative definitions in a dictionary I selected at random: "activity engaged in for diversion or amusement"; "a procedure for gaining an end: TACTIC"; "a physical or mental competition conducted according to rules with the participants in direct opposition to each other"; "a field of gainful activity: LINE <the newspaper *game*>"; "any activity undertaken or regarded as a contest involving rivalry, strategy, or struggle <the dating *game*>."[13] Where does our willingness to call something a game stop? The insight from the metaphor theorists discussed in Chapter 3 is helpful here. Our images of games precede the attempt to use

ESSAYS IN JURISPRUDENCE AND PHILOSOPHY 21 (1983); David Lewis, *Scorekeeping in a Language Game*, in PHILOSOPHICAL PAPERS 233 (1983); JOSEPH RAZ, PRACTICAL REASON AND NORMS (1999).

10 SEARLE, *supra* note 9, at 33.
11 SCHAUER, *supra* note 9, at 6–7.
12 June Carbone, *Back to the Future: Intellectual Property and the Rediscovery of Property Rights—and Wrongs*, 46 ST. LOUIS U.L.J. 629, 630 (2002).
13 MERRIAM-WEBSTER'S DELUXE DICTIONARY 753 (10th ed. 1998).

language to define them. We should know better than to attempt to find a common thread or denominator for all usages of "game" or for all usages of "model." There may be multiple idealized conceptions of "game" having different prototypical examples. The conceptions may conflict, creating the kind of Venn diagram overlap we saw in Chapter 3.

The philosopher Ludwig Wittgenstein anticipated the metaphor theorists' intuition that language is itself a mental process in which we only secondarily define categories of related but different images. Wittgenstein used the word "game" itself to demonstrate that the different usages of a word resemble each other as do members of a family, but are not identical. As to "game," for example, Solitaire is one, so the definition cannot turn wholly on there being more than one participant; tic-tac-toe is a game, but it is hardly amusing; being in the newspaper or the investment banking game is one's life, not a diversion. There is nothing common to every usage of "game," but instead there are "similarities, relationships, and a whole series of them at that."[14] Each example bears a similarity to the last, but each is slightly different. At the extreme, something like picking up the dogs' dishes, taking them to the basement, filling them with kibble, and setting them back down in front of the dogs is not a game. We could agree something that looks like feeding the dogs could be a game (i.e. the first dog to reach the dish gets fed first), but the point, as in metaphor theory, is the absence of a defined frontier to the concept.[15]

On the other hand, what is a model? That same dictionary says a model is, alternatively, "a usu. miniature representation of something; also: a pattern of something to be made[;]" "a person or thing that serves as a pattern for an artist; esp: one who poses for an artist[;]" "a description or analogy used to help visualize something (as an atom) that cannot be directly observed[;]" "a system of postulates, data, and inferences presented as a mathematical description of an entity or state of affairs[.]"[16] One idealized conceptual model of a *model* is as a representation or a pattern of something else. A prototype would be something like the laws of physics, where the model is simpler than the reality. Its purpose is to capture what is important about the reality in a way that helps us make sense. Models themselves bear a family resemblance to theories. My boyhood creation of a miniature Mercury space capsule with plastic parts and cement was a model but not a theory; the most successful theory in the history of science, that of quantum physics, is known as the Standard Model.

Modeling from complexity to simplicity is most apparent in the most deductive of systems: computer science. There, the complexity of a sequence is an indicator of the cost of generating the sequence in memory storage (space) and

14 WITTGENSTEIN, *supra* note 1, at 27ᶜ.
15 *Id.* at 28ᶜ–29ᶜ.
16 MERRIAM-WEBSTER'S COLLEGIATE DICTIONARY 746 (10th ed. 2002).

in central processing unit expenditure (time).[17] The point of a model is to take the many bits of information available in a universe, and to construct an explanation (algorithmic in the case of a computer) that has a fair probability, in far fewer bits, of being able to replicate the actual universe of inputs.[18] We accept the explanatory power of models just as we accept the explanatory power of theories. It is because we assume a certain amount of coherent order or purposiveness to the universe through more and more general unifying principles. That is what Langdell thought he could find by scouring the case law, as we explored in Chapter 3.

Games and models bear a family resemblance. Each is a construct of constitutive and regulative rules. The rules of Scrabble® are set forth in a booklet or printed on the inside of the box cover. The rules can change, but only if we make express accommodations (ground rules, so to speak). As we move from the core of a game as concrete and real as, say, Scrabble® or football to language or aspects of the law as a game, we gain and lose attributes of what makes the thing being described as prototypically game-like. Nevertheless, there is a difference at the prototypical extremes of game-playing and model-making. Even when we are talking about something as ephemeral as the law game or the language game, what establishes the family resemblance is that the game still involves players. I have in mind the 1982 movie *Tron*, in which Jeff Bridges's character hacks into a computer game, is sucked into the program, and becomes an actual participant in the virtual battle.[19] He transformed from modeler (programmer) to player (gladiator). In short, in addition to rules, we can say the game is real if we have players *in* it, and not merely using the idea of a game as a model to explain something else.

In contrast, at the other end of the polarity, the essence of a model is third-person objectivity. The modeler is not a game player. She is observing a complex slice of reality and using a tool to reduce it to something shorter, simpler, and more understandable, at least as to the point she wants to make. It seems to me no coincidence that we often use games as models. Seeing a particular complex reality in the form of the game simplifies and explains it. Moreover, using the game as a model permits the objective observer-modeler to teach or explain the actions of the player.

In the continuum of family-related games and models, the prototypical game requires the player to have some subjective understanding of the rules, an internal point of view, whether or not the player has thought about whether the activity is a game. Let's assume we set up a small wooden maze with a start and finish line. If we were to place mice at the start and declared the first one over the finish line to be a winner, would the mice be players? Unless the mice have an internal

---

17 F.T. Arecchi, *Complexity, Complex Systems, and Adaptation*, 879 ANNALS N.Y. ACAD. SCI. 45, 46 (1999); *see also* MELANIE MITCHELL, COMPLEXITY: A GUIDED TOUR 98–100 (2009).

18 Arecchi, *supra* note 17, at 48.

19 TRON (Walt Disney Productions 1982).

point of view, I think not. If there is "gameness" to the activity, it comes from the internal point of view of the observers of the mice, not the mice themselves. On the other hand, it's entirely conceivable that running mice through mazes serves as a model that helps explain something else. In that case, the internal point of view toward the game of either the mice or the observer is irrelevant.

The implication is that there something common to usages of the "game" concept, i.e. that the thing so categorized is real. In contrast, there is something common to usages of the "model" concept, i.e. the thing so categorized stands in for something else. When I'm watching rugby, I'm seeing a game. When I'm looking at a marginal cost and revenue graph, I'm seeing a model. The latter is a system of postulates, data, and inferences that are representations of something else. The graph does not have "thingness" in the same way that the rugby game does. But the usages blur as we move from the polarities of the continuum toward the middle. The prisoner's dilemma, undoubtedly a game (particularly if you happen to be one of the prisoners), is used as a model, and the dictionary definition of a model includes the person or thing that serves as the object of the artist's work. The same could be said of our mice in the maze.

If we see the construct of rules as a game, at least some variations of the concept will include an *explicit* purpose from an internal point of view: to win or to succeed under whatever conditions constitute success in the game. Without engaging in too much amateur psychology, it is entirely reasonable that the competitive sorts who become lawyers might equate achieving the implicit purpose of what ought to be a model with the achievement of success in a game. We will explore that issue in the next section.

Games and models in law

Here are some examples of games and models as they appear in the law.

Litigation

The most obvious example of game-like structure in law is the process of litigation itself. Whether it is criminal, civil, or administrative, the process has players, teams, procedural rules, referees, penalties, winners, and losers. There are strategies and tactics. There is an order of play. There is dramatic tension as the judge asks the jury foreperson, "How do you find on the sole count of the indictment, murder in the second degree?" The analogies to other games come so easily as to be silly. In tennis, for example, the server begins play by tossing a ball into the air and, before it hits the ground, striking it with the racket so that the ball travels in the air across the net and bounces in the service court. In civil litigation, the plaintiff starts the game by filing a complaint that comports with the local court rules and satisfies the substantive pleading requirements of the Federal Rules of Civil Procedure. I could go on, but the point is so obviously true. Not surprisingly, trials are a common plot device in entertainment, precisely because they are so much like games.

Commercial law

Litigation as game is obvious. What may be less obvious is the extent to which games and models show up in the substantive law itself. Contrast Article 9 of the Uniform Commercial Code, governing security interests in personal property with Article 2 of the Uniform Commercial Code, dealing with transactions in (mostly sales of) goods. Even teaching Article 2 (and, to a large extent, contracts) is, to a long-time practitioner like me, a somewhat archaic exercise. In my experience, most real business disputes are about interpretation, and not things like offer and acceptance or consideration or defenses. In contrast, I had never taken a secured transactions course in law school, and dealt with Article 9 only cursorily in practice. To my surprise, I found the process of learning it and teaching it to be immensely satisfying, far more so than Article 2.

I concluded that the reason had to do with Article 9 being a game with thing-ness. The rules in Article 9 actually create a thing, a game, out of whole cloth. The key construct in the game is the security interest, which would not exist but for its definitional creation in the Uniform Commercial Code.[20] Depending on your particular interest as debtor, secured creditor, unsecured creditor, or trustee in bankruptcy, you win the game by creating an enforceable security interest, or by defeating the security interest.[21] The game has rules of conduct and procedure, but it is as much a game as football, which would not exist but for the establishment of foundational rules that set the field, the points for a touchdown, what constitutes a first down or clipping, and so on.

In contrast, the rules governing sales contract in Article 2 of the Uniform Commercial Code, and in the law of contracts generally, are "about" an antecedent and independently existing practice—the social relationship of promising—and therefore more like a model of something else. As an example, consider Section 2-207 of Article 2, the infamous provision dealing with the "battle of the forms" as an example. The drafters of the Uniform Commercial Code observed a morass of communications out of which the parties might well have thought they had an agreement, but courts applying the classical rules of offer and acceptance (the "mirror image") would not. Section 2-207 does not say "this is what you must do to create a contract" in the same way Article 9 spells out precisely what you must do to create, attach, and perfect a security interest. Instead, Section 2-207 tries to create a model of what is going on, and to interpret the parties' moves and counter-moves in the context of the model.

---

20 A "'[s]ecurity interest' means an interest in personal property or fixtures which secures payment or performance of an obligation." U.C.C. § 1-201(35) (1977).
21 For example, U.C.C. § 9-336(a) (2000) defines commingled goods as those "physically united with other goods in such a manner that their identity is lost in a product or mass." The rules of the game are that the secured party loses its security interest in goods that become commingled goods.

Business association law

Much of business association law has a game-like quality in much the same way. What we do in setting up a limited liability organization, like a corporation, a limited liability company, or a limited partnership, is not unlike arranging the playing pieces when we begin a board game like Monopoly®. With a set of constitutive rules, we create the playing field (filing the certificate of incorporation or organization, designating the number of seats on the board, creating offices, authorizing and issuing shares or units), identify the players by role (officer, director, shareholder, member, limited partner), and give them their playing pieces (shares, units). There are plenty of regulative rules authorizing, permitting, and prohibiting particular acts by particular players; they are found in the state and federal law, the charter, the operating agreement, or the bylaws.

In contrast, general partnership law begins, at least, with model-like aboutness. The law has an image of what it means to be a general partner, and imposes legal obligations on the parties if what they do is to act like general partners, whether or not they intend to do so.[22] Interestingly, general partnership law illuminates some of the nuance in the game-model distinction. Partnership law does not forbid the parties to opt out of the model and into games they create themselves. It is certainly possible for lawyers as game-creators to construct a more game-like arrangement through the partnership agreement. But in the default situation, general partnership is something of a game-model hybrid, because only by having been so deemed does the arrangement take on some "thingness." Hence, we have the long-standing debate over whether partnerships are entities (i.e. things in themselves) or merely contractual aggregations of assets (i.e. a legal model that is about what the parties have done).[23]

Contracts

Contracts are the most interesting subjects, at least the substantive law, of my game-model metaphor. Like an electron, which in physics sometimes looks like a wave and sometimes looks like a particle, a contract is an elusive thing. Sometimes it is a model, and not real. It is a model because it is an expression of what is essential about the underlying transaction it reflects, but necessarily in fewer bits of information than the whole of the deal. It is a map of the transaction in the same way that the diagram in Google Maps is a diagram of Cambridge, Massachusetts. If the map contained as much information as the reality of all of Cambridge, it would lose its utility as a map. The same is true of contracts, even

---

22 *See* Uniform Partnership Act § 202(a) (1997) (defining partnership as "the association of two or more persons to carry on as co-owners a business for profit forms a partnership, *whether or not the parties intend to form a partnership*") (emphasis added).

23 *See, e.g.,* Alfred D. Youngwood & Deborah B. Weiss, *Partners and Partnerships—Aggregate vs. Entity Outside of Subchapter K*, 48 TAX LAWYER 39 (1994).

those as lengthy and complex as the multi-hundred page volumes it takes to document a billion-dollar business acquisition. Perhaps a dozen lawyers are involved in drafting the agreements, but the deal and the resulting business integration involve hundreds or thousands of people and everything they know.

Sometimes the contract drafters intentionally create a game within the contract. A contract can be a model that seeks to predict future events and the exercise in pure lawyering is to dictate the legal consequences resulting from those events. It is akin to writing a document that predicts moves and counter-moves in a chess game. I once negotiated a lease that dealt with the following situation. Tenant leased commercial space in Building 1 from Landlord, but wanted to downsize. Landlord had alternatives both in Building 1 and a proposed new Building 2. The final contract created a game with a progression from Tenant resident in its present space to six possible outcomes too detailed to bother replicating here. At each step, the possible outcomes in the real world grew exponentially, but the flow chart implicit in the contract charted only a select few from which either party could make choices. At some point, the flow chart became too complex and the solution at that point was to have the game end by declaration of a breach or the right to walk away rather than to make another choice.

Another example is the post-closing adjustment typically found in a business acquisition agreement. The buyer will undertake due diligence on the present state of the business it is buying. The centerpiece of that effort is usually a balance sheet from the most recent year or quarter end, called the Reference Balance Sheet ("RBS"). The RBS will have been the focus of due diligence because the seller will have prepared one in the ordinary course of its business, and it is the best evidence of the seller's own view of the business's financial condition. But the parties recognize that both the RBS and the contract description of business assets being sold and liabilities being transferred are models. In the model, the net book equity in the RBS becomes a numerical proxy for the value of the business upon which the parties negotiated between the price of the business.[24]

There is, however, invariably a gap between the date of the RBS and the actual closing date. Hence, the numerical proxy may become obsolete due to the changes in the financial condition over the period of that gap. To deal with this, the parties often include what is known as a post-closing price adjustment provision. Shortly after the deal successfully closes, the parties prepare *another* balance sheet, known as the Closing Balance Sheet ("CBS"), effective as of the closing date. The net difference in book net equity between the CBS and the RBS will correspond dollar for dollar to an adjustment in the purchase price. For example, assume the net book equity of the business on the RBS was $200 million and the purchase price

---

24 There is no necessary relationship between the net book equity and the price. The net book equity is an accounting calculation under generally accepted accounting principles. It generally reflects historical costs of assets, not market values. Price is a negotiated market transaction between a willing seller and a willing buyer. Hence, for example, the net book equity of a business sold for $500 million could be $98 million or $500 million or $1 billion.

was $500 million. At the closing, buyer would have transferred $500 million to seller. The parties then prepare the CBS which shows net book equity of $215 million. In that event, the buyer would owe the seller an additional $15 million in purchase price. If the net equity decreases, then the seller would have to refund some of the purchase price back to the buyer.

In drafting the post-closing adjustment, the parties are setting the constitutive rules for a game in which there can be a payoff to the seller or the buyer. In addition, there are regulative game rules. Either the seller or the buyer has the right to prepare the CBS. The other party will have the right to object within a certain period of time. Often there are rules that attempt to ensure that the same principles used in calculating the RBS are used in calculating the CBS. The game rules specify who the referee will be in the event of a dispute (usually one of the big accounting firms not already associated with the parties).

Sometimes the process of creating any contract model itself becomes a lawyers' game, usually to the great frustration of the businesspeople. It's a fair observation that many deal lawyers like to win "points" in the negotiation of the contract merely for the sake of winning points in the contract negotiation game. I confess that, when I was a general counsel and therefore the client, I simply left the negotiating room when our retained lawyers were fighting over the representations and warranties in the acquisition document. I knew they would fight about them anyway, whether the result of the fight made any difference and whether I instructed them not to fight about it. It was pure lawyering at its finest: if *this* ever happens, we want to make sure we have documented *that* will be the legal consequence. As I had already concluded the likelihood of *this* or *that* was close to zero, I would find an empty office and focus on something more important.

Conflating games and models

The core concepts of game and model thus differ in two critical respects: first, a game has independent reality, and, second, a game involves players and not merely observer-modelers. Here I want to explore the bad news: (a) there is a pragmatic consequence to confusing games and models, with accounting systems and financial reporting being a prime example, and (b) there is a difference between, on one hand, using a model to make "scientific" causal explanations about game players we may be observing and, on the other, understanding the causal reasons why game players act the way they do. What we ought to do is reflect on the conflation of games and models and their relationship to pure lawyering, and hence be better lawyers and counselors as a result.

Gaming instead of modeling

The example par excellence of confusing a model with a game comes from the way in which lawyers can be involved with financial accounting and reporting.

The process by which a public company reports its financial condition is governed by a complex set of rules ranging from the organization of the categories in the statements to the footnotes explaining the status of litigation, to how widely it must distribute the conference call in which the CEO speaks with analysts on the day after the periodic earnings have been released. The rules themselves come from standards adopted by the public accounting profession and are known as "generally accepted accounting principles" ("GAAP"), state corporate laws, and federal securities law statutes and regulations that incorporate GAAP rules.[25]

GAAP itself has language-like and game-like constitutive rules. Observers have noted that it has different dialects, definite and indefinite rules, and is subject to evolution and change in response to the changing needs of society.[26] It grows organically, like a language, as the result of practice.[27] The rules are "man-made" in that there is nothing necessary about accounting rules. It is an arbitrary system.[28] But GAAP financial statements *model* business results, among other things, in the same way the curves of microeconomics *model* a firm's price and volume decisions, among other things. Both simplify and explain an antecedently existing and far more complex form of behavior—namely, a business.

The ultimate goal of the financial accounting exercise is to present a model of the current state of the business accurate to within acceptable tolerances. It is still, however, a model, and thus will necessarily be different from the underlying reality of the business. For example, one part of the GAAP exercise requires management to certify, and the auditors to confirm (in accordance with generally accepted auditing standards) that the written financial statements fairly present as a whole, in all material respects, the financial condition of the company. Certification of "fairly presents" has a shared meaning in the rules and principles that constitute the language of GAAP. Both the accounting profession and the courts recognize, however, that GAAP is not the exclusive, nor necessarily even the best, language by which we communicate the state of a business.[29] The fact that the financial statements comport with GAAP (and fairly present the financial condition) is not a defense to securities fraud, for example, if the managers otherwise engaged in fraudulent transactions within the company.[30] To put it another way, the financial statements may or may not correspond to another reality that is the true state of the business in a way that satisfies legal and community standards.

---

25 *See* AUDITING STANDARDS BD. AU § 411; BARRY J. EPSTEIN, RALPH NACH, & STEVEN M. BRAGG, WILEY GAAP 2007: INTERPRETATION AND APPLICATION OF GENERALLY ACCEPTED ACCOUNTING PRINCIPLES 1 (2006).

26 ROBERT N. ANTHONY, DAVID F. HAWKINS, & KENNETH A. MERCHANT, ACCOUNTING: TEXT & CASES 8–9 (11th ed. 2004).

27 Epstein, et al., *supra* note 25, at 1–2.

28 *Id.* at 13.

29 *Id; see also* ROBERT B. DICKIE, FINANCIAL STATEMENT ANALYSIS AND BUSINESS VALUATION FOR THE PRACTICAL LAWYER 99 (1998) (financial statement earnings are not the same as value, but earnings are a surrogate for value because they are easier to measure).

30 United States v. Simon, 425 F.2d 796, 805–06 (2d Cir. 1969).

How can that happen? Although the constitutive and regulative rules of accounting exist to model the reality of the underlying business, they can also be game-like. There are players. The very nature of accounting is to keep score, and winning means showing more profits. The rules can be arbitrary and they are subject to interpretation. Game players have to decide how far they are willing to push their interpretations in pursuit of winning the game.

How might one play the accounting game? On the revenue side, "net income" on a profit and loss (income) statement is not the same as "cash flow" on the cash flow statement. This is because one of the underlying assumptions of GAAP is the matching principle: revenue reported in a given period should more or less match the costs actually incurred to generate it. Hence, GAAP uses the accrual method to match revenues with the appropriate (at least within GAAP) expenses within periods like quarters and years.

Here is a hypothetical example. Assume for the year 2014 that Amalgamated Widgets, Inc. had only the following dollar inflows and outflows. It bought a new $50,000 machine with a useful life of ten years. It used the machine to generate $10,000 of revenue in 2014, $2,000 of which customers didn't pay until 2015. On the profit and loss statement for 2014, the correct expense for the machine should be the extent to which it got "used up" during the year. If we "depreciate" the machine ratably over ten years, the machine expense in 2014 on the income statement was $5,000, even though Amalgamated shelled out $50,000 in cash.[31] Moreover, if Amalgamated charged customers $10,000 for services rendered in 2014, it had "revenue" on the 2014 income statement even though it received $8,000 of the cash during the year and extended credit to its customers (as an "account receivable") for the other $2,000. Hence, even though Amalgamated had a negative *cash flow* in 2014 of $42,000 ($50,000 cash outlay for the machine less the $8,000 cash received for services), under GAAP it had an *income statement profit* of $5,000 ($10,000 revenue less $5,000 machine expense).

GAAP has a salutary purpose. As financial analysts have observed, "[n]et income is just an opinion, but cash flow is a fact." [32] Nevertheless, $5,000 of net income during the period really *is* a better measure than cash flow for assessing Amalgamated's ability to take finite inputs and turn them into more valuable outputs. Moreover, in theory, somebody familiar with GAAP rules looking at Amalgamated's fully GAAP-compliant set of financial statements would know there was a difference between the cash flow and the net income and be able to decide if the difference were meaningful. Just like a pilot uses information from instruments to interpret the reality of the situation in flight,

> a person who is to make intelligent use of accounting information must under-
> stand what a given accounting figure probably means, what its limitations

---

31 Anthony, et al., *supra* note 26, at 200.
32 PABLO FERNÁNDEZ, VALUATION METHODS AND SHAREHOLDER VALUE CREATION 169 (2002).

are, and the circumstances in which it may mean something different from the apparent "signal" that it gives.[33]

The danger of a model becoming a game comes from the fact that the model is significantly more complex than this simple example shows. In video game terms, my example is to actual accounting as the game Pong was to actual tennis. There are many rules and somebody has to interpret and apply them.

Let's return to the depreciation of the $50,000 machine, for example. When we use a depreciation method, we are reflecting only a *model* of the extent to which the asset is used up. In practice, the business has to predict the useful life of the machine, predict its salvage value at the end, and adopt a method of depreciation. For simplicity's sake, I assumed the machine was used up at the end of ten years, and divided $50,000 by ten. This is called "straight line" depreciation. While the business could adopt my method, it might also select an accelerated depreciation method on the theory that the machine is more valuable when it is newer. In any case, it's an inexact judgment call based on what should be good faith estimates.[34]

Depreciation is just one of the many examples of inexact judgment calls under GAAP rules. Here is another. Recall that at the time Amalgamated provided the $10,000 worth of services, it extended $2,000 in credit to its customers. It recorded the customers' obligation to pay, the account receivable, as something valuable to which it had a legal right and therefore as an "asset" on the balance sheet. But it also might have recognized that customers do not always pay. GAAP permits Amalgamated's managers to estimate an allowance for bad debt (say, 5 percent of the sales price), which it may record and reflect on the balance sheet as a subtraction from the accounts receivable assets.[35] Hence, the revenue the business records on the books is a guesstimate (and even an educated one) of the ultimate benefit of the sale to the business. The recorded revenue represents the sales price of the services rendered and the invoice sent to the customer, but it is merely an estimate of how much cash the business will ultimately receive.

One of the most egregious, notorious, and consequential abuses of this kind of judgment call occurred at Enron in the late 1990s and early 2000s. Enron itself influenced the drafting of the accounting rules with respect to how companies in the energy trading business reported the financial impact of their sales. Enron would contract with utilities to supply power in the future at a fixed price set by the present contract. Enron based its business model on its purported ability to find sources of energy in the future at prices *less* than the contract price. As with estimates of bad debt, the rules permitted Enron to make estimates of future energy prices, and to report as current income the difference between the present

---

33 Anthony, et al., *supra* note 26, at 7.
34 *Id.* at 201.
35 *Id.* at 121–22.

known fixed prices and the future estimated costs. (This estimate of the present value was known as the "mark to market" technique.)[36]

The problem was not that the rules permitted estimates of future costs. GAAP regularly permits estimates. One such instance involves lawyers. Sometimes GAAP requires that a contingency of a future loss, that is, of one not certain to occur, be reported as an expense in the current period. This requires a prediction of the likelihood that a contingent event will occur and an estimate of the contingency's dollar significance. The rules are set forth in *Statement of Financial Accounting Standards* 5 ("FAS 5") promulgated by the Financial Accounting Standards Board. Under FAS 5, the accounting profession uses the word "probable" to indicate one of three different states of likelihood—the other two are "reasonably possible" and "remote"—that future events will confirm the incurrence of a liability.[37] "Probable" is defined as "[t]he future event or events [that] are likely to occur." In short, telling an auditor that the company has a better chance of losing a case in which the amount of the loss can be estimated is tantamount to incurring the expense not in the future, but today. If an event is probable and the amount of the loss is reasonably estimable, FAS 5 requires that the obligation be booked as a liability on the balance sheet. By the nature of double-entry accounting, it will also have to be recorded as an expense on the income statement. Hence, booking a contingent loss in a given period reduces a company's reported earnings—something not usually considered a good thing.

In the insurance industry, as another example, the companies' revenues consist in part of the premium they receive for policies. Companies, through actuarial analysis, can also predict with some confidence that they will be liable in the future for claims arising out of the policies they have just issued and the revenue they have just received. To oversimplify a bit, an insurance company reports its profits in the present period as its revenues during that period less "reserves," which represent the costs the company estimates as future expenses from both known and unknown ("incurred but not reported") claims. Those reserves come about by way of estimates, albeit sophisticated ones. But under-reserving has been the downfall of many a now-defunct insurance company. The collapse of AIG in the financial crisis of 2008–09 was just such an instance. Effectively AIG sold insurance, called "credit default swaps," purportedly protecting buyers of bonds based on subprime mortgages against the bond issuer's default. AIG collected the premiums, but didn't book or retain sufficient reserves against the massive defaults that in fact took place.

Similarly, the "mark to market" rules permitted Enron to make estimates, and Enron responded by being regularly (and allegedly knowingly and deliberately) over-optimistic about energy prices falling in the future. To invoke another metaphor, it may well have been that the relationship of the rule to the business

36 Floyd Norris & Kurt Eichenwald, *Enron's Many Strands: The Accounting; Fuzzy Rules of Accounting and Enron*, N.Y. TIMES, Jan. 30, 2002, at C6.

37 AICPA PROFESSIONAL STANDARDS (1987), AU § 337C, at 407.

was like putting candy within arm's reach of a child but stating the rule that it is not to be eaten. Nevertheless, given that Enron's executives were adults not children, the problem at Enron was not so much the rules, but the temptation. Enron stretched the rules as a matter of game playing to the extent that the financial statements were no longer a reliable model of any reasonable independent reality about energy sales. When investors stopped believing that the financial model accurately reflected Enron's value, the company collapsed, with all the attendant consequences.[38]

The extent to which GAAP is supposed to be a model should now be apparent, but the limitations of the model allow it to be played as a game. The crux of the problem comes from a paradox built between the way the rules of the accounting model versus the way it gets used. The point of the model is to have consistency both from year to year in the case of specific companies, and from company to company for purposes of comparison. Thus, one of the objectives of GAAP is to avoid, as much as possible, the kind of deliberate or innocent variations that arise out of estimates and predictions, and to rely on empirically sound historical data. Another GAAP objective is to be conservative; that is, to have the model underestimate assets and overestimate liabilities. Hence the general rule under GAAP is that assets get recorded at their historical cost. That value does not change over time on the financial statement, even if the market value of the asset changes, absent a legitimate transaction involving the asset. The paradox occurs because any moderately knowledgeable businessperson or investor knows that the present financial statement "book" value of a company's common stock, based on historical data, most often bears little or no relation even to the *present* market price of the company's shares as reflected on the stock exchange. Yet even recognizing this fact about the model, everybody, including investors and analysts, uses the information the financial model provides to infer something about the future prospects of the company.

The audit process does not resolve the paradox, and in some ways reinforces it. Even when GAAP rules permit managers to make assumptions or estimates, they are not supposed to be willy-nilly. The public accounting firms who audit the financial statements are metaphoric referees. The objective of the ordinary audit, according to the auditing profession, is "[t]o express an opinion on the fairness, in all material respects, with which the financial statements present financial position, results of operations, and cash flows in conformity with generally accepted accounting principles or another comprehensive basis of accounting."[39] This does nothing to resolve the "past-present-future" paradox. In terms of its use as a predictor, the auditor's clean opinion is a tautology, a meaningless circularity. All the auditors are certifying is that the largely historical financial statements satisfy the present rules for largely historical financial statements.

---

38 Norris & Eichenwald, *supra* note 36.
39 Michael J. Ramos, Wiley Practitioner's Guide to GAAS 1, 2 (2007).

It is hardly surprising, then, that the financial reporting system, which all but describes itself as a game removed from any other underlying reality, comes to be viewed by the players as a self-contained game and not a model. One of the reported comments from a member of the Emerging Issues Task Force, an accounting industry group under the supervision of the Financial Accounting Standards Board ("EITF"), which creates GAAP, was that the EITF made the correct decisions about the form of accounting Enron used for energy trades. He added, however, "if you are telling me that somebody who wants to game the system can do it, you probably have a lot of evidence to support that."[40] Moreover, just as a basketball coach "works" the referees from the sideline to influence the referee's interpretation whether certain acts constitute a foul, Enron appears to have "worked" the now defunct auditor, Arthur Andersen, to approve the aggressive accounting.[41]

The tactics need not reach the Enron level, but there is still plenty of opportunity to play the game. GAAP earnings are what Wall Street analysts (if not the company itself) use as an important present surrogate for their inferences of future earning power. The analysts calculate and publish their predictions for the company's future earnings (known as "targets"), and there is internal and external pressure to meet those targets.[42] Consider several different circumstances, perhaps some of which are less egregious than what Enron did.[43] First, knowing that current sales will not get to the earnings target, and feeling the pressure from the CEO and CFO, one of the business managers takes advantage of the arbitrary periods in financial reporting by actually holding back expenses (e.g., barring all travel for the remainder of the year) or actually bringing forward revenue (e.g., "stuffing the channel" by offering extended credit terms for sales made to customers in the present period).[44]

Second, the next quarter, even with manipulation of the actual sales and actual expenses, the results come up to the CFO and are disappointing. To improve the results, she takes two actions. She decides that crib inventories, heretofore expensed, are really capital expenditures, because they are rarely used in the year in which the inventory is purchased. The CFO thus issues the following statement: "Crib inventories are all capital expenditures." GAAP is complex, time is short, resources are limited, the CFO ought to know what she's doing, and divisional controllers proceed to capitalize crib inventories. The effect, as the CFO expected, is to increase earnings in the current period. She also concludes that the company has been over-estimating the likelihood of non-payment of invoices, and so she

40 Comment of Edward W. Trott, *reported in* Norris & Eichenwald, *supra* note 36.
41 *Id.*
42 Michael R. Young, *The Origin of Financial Fraud*, in ACCOUNTING IRREGULARITIES AND FINANCIAL FRAUD 11 (Michael R. Young, ed. 2000).
43 *Id.* at 6–10. I have borrowed from and enhanced the very helpful hypothetical presented there.
44 *Id.* at 7–8.

reverses a portion of the bad debt reserve. (Recall that 5 percent or so of each sale goes into this reserve as a cushion, against which actual bad debts are to be charged.) This practice is also known as "smoothing earnings," by which companies deliberately manipulate the revenues and costs in the various period buckets so as to conform to earlier predictions, either from management or from analysts.[45]

Third, in the next quarter, even after manipulating the actual sales and costs, and even after the accounting adjustments of the previous quarter, the net income numbers still fail to meet expectations. The CFO expects their announcement to have a negative impact on the stock. So she takes out her pencil, erases the revenue number, and writes in an amount that is 20 percent greater. This is fraud: "[a]n intentional act that results in a material misstatement in financial statements that are the subject of an audit."[46]

What we have here is a continuum that ranges from the legal (but possibly nonsensical) manipulation of the period accounting, to aggressive interpretation of the GAAP reporting rules, to, finally, an out-and-out lie. It is the process of turning what we all understand to be a model into a game. I leave to the rich literature in sociology and criminology the process by which those in the business might well rationalize from the legal manipulation to accounting manipulation to the out-and-out lie.[47]

Let us instead return to a simple concept of the game. What precisely is the company's obligation in presenting its financial statements? Is it to model the state of the business? Or, in the spirit of the tautology, is it to present its financial statements? Thinking about the financial statements as a game rather than a model may keep us from out-and-out lying, just as the rules in baseball against corked bats may keep players from using blatantly illegal equipment. But it is well known that umpires in baseball allow the "phantom double play" in which the second baseman or the shortstop taking the throw at second base never actually steps on the base to make the put-out (a concession no doubt to the fact that a runner is

45 *Id.* at 8–9. *See* Michael C. Jensen, *The Puzzling State of Low-Integrity Relations between Managers and Capital Markets (PDF Files of Slides)* (Barbados Group, Working Paper No. 5-05, 2005), http://ssrn.com/abstract=783604; Lawrence A. Cunningham, *Rediscovering Board Expertise: Legal Implications of the Empirical Literature* (GWU Public Law and Legal Theory, Working Paper No. 363, 2007), http://ssrn.com/abstract =1024261.

46 *See Statement on Auditing Standards* 99, in CONSIDERATION OF FRAUD IN A FINANCIAL STATEMENT AUDIT (2002).

47 *See, e.g.*, GILBERT GEIS & EZRA STOTLAND, WHITE-COLLAR CRIME: THEORY AND RESEARCH (1980); Nancy Reichman, *Insider Trading*, in 18 BEYOND THE LAW: CRIME IN COMPLEX ORGANIZATIONS (Michael Tonry & Albert J. Reiss, Jr., eds. 1993); VICENZO RUGGIERO, CRIME AND MARKETS: ESSAYS IN ANTI-CRIMINOLOGY (2000); NEAL SHOVER & JOHN PAUL WRIGHT, CRIMES OF PRIVILEGE: READINGS IN WHITE-COLLAR CRIME (2001); EDWIN SUTHERLAND, WHITE COLLAR CRIME (1949); Gresham M. Sykes & David Matza, *Techniques of Neutralization: A Theory of Delinquency*, 22 AM. SOC. REV. 664, 666 (1957).

hurtling into the fielder at a high rate of speed). We can rationalize the aggressive interpretation of the accounting rules in the same way.

Into this morass wades somebody who has been told that his or her job is to think like a lawyer. My concern is the amorality of pure lawyering, which I've characterized as the conversion of real-world narratives into legal consequences. Here the problem is its potential for inappropriate acquiescence in, or abetting of, gaming or modeling. When we are actually practicing law, and involved with financial accounting, we may well be obliged to step back from the process of pure lawyering and engage in the very pragmatic exercise of deciding: (a) what is true, and (b) what is the right thing to do.

The related metaphors of games and models can be helpful. Is it appropriate to modify results in a press release so that they don't conform to the GAAP model? It turns out that the rules of the game permit the use of a different model. Even analysts want GAAP results to be modified to better understand the ongoing state of the business. What sophisticated observers of publicly-held companies and consumers of public company financial information—the stock analysts— want information, but only that which is evidence of a particular value, defined loosely as the future earning power of the company. GAAP takes account of many historical events that do not impact this value, and companies and analysts, on their own, have long manipulated GAAP to understand it. We can advise our clients this is permissible as long as the company fulfills the requirement that pro forma results be reconciled to GAAP.[48]

But there are areas in which accounting continues to be a game consisting of arbitrary constitutive rules that have to be interpreted. The most direct instance of a lawyer's regular invitation to play the game is in the assessment of litigation loss contingencies. We saw earlier that GAAP, under Standard 5 of the Financial Accounting Standards Board requires a contingent loss to be recorded as an expense (and not merely footnoted) if it is "probable" and "estimable" under the accountants' definitions of those terms. Lawyers, on the other hand, use the loose language of probability to convey a sense of the outcome to their clients on a regular basis: "Your odds of winning are 50–50, 60–40, one in ten, etc." The result is an uneasy truce between the legal and accounting professions, which the American Bar Association (ABA) has attempted to explain in its *Statement of Policy Regarding Lawyers' Responses to Auditors' Requests for Information*:

> Generally, the outcome of . . . litigation cannot be assessed in any way that is comparable to a statistically or empirically determined concept of "probabil-ity" . . . . Lawyers do not generally quantify for clients the "odds" in numerical terms; if they do, the quantification is generally only undertaken in an effort to make meaningful, for limited purposes, a whole host of judgmental factors

---

48 Conditions for Use of Non-GAAP Financial Measures, SEC and Exchange Committee Release No. 33-8176, 2003 SEC LEXIS 193, at *7 (Jan. 22, 2003).

applicable at a particular time, without any intention to depict "probability" in any statistical, scientific or empirically-grounded sense.[49]

Each year, and some times each quarter, the company's auditors will meet with the general counsel to discuss pending cases. The auditors, speaking the language of FAS 5, will ask how probable it is that a particular case will come out badly, and if so, for how much. A general counsel might be inclined to play the financial statement game. She understands the difference between legal and accounting language of contingency. If she merely calls the adverse outcome "reasonably possible," the case will be disclosed in the contingency footnote but not reflected as a charge. But does the company want the case reflected as a charge? Is this an opportunity to smooth the earnings because we happened to sell an asset and have a one-time gain (which we excluded from the permitted pro forma anyway) against which to set it off? Does it make any difference in terms of the underlying reality of the business? Will the analysts discount the significance of the one-time loss, either now or in the future, just as they discount a one-time gain?

The general counsel, having been trained to think like a lawyer, might turn to the CEO or CFO, and legitimately state, "Tell me how you want it to come out on the income statement, and then I will answer." Whether the lawyer makes that statement, however, will have to be based on some means of judgment other than the process of pure lawyering.

Modeling instead of gaming

Imagine you are a visitor from outer space, knowing nothing of our culture, and happen to land next to a cricket game. An American can experience this feeling by sitting in a London pub with one playing on the telly, and conversely, non-Americans need merely watch baseball. Having no predisposition, could you give a complete explanation of what was going on? Imagine instead you landed in Hong Kong next to a park in which old men were practicing tai chi stances. Would you understand what they meant? These little thought experiments mean to demonstrate that there is a significant difference between an observer using models to make "scientific" causal explanations about the activity they may be observing, on one hand, and understanding the causal reasons why the actors are acting that way, on the other.

I once worked with someone who, outside the office, was a person of exquisite common sense, kindness, and values. For some reason, many of those attributes, particularly the common sense about human nature, seemed to fall away in the office. For example, we were working on a deal that was sensitive and the issue was maintaining confidentiality. The problem, of course, is that it is exceedingly difficult to keep the fact of a deal secret. Even if people do not talk about it, there

---

49 *Id*. at 409–10.

are patterns of activity (certain groups of executives traveling at the same time to particular destinations, particular conference rooms being taken, the way certain visitors to the offices are greeted, various information requests, etc.) that make it clear to even the moderately observant non-involved employee that something is going on. I suggested one day that we should think of this in terms of a family situation in which the parents need to talk about something but keep it from their naturally curious children. The executive shut me down with a theory about human nature expressed in words to the effect: "That's ridiculous; everybody here is an adult and should be dealt with like an adult."

At the time, I thought it was wrong to conclude that human behavior changed merely because we were operating within a large business corporation. From my present academic perch, I think now that it was a reflection of how modern professionals, and the academies that train them, have assimilated the theoretical models of science and social science to explain human behavior. Lawyers' professionalism, from Langdell on, has been the manifestation of a process "which Max Weber called 'rationalization,' the ominous tendency in European civilization for impersonal calculations of least cost and maximum efficiency to enter, and finally dominate, every sphere of life."[50]

But our clients aren't just mice in a maze to be observed and acted upon. To be effective as lawyers and managers, we need to understand what we are observing as the behavior of humans who have intention and purpose, and act within context. It is not enough merely to engage in law-like, descriptive assessments about how people behave, à la Carl Hempel. The historian Thomas Haskell captured how a rational and objective scientific explanation of an event can nevertheless fail to convey the correct meaning. A client, for example, has described an altercation in which he hit somebody in the face. The scientific explanation—"my muscles contracted and the end result was the propulsion of my fist into his nose"—is impertinent. The meaningful explanation is a narrative about the reason for the action—"he pissed me off and I punched him."[51]

Once again, the game and model metaphors are a helpful way to think our way out of pure lawyering. One of the core skills of a transactional lawyer (not often taught in law school, by the way) is as modeler. The underlying deal is a negotiating game going on between the parties. The contract is a model that is *about* that game because, as noted earlier, it expresses fewer but essential bits of information regarding the underlying reality of the deal.

What contracts do, however, is reify the game into an objective model that may or may not have reflected the subjective desires of the individual parties. In the lawyers' contract writing game, it may well be, as in the last paragraphs of the lease I described, the drafters have reached the limit of their ability to model reality in the transaction game. Or a provision in the contract may not have been a model

50 *See* THOMAS L. HASKELL, OBJECTIVITY IS NOT NEUTRALITY: EXPLANATORY SCHEMES IN HISTORY 74 (1998).

51 *Id*. at 12–24.

of anything, but in fact a dummy provision inserted without meaning so that the deal would close. And then life goes on. Contracts no longer reflect the present business reality. The contracting parties play a new set of games. If we were merely objective observers considering human behavior à la Hempel, we might wonder why the contract never got used—the pure lawyering of good contract drafting created private law under which Party X had a breach of contract claim against Party B for failing to show up with the widgets at Time T.

Here is where, as lawyers, we need to get beyond the refined logic and reductive models of pure lawyering. Our clients may or may not care whether the situation or their desires line up with their legal rights. Business people have a way of understanding that the goalposts move from time to time, and that not standing on one's contractual rights is a kind of grease that lubricates business relationships. Lisa Bernstein's research into contracting practices of Southern cotton-brokers reflected what I suspect is common across most industries: there is a highly moral attitude toward contractual promises, and the Holmesian pure lawyering consequence of "promise or pay" is not an acceptable moral or business stance.[52] When a cotton seller is going to breach his contract, and so advises the buyer, the buyer is going to want to know the reason—the justification for the breach— because that will likely determine whether the reaction is one of enforcement or accommodation. If the breach is not an exercise in bald-faced opportunism, the more likely result is a negotiation, a split of the benefit, and an amicable compromise. That is, the non-breaching party is more likely to be satisfied by getting a piece of the action than by litigating the matter to a conclusion.

"To spot the gist"

Douglas Hofstadter observed of human brains what is true in spades for effective lawyers: their "main business [is] to take a complex situation and to put one's finger on *what matters* in it, to distill from an initial welter of sensations and ideas what a situation is really all about. *To spot the gist*."[53] When we try to unpack "spotting the gist" (i.e. think about thinking), it is helpful to consider the two polarities we used to distinguish modeling and game-playing. First, there is the polarity of the descriptive versus the normative. Modeling is a descriptive exercise, because we want to get to the gist of what matters with as little information as possible that is still an accurate prediction of the real world. Game-playing is a normative exercise, because we are in the game and need to decide what we ought to do. Second, there is the polarity of objectivity versus subjectivity. Modeling is objective; game-playing is subjective.

52 Lisa Bernstein, *Private Commercial Law in the Cotton Industry: Creating Cooperation through Rules, Norms, and Institutions* (John M. Olin Program in Law and Economics Working Paper No. 133, 2001), http://chicagounbound.uchicago.edu/cgi/viewcontent.cgi?article=1379&context=law_and_economics.
53 DOUGLAS HOFSTADTER, I AM A STRANGE LOOP 277 (2007) (emphasis added).

Business people and their lawyers tend to be doers, not abstract theorizers. They absorb and synthesize data about the world, using it to predict the impact of decisions, and then make decisions not only about what they might do, but what they ought to do. It is a continual process of modeling and game-playing. My thesis is simply that, in addition to the process of pure lawyering, there are other ways of making sense of what is and what ought to be, and the possibility of error exists when they are inappropriately applied. Sometimes we are modeling as when we write contracts; sometimes we are game-playing as when we are negotiating. Spotting the gist means determining whether there's a model inappropriately being treated as a game, or something that is really a game being misunderstood because the observer has looked at it through the lens of an inappropriate model.

It would be easier to spot the gist as between games and models if there were an algorithm or even a good rule of thumb for knowing which would do a better job of understanding a problem. The real world does not work that way. There is no rule for the application of a rule. Coming to believe that a model of the world, like a contract, really *is* the world, or seeing financial reporting as a game to be played are both category errors to which lawyers (and their teachers) can fall victim if they are only engaged in pure lawyering.

5 Causation and Blame

"Stuff" happens

Even though causation is an element in almost every theory of legal liability, most law school curricula relegate its study to a relatively brief discussion of "proximate cause" in torts. What concerns me is the difference between cause-and-effect for purposes of what we know as in science versus how we train lawyers to think about the subject. Causation in pure lawyering, particularly its purest form, advocacy, isn't about knowledge or truth. Rather, its purpose in the logic of legal theories is to assign responsibility and determine who bears the liability for (to keep this G-rated) stuff happening that somebody didn't want to happen.

Getting beyond legal reasoning means being able to think about causation in a world where sometimes somebody really is to blame and where, at other times, well, stuff just happens, and attributing blame is not particularly helpful. For example, all of my children are Type 1 diabetics, an autoimmune disorder. The scientific theory, still not conclusive, is they have it because they had a genetic predisposition putting them at risk.[1] Being at risk genetically, however, does not necessarily mean one will get Type 1 diabetes; if an identical twin has the disease, there is still only a 50 percent chance the other twin will get it.[2] Something else, either a virus or an environmental factor, then triggers the disease. Some combinations of their gene and a trigger resulted in a reaction in which my children's immune systems attacked and destroyed the insulin-creating beta cells of the pancreas.

Both the genes and the triggering factors are, in one famous test for natural or factual causation, a necessary part of a complex of conditions sufficient for an outcome.[3] I have an intuitive sense, however, that the genetic predisposition is more "important" because we are more likely to cure permanently the problem

1 LAURA DEAN & JO MCENTYRE, THE GENETIC LANDSCAPE OF DIABETES (2004), http://www.ncbi.nlm.nih.gov/books/NBK1667.
2 AMERICAN DIABETES ASS'N, GENETICS OF DIABETES, http://www.diabetes.org/diabetes-basics/genetics-of-diabetes.html.
3 Anthony Honoré, *Causation in the Law*, STANFORD ENCYCLOPEDIA OF PHILOSOPHY, http://plato.stanford.edu/archives/win2010/entries/causation-law.

of Type 1 diabetes by fixing it than by changing the environment in which diabetes-predisposed people exist. Hence, the focus of current research is the development of vaccines that affect the immune system's inclination to attack the beta cells.[4] Why doesn't this carry the same aura of animate responsibility as when we assess the equivalent mix of causes in a tort case? Both involve the *fact* of actual cause in a descriptive sense, but not the same aspiration to the correction of an injustice. We understand the words "attack" and "destroy" to be metaphoric because we don't believe cells have will or intention. Rather, "the focus is on selecting from the whole complex the particular condition or conditions that best explain a given outcome."[5]

Compare this to one of the most notable examples of the relationship between causation and blame in recent history, the Financial Crisis of 2008–09. That global meltdown, triggered by a collapse in housing prices and consequently the market for bonds backed by subprime mortgages, was, by most accounts, a systemic breakdown. While I don't discount the reality that there were lots of folks out to make a lot of money as quickly as they could, and that Wall Street bankers were an easy (and perhaps deserving) target, sorting out the causes has not been a simple matter.[6]

Nevertheless, when something goes terribly wrong and lots of people suffer, a "perp walk" in which a corporate executive gets led from a Manhattan office tower in handcuffs provides, in the modern parlance, "closure." Not only do we know why the bad thing happened, we have settled the score with whomever was responsible, and thus have achieved that intuitive repair of the world that Aristotle called "corrective justice." In many quarters, there is the frustration that no Wall Street investment bankers have gone to jail for "causing" the crisis.[7] Why hasn't some prosecutor used the modus ponens logic of pure lawyering to convert the narrative of the disaster into: (a) the "if-then" major premise of a criminal statute, (b) the minor premise that the antecedent conditions of the "if-then" rule were present in the narrative, and (c) the outcome of guilt that must necessarily flow from it?

With respect to the Financial Crisis, if prosecutors charge brokers or bankers with a crime, or plaintiffs' class action lawyers pursue tort or securities law claims, the legal process constitutes a means of redressing a consequence of a bad act that in a just world *ought not* to have occurred. When lawyers litigate criminal or tort cases, the empirical or descriptive inquiry is not about the law itself, but

---

4 *Diabetes Cure*, DIABETES.CO.UK, http://www.diabetes.co.uk/Diabetes-Cure.html (last visited Aug. 14, 2016).

5 Honoré, *supra* note 3.

6 The most dispassionate and soundest assessment of cause-and-effect in the Financial Crisis I've read is ALAN S. BLINDER, AFTER THE MUSIC STOPPED: THE FINANCIAL CRISIS, THE RESPONSE, AND THE WORK AHEAD (2013).

7 Gretchen Morgenson & Louise Story, *In Financial Crisis, No Prosecutions of Top Figures*, N.Y. TIMES (Apr. 14, 2011), at A1.

whether completed historical events satisfy the "if" elements of the crime or tort. The application of the law to those facts, however, is pure normativity—a judgment about what ought to have been and who is to blame for what it was or wasn't. And, if by thinking like a lawyer, one can make a colorable claim that the investment bankers fulfilled all the elements of some crime or tort, including that the crime or tort caused harm, one stands a chance of getting a conviction or damages.

Even in the more mundane practice of business dispute resolution, the idea of blame seeps in, but in a subtler way. Before deciding that it wasn't for me, I spent ten years as a big law firm litigator specializing in, among other things, cases turning on the interpretation of complex contracts. It turns out that the standard introduction to contract law in the first year of law school devotes only a small sliver to interpretation. I suspect this is because there's only so much you can say generally about interpretation and then everything turns on the individual case circumstances. In practice, by contrast, the vast bulk of contract litigation is not about offer-and-acceptance, or consideration, or promissory estoppel and other staples of the curriculum, but whether the not-particularly-clear language the parties used in the past favors the desired outcome of one party or the other in the present. And our litigators' after-the-fact assessments of transactional lawyers was normative, if not arrogantly judgmental and derisive. I can't now count or even remember the number of times we litigators, with the luxury of hindsight, would say about an acquisition agreement, or a long-term coal supply contract, or a commercial lease, "What in God's name were the lawyers thinking when they wrote this thing?"

That was because we had unbounded faith in the power of lawyerly rationality to predict the future, and to capture its vagaries in contract provisions. What I figured out later was that: (a) things frequently just manage not to get covered because the reality of the world was too complex to map in *any* contract, and (b) in reality, in their scramble to nail everything down twenty minutes before the federal wire transfer machinery shut down for the weekend on a Friday afternoon, meaning that the cash couldn't flow and the deal couldn't close, the lawyers weren't trying to map anything; what was more important at the time was getting to see the money change hands.

In the balance of this chapter, we will examine the differences between conceptions of causation in law and the sciences, consider some aspects of lawyering in which putting aside the former and adopting the latter makes sense, and reflect on the difficulties in doing any of that. Attributing blame and responsibility through the translation of a historical set of events into a legal outcome in which the actions of the defendant caused the injury to the plaintiff is at the heart of pure lawyering. Pure lawyering rejects "stuff happens" for a normative judgment of blame and responsibility. It means thinking about causation as between actors as a matter of justice. It is *not* scientific. Think about the diabetes gene and the triggering environment. Treating them as a matter of justice smacks of an atavistic return to a world governed not by physical laws but God's will. But the blaming nature of causation in law is subtly atavistic in the same way.

Sometimes there is no alternative but to cast blame, and like generals forced to go to war, we pick up and use the weapons of pure lawyering. But a lot of what we deal with, particularly in planning, policy, and counseling, is "stuff happens," and it takes getting beyond legal reasoning to do that.

Causation in law and science

Causation in standard legal doctrine

In considering pure lawyering with respect to "stuff happens," the main task is to understand what lawyers and legal scholars usually mean by causation. In lawyering, the term most often doesn't mean what scientists and philosophers (other than of law) mean when they use the same word.

Causation is one of the more difficult pieces of pure lawyering to nail down. It is the element within a legal theory that links the breach of a duty to the injury. For example, under tort law, Mary may have a duty of due care when driving a car, and she may have violated it by running a red light, but if her negligence didn't *proximately* cause Joe's injury when she hit his car, she won't be liable for damages. The first step is actual or natural causation. Did the wrongful act actually have something to do with the harm? In simple tort cases, except for odd and rare situations that are fodder for casebooks, like two hunters shooting at quail simultaneously in the direction of a third hunter, but only one of them hitting him,[8] the scientific or natural causation isn't the interesting issue. In complex cases, it *can* be interesting. Some kinds of cases are no longer scientifically simple. Dozens of companies made asbestos products, but we will never be able to tell which company's product actually harmed the plaintiff. Or patients take a mix of drugs and have an adverse reaction. Sorting out which drug actually caused it is difficult or presently impossible.

Nevertheless, just showing that something actually or naturally caused harm, whether the tort case is simple or complex, isn't enough to establish legal liability. Even in simple cases, we take for granted that there are infinite "but for" causes for the traffic accident in which Mary ran a red light and hit Joe. Joe, the victim, was as much a "but for" cause as Mary in the sense that if he had not been in the intersection Mary would not have hit him. More remotely, if the officer at Ellis Island had refused admission to Joe's great-grandmother, the accident would not have happened. Determining that a cause is proximate means that it has legal rather than merely actual or natural significance.

In the prototypical tort claim, a lawyer needs first to establish or refute the elements of a duty and its breach. In the car accident case, the modus ponens inference of pure lawyering for those elements is a matter of finding the right facts, p, for the minor premise, which, when combined with the "if p, then q" major

8 Summers v. Tice, 199 P.2d 1 (Cal. 1948).

premise, leads deductively to the conclusion that Mary is liable or not. If Mary didn't drive reasonably in light of the foreseeable consequence of not driving reasonably, then she didn't act with due care, i.e. negligently. One can imagine the evidence of negligence: she was texting while driving, for example. Or she sped up to get through the yellow light.

The next "if-then" sequence is the element of the causative link: "if her negligence proximately caused the injury, she is liable to Joe." Now there are all sorts of facts that might help in establishing "if *p*" facts of causation, but what are they? It would probably be an easy case, a matter of common sense, that she's responsible but for the following uncomfortable set of facts. It turns out that Joe wasn't wearing a seat belt, and we can be fairly sure that had he been wearing one, he would have escaped unscathed, notwithstanding the damage to the car. But it turns out that Joe had just left Moe's Bar, his blood alcohol level was .21 percent, and he was too intoxicated to remember to fasten his seat belt. The collision wasn't enough to set off the air bag, but it was enough to cause him to bounce around the dashboard and sustain a significant closed head injury.

Joe v. Mary is still a relatively simple case. Other than some imagined counterfactual narrative in which somebody else's car also hit Joe, Mary was a "but for" cause of the injury. But did she *proximately* cause it? As we will see, legal philosophers have tried to come to a general understanding of causation in law, particularly in complex tort cases, offering typologies of both natural/factual causation and the normative weighting of relative causes when there are multiple influences.[9] And cause-in-fact might well be a very real issue to litigate, for example, under an insurance policy where the contractual duty is to cover losses from "fire," and the insurer refuses payment on the basis that there was a fire but wind caused the damage. Or in a warranty claim where there is an exception for coverage in the event of "abuse," did the abuse or some other factor cause the item not to work? In a patent case, a chemical company holds a patent on Compound A. The claim is that another company's process for making Compound B infringes the patent because, at least in theory, Compound A exists momentarily in the reactor.

Whether "cause-in-fact" or "proximate cause," causation in the law still comes down to the justice or justification of remedies and punishments. To suggest that legal causation is "causation" is to impute a kind of objective science to it, when in practice legal causation of any kind is based on a normative assessment of the particular "oomph" between the deed and the outcome relative to all the events or non-events that led up to the outcome. Legal causation is a throwback to a time when religion, not science, dominated explanations of the natural world, and there was no difference between natural or actual causation, on one hand, and moral blameworthiness, on the other. Let's explore why.

---

9 *See, e.g.,* Honoré, *supra* note 3; Richard W. Wright, *Causation in Tort Law,* 73 CAL. L. REV. 1735 (1985); Lawrence B. Solum, *Legal Theory Lexicon: Causation,* LEGAL THEORY BLOG, http://lsolum.typepad.com/legaltheory/2016/04/legal-theory-lexicon-causation.html.

Causation without metaphysics: the scientific aspiration

Natural causation as equivalent to moral blame goes back thousands of years. If you believed in an all-powerful God, there really wasn't going to be a difference between how things ought to be and how they actually were or turned out to be. If somebody suffered, it wasn't random. To compress thousands of years into a couple sentences, in Deuteronomy, the causative link between morality and good fortune was clear: "keep His commandments . . . that you may thrive and increase . . . . But if your heart turns away . . . I declare to you this day that you shall certainly perish."[10]

By the early Enlightenment, philosophers like Leibniz wanted to understand through reason rather than mere commandment the linkage between natural causation and moral blame. Leibniz's *Theodicy* (a word he invented) was a reasoned justification of God's goodness. The so-called "principle of sufficient reason" is that there is a reason for everything that happens, naturally or morally. Hence, if we simply think hard enough, the connection between the "is" of the real world and the "ought" of how things should be will become clear. Moreover, the upshot of Leibniz's defense of God is not that there is no evil in the world, but that what happens for better or worse is still the "best of all possible worlds."[11]

The Enlightenment sea change in thinking about cause-and-effect in the world at large was to eliminate its deism and to reject theodicy. It meant rejecting as well animate reasons (e.g., God's will) for the occurrence of natural events. Among secular thinkers at least, the great earthquake of 1755 which destroyed Lisbon, perceived as a "good" city, shook the foundations of Leibniz's principle of sufficient reason. It's no coincidence that Voltaire's *Candide* mocks Leibniz as the addled but optimistic Dr. Pangloss, who is capable of explaining why his own syphilis is necessary in the best of all possible worlds, and has Pangloss and Candide sail off to Lisbon where, among other things, they experience the earthquake.[12]

The most significant and permanent deflation of causation as having anything to do with sufficient reasons (or reason itself) came from the philosopher David Hume. He rejected the idea of any metaphysical "glue" (secular, deistic, or otherwise) of causation that is accessible through reason. What we perceive as causation is rather our experience of constant conjunction of events in relation to each other. There's no substance or other reality of causation when we see one billiard ball strike another. There's no reason why a billiard ball couldn't fly off into the stratosphere when hit by another one, but it's never happened.[13] All we

---

10 *Deuteronomy* 30:17–18 (ETZ HAYIM TORAH AND COMMENTARY, David L. Lieber, ed. 1999).

11 SUSAN NEIMAN, EVIL IN MODERN THOUGHT: AN ALTERNATIVE HISTORY OF PHILOSOPHY 18–27 (2002).

12 *Id.* at 143.

13 DAVID HUME, A TREATISE OF HUMAN NATURE 205–25 (Penguin 1969) (1739–40); NEIMAN, *supra* note 11, at 154–55; Wright, *supra* note 9, at 1789–90.

can know is that there are regularities and "laws of nature are nothing more than true universal generalizations."[14]

Admittedly oversimplified in light of the extensive philosophical discourse on the subject of causation, that is still the essence of the scientific orientation to natural/actual/factual causation. The most extreme view arose in the early 20th century among the so-called "logical positivists" or "verificationists." They rejected metaphysics entirely as meaningless, and contended the only meaningful science arises solely from first-person empirical observation and logical deduction.[15] While logical positivism no longer holds much sway, it is probably fair to say that most scientists studying the physical or natural world still believe "when someone asks why, we assume that he means it in a scientific, non-metaphysical sense."[16]

I am not arguing that applied physical or natural science never involves, as in law, the relative weighting of multiple causes. Often it does. If we are solving a problem like Type 1 diabetes, prioritizing research grants may well involve the judgment that focusing on the genome rather than the environment will be more productive. The same holds for business or policy decisions. Assume you are a widget manufacturer running a production line involving six processes, labeled A through F. Fifteen percent of the widgets are defective when they finish with Process F. You do some testing and conclude that half of the defects come from Process B, a quarter from Process C, and the rest spread evenly among the others. If your resources are limited, your brief experiment into causation tells you that the first thing you ought to do is fix Process B and then Process C.

Sometimes the physical or natural scientific issue is unsettled, has significant political implications, or gets clouded by what people on either side of the debate *want* to believe. If you are the Environment Protection Agency, and you are deciding whether to permit the use of the only chemical flame retardant that works cost-effectively in preventing sofa fires (a real problem, by the way), but the chemical may have a long-term effect on a certain species of fish, you will want to understand the causal relationships before you make a policy decision. But chemical manufacturers and environmentalists may not agree on the normative choice. Even when climate scientists no longer debate the fact of climate change, they can still argue about what to do about it.[17] Nevertheless, the pure science really ought to be devoid of either animate God-like or other sufficient reasons *why* things cause other things to happen. All we are interested in are the regularities

14 MARTIN CURD & J.A. COVER, PHILOSOPHY OF SCIENCE: THE CENTRAL ISSUES 879–80 (1998).
15 ALEXANDER ROSENBERG, PHILOSOPHY OF SOCIAL SCIENCE 10–11 (1995).
16 Rudolf Carnap, *The Value of Laws: Explanation and Prediction*, in CURD & COVER, *supra* note 14, at 678.
17 For example, I was surprised to see an op-ed piece in the *Wall Street Journal* that actually acknowledged that global warming was a problem, but counseled a thoughtful assessment whether potential negative effects on human life would be offset by a reduction in deaths due to cold. I suspect somebody thinks there is a knock-down response to that. Bjorn Lomborg, *The Overheated Climate Alarm*, WALL ST. J., Apr. 7, 2016, at A15.

by which we reason inductively to theories and then laws of nature. If we can isolate carbon emissions as having a causal relationship to global warming, then we ought to do something about carbon emissions.

When social scientists deal with "why" issues of causation, the line between causation and blame gets murkier. We are no longer dealing with things like beta cells, in which the idea of animate cause is clearly metaphoric. When we try to explain human activity, we can be talking about sufficient *reasons* rather than mere regularities in the following way. If you ask your child why she wrote with crayon all over the wall, and she answers, "Because my brain stimulated nerve impulses that prompted my muscles to contract, my fingers to grasp, and the crayon to approach the wall with a force equal to its mass times acceleration," you might think about getting the application to Stanford ready, but the answer would be impertinent. That is because you asked for what Max Weber would have called the attributive answer, the *reason*, the intention or motive, as cause, and your child gave you the nomological-deductive answer, the biology and physics, as cause.[18]

The appropriate reconciliation of these two different kinds of causal explanation is a problem in social science. The subject isn't just individual human activities, but things that happen in human-created institutions. Scientific causality should be devoid of all notions of intentionality, it is thought, even if the system being studied seems to have a purpose. In an earlier chapter, I talked about the apparent purposiveness of a physical feedback system like a thermostat or a toilet float to have the intention of seeking equilibrium. Or we think of the antibodies attacking the pancreas to cause Type I diabetes. We don't have any problem understanding those images of physical systems as mere metaphor. It is harder to separate out human purposiveness when we are thinking about or studying human institutions or markets.[19] Nevertheless, it is absurd to ascribe intention or purposiveness to, for example, markets for labor or subprime mortgages. In that context as in physical science, "[e]nd-seeking is a property that adds no explanatory content—everything that happens does so because of the arrangement of causal mechanisms such as the feedback mechanisms that do the work of directing the system toward the end state."[20]

For example, economics is the social science par excellence. It is "traditionally the most formal and abstract of the discourses about human interactions."[21] If it is a *science*, then it ought not to speculate why things are happening in a

---

18 THOMAS L. HASKELL, OBJECTIVITY IS NOT NEUTRALITY: EXPLANATORY SCHEMES IN HISTORY 15–16 (1998).

19 *See* Stephen P. Turner, *Cause, the Persistence of Teleology, and the Origins of the Philosophy of Social Science*, in THE BLACKWELL GUIDE TO THE PHILOSOPHY OF THE SOCIAL SCIENCES 30 (Stephen P. Turner & Paul A. Roth, eds. 2003).

20 Turner, *supra* note 19, at 35.

21 Hans Kellner, *"See Also Literary Criticism": Social Science Between Facts and Figures*, in BLACKWELL GUIDE, *supra* note 19, at 248.

metaphysical sense, but simply explain or predict regularities. For example, if marginal costs exceed marginal revenues, generally the firm will shut down production. If interest rates go down, generally demand for houses will go up. If demand for labor goes up, so will wages. As Paul Krugman observed, "the amorality of the market economy is part of its essence, and cannot be legislated away."[22]

Recall, however, as discussed in Chapter 3, that science is theory-laden, and the economic theorists themselves may have normative biases that impact their abductive leaps to hypothesis and theory. Consider, for example, the economics of minimum wage laws. We ought at least to be able to agree as a descriptive matter about the effect of minimum wage laws before debating their desirability as a matter of policy. It is, however, not so easy, even for something arguably at the level of an introductory microeconomics course. Under neo-classical microeconomics, an unregulated market for labor will reach equilibrium at a wage rate and employment level that clears the market. Everybody who wants a job will be employed, but the wage level may be lower than they would like. The impact of imposing a minimum wage floor, as the theory predicts, is that employers who would otherwise hire at lower wages will not, and the result will be increased unemployment. But there is no universal agreement either on the actual effect in the real world, nor on the policy choices.[23]

Nevertheless, even in a world where Republicans and Democrats blame each other for everything, including what ought to be beyond debate, the aspiration in the social science itself still is to objective and non-metaphysical causation, even if the science is providing factual support for normative arguments.

Causation with metaphysics: the legal version

Law is different. Even when the study of law is, as Langdell suggested, conceived of as a science, its treatment of causation runs counter to the anti-metaphysical aspiration of objective science. Most law professors today would not, I think, object strenuously to H.L.A. Hart's "internal point of view" thesis: what makes something law is not merely that we can observe objectively the actors following certain norms, but that the actors themselves understand subjectively that they are supposed to follow them.[24] To modify Hart's example slightly to make the distinction even clearer, if one were to observe a stop light at a lonely intersection between three and four o'clock in the morning, one would likely see individual cars stopping regularly for red lights, even though there was no reason other than the red light itself to stop. One can imagine safety or self-preservation as an explanatory cause of stopping coinciding with red lights, in addition to hypothesizing the red light "as a natural *sign that* people will behave in certain ways, as

---

22 Paul Krugman, *The Living Wage: What It Is and Why We Need It*, WASH. MONTHLY, Sept. 1, 1998, http://economistsview.typepad.com/economistsview/2006/06/paul_krugman_th_2.html.
23 *Id.*
24 H.L.A. HART, THE CONCEPT OF LAW 56–57 (2d ed. 1994).

clouds are a *sign that* rain will come." But the only way to understand why some-body stops at the red light at three a.m. with nobody else around is to understand Weber's *attributive* cause: that the somebody regards stopping at the red light as an obligation.[25]

Because the very nature of law involves understanding what the actors think, legal causation necessarily reincorporates a kind of explanatory glue, addressing relativities of causative importance in *singular* rather than *generalized* cases that science doesn't want or need to address. As noted above, there is a place for using *generalized* understandings of relative cause-and-effect from physical or social science to set normative business, social, or legislative priorities. In business, if applying our limited resources to Input A reduces bad output by 60 percent, compared with the next best solution, Input B, in which applying the same resources reduces bad output by 30 percent, we should choose to affect Input A. In legislation like the Dodd-Frank Act, which deals, among other things, with regulation of banks that are too big to fail, do the measures contemplated by the Act really work better than the operation of the markets?

I am hard-pressed, however, to think of a reason why *scientifically* and *descriptively*, we need to understand in the *singular* case of Joe's closed head injury whether Mary's negligence is more significant than Joe's unfastened seat belt. It is, on the other hand, highly relevant to the *normative* task of determining whether Mary has to pay damages to Joe and, if she does, how much. Yet the algorithm for causation in that mundane aspect of lawyering is a strangely loose approximation in the midst of the aspiration to science. If causation were wind direction, we'd love to have a sophisticated sensor, but all we get is a wet thumb in the air. The reason is because attribution of singular causation is simply not capable of scientific measurement.

The modus ponens sequence of the pure lawyering logic in causation will look something like this:

(1) If Mary's negligence proximately caused Joe's injury, she is liable for damages.
(2) Mary's negligence proximately caused Joe's injury.
(3) Therefore, Mary is liable for damages.

But what is the rule for determining if something is proximately caused by something else? Using a typical standard jury instruction in civil tort cases, let's posit this as a major premise:

(4) If the negligence was a substantial factor in bringing the injury about, then it is a proximate cause of the injury.[26]

25 HART, *supra* note 24, at 90; HASKELL, *supra* note 18.
26 CONN. CIV. JURY INSTRUCTIONS § 3.1-3.

Assuming we have any idea what "substantial factor" means, we now have the rule (such as it is) the jury must apply in determining whether Mary's negligence must result in liability to Joe.

How do we deal with Joe's own negligence in drinking and not fastening his seat belt? The rules permit Mary to assert that as a cause of Joe's injury and to reduce her liability accordingly. The rule, again derived from a typical standard jury instruction, looks something like this:

> (5) If the plaintiff's own negligence proximately caused his injury, then the defendant's liability to the plaintiff in damages must be reduced by any percentage not caused by defendant's negligence, but rather caused by plaintiff's negligence.[27]

Mary's strategy may well be to concede she was negligent, but to base her defense on relative causation: her negligence wasn't a substantial factor in Joe's injury because the evidence has shown that he would have walked away unscathed if he had merely fastened his seatbelt. In practice, the jury instruction no doubt works fairly well. I can only assume that jurors use common sense to make a relatively arbitrary determination like Mary is 25 percent and Joe is 75 percent responsible.

The comparative causation issue is significantly harder for legal theorists who would like to get beyond mere common sense as the explanation. When multiple events factor into a consequence, as they always do, how do you measure their relative importance as factors when causation itself is such an approximate concept? Is there something more than random intuition or even social policy to the attribution of relative causal significance to the defendant's action out of all the possible factors that led to the injury?[28] Some of the most recent scholarly commentary on causation acknowledges there is still considerable confusion caused by language that covers causation in the sense of working out descriptively the laws of nature *and* in the normative ascription of moral and legal responsibility.[29] For example, over-determination is the fancy term for a circumstance in which one effect has two sufficient causes. Mary's car hits pedestrian Joe while at the exact moment he has a massive myocardial infarction. Either the brain injury from the collision or the heart attack, if one had occurred without the other, would have killed him. Working through this means parsing natural causation into the logical alternatives of necessity (was it necessary for cause X to have occurred for Y to result?) and sufficiency (was cause X sufficient on its own to result in Y?), and

27 CONN. CIV. JURY INSTRUCTIONS §§ 3.5-1 and 3.5-7.
28 H.L.A. HART & A.M. HONORÉ, CAUSATION IN THE LAW 22–23 (1959).
29 Richard W. Wright, Florence G'sell, & Samuel Ferey, *Introduction*, 91 CHI.-KENT L. REV. 445, 446 (2016).

even more fine-tuned delineations in which the necessity or the sufficiency is "strict," "strong," or "weak."[30]

Nature doesn't care if Joe died because of a brain injury or a heart attack, but lawyers seeking to ascribe responsibility or blame in a normative system do. To make the point, let's take a look at two of the most prominent systematic treatments of legal causation over the last sixty years or so: *Causation in the Law* by H.L.A. Hart and Tony Honoré ("Hart-Honoré") in 1959[31] and Michael Moore's *Causation and Responsibility*[32] almost fifty years later. Both of these seminal works demonstrate to me that it is almost impossible to think about legal causation without putting aside scientific dispassion. You can use an unscientific and intuitive rule of thumb, as with the application of the comparative negligence jury instruction. Or you can readopt some of that metaphysical glue that science worked so hard to make irrelevant.

Hart-Honoré's treatment of causation aspired to science, and abjured any discussion of metaphysics. (That is consistent with Hart's more general view that the source of authority of positive law is not metaphysical, but empirical and social.) Hart-Honoré began by distinguishing the broader philosophical issues of causation, including, among other things, the Humean rejection of metaphysical causation in favor of causation simply as the generalization from uniform sequence.[33] They acknowledged that causation for lawyers was a different kind of inquiry, one that largely accepted the search for physical explanation, as in the Mary-Joe accident, which raised few perplexities.[34]

But rigorously explaining, much less quantifying, that loosey-goosey normative exercise of assigning relative importance to one cause or another in the case of a single injury *is* perplexing. There is no mechanical or scientific way of valuing the causal significance of the relative factors. Hence, Hart-Honoré characterized the legal sense of causation more in the attributive, common sense causal notions of the "historian, the lawyer, and the plain man."[35] In Chapter 3, I mentioned Dean Scott's bête noire, the "wise man," substituting for rigorous theory in analysis of law. This idea of causation hearkens back to the wise man over theory.

Hart-Honoré relied on a kind of folk psychology for distinguishing "but for" conditions (like the fact that the Department of Motor Vehicles allowed Joe to drive a car) from cognizable legal causes.[36] The gist of their argument was that legal cause differs fundamentally from "but for" cause when abnormal events or voluntary human actions "bring about disturbances or deviations from the

---

30 Richard W. Wright & Ingeborg Puppe, *Causation: Linguistic, Philosophical, Legal and Economic*, 91 CHI.-KENT L. REV. 461 (2016).
31 HART & HONORÉ, *supra* note 28.
32 MICHAEL S. MOORE, CAUSATION AND RESPONSIBILITY (2008).
33 HART & HONORÉ, *supra* note 28, at 14.
34 *Id*. at 8.
35 *Id*. at 11.
36 *Id*. at 30–31.

normal course of things."[37] Like the authority of law itself, causation is social—"truth by convention"—and not metaphysical.[38] The concepts of intervening and superseding causes in the law have their sources in the unreflective usages of ordinary language.[39] Because people tend to talk about it that way, the law should regard voluntary human actions and abnormal natural events as breaking the chain of the causal responsibility of earlier actors. The metaphor of breaking the chain isn't based on any physical reality, but simply reflects how people ordinarily conceive that some moral causes supersede or intervene as against others.[40] In the folk psychology approach, the 25–75 percent split our hypothetical jury dished out in the *Joe v. Mary* case was probably pretty reasonable.

Moore, on the other hand, thought the Hart-Honoré treatment of the attribution of relative causal significance *was* metaphysics, and mistaken metaphysics at that, no matter how they happened to characterize it.[41] Why should the law adopt this homely and unsophisticated view of such a perplexing philosophical issue? Refining concepts of legal causation ought not to end just because Hart-Honoré think relative cause is derived from the "ordinary notion." Rather, argued Moore, we need at least to look at what it means actually to cause harm, not just the conventions ordinary people use when they talk about it.[42]

Moore thought the "ordinary notion" approach causes conceptions of causation "to be fixed by the conventions of present usage . . . . It thus purports to cut off scientific theorizing about such nature on the grounds that anything ordinary thought does not already recognize as causation cannot be causation."[43] His problem with the Hart-Honoré conception of causation was not that it incorporated some metaphysical glue into the attribution of relative responsibility. It is rather that they employed bad metaphysics—the metaphysics of the Stone Age, he called it, an acceptance of brute inexplicability in which something in the chain of events throws off our ability to trace an effect to the real cause.[44]

Moore wasn't advocating a return to the causal (and equally brute) metaphysics of Deuteronomy or Leibniz, to the effect that whatever science cannot explain, God, the Uncaused Cause, does. He was, rather, simply optimistic about the human capability for understanding. There is enough yet to be discovered in the physical sciences to avoid the metaphysical questions at the far end of cosmology; the problems of human interaction and human systems almost always require

---

37 *Id.* at 37–38.
38 MOORE, *supra* note 32, at 259. It is also consistent with Hart's rejection of Kelsen's neo-Kantian metaphysics when thinking about the ultimate source of positive law. The Rule of Recognition is what people agree it is.
39 *Id.* at 256.
40 HART & HONORÉ, *supra* note 28, at 69.
41 MOORE, *supra* note 32, at 254–79.
42 *Id.* at 259.
43 *Id.*
44 *Id.* at 260.

that the observer take stock of what she assumes to be axiomatic.[45] The problem is that Hart-Honoré avoided foundational questions entirely, and in their own way (as Moore correctly observes) simply foreclosed the path to possible "explanatory bedrock." Moore didn't want to rule out the possibility that there *is* a scientific reason for deeming one cause to be more significant than another, even if we can't think of any right now.

As an alternative, Moore constructed his own metaphysics of causation. I won't belabor the topic here except to say that he was more willing to accept or anticipate scientific "but for" relationships as sufficient bases for the attribution of responsibility.[46] I don't find it very satisfying. His construction strikes me instead as more evidence of the intractability of the translation of scientific or natural causation to the social institution of law. In other words, Moore hasn't given up hope that we will find a scientific or empirical basis for our normative intuitions—the same merging of the "is" and the "ought" that characterized theistic pre-Enlightenment ideas of causation. Like Hume and Kant, I don't believe "is" and "ought" will ever be merged. Hence, I don't see us getting to a scientific split of the *Joe v. Mary* responsibility any time soon.

Hart-Honoré simply put aside metaphysics in favor of a kind of folk understanding of causal relationship. Moore's discussion of the metaphysics of causation was an attempt to reach a foundational truth about relative significance somewhere between nomological-deductive cause and attributive cause, but rejecting out of hand the possibility of "uncaused" human agency as the source of the perplexing irreducibility of the problem.[47] Moore appeared to agree it is a truism that all *singular* causal relationships, the kind with which the law is concerned in individual cases, have to reduce in some sense to Humean *generalized* inductive laws. What he really wanted to do was resolve the paradox of the internal point of view, avoid the libertarian metaphysics of human free will, and reconcile once and for all nomological-deductive and attribute cause.[48]

This, then, is the current state of affairs in the theoretical metaphysics of the *legal* approach to causation. We'd love for it to be like science, but it's not. In contrast to science, pure lawyering *re*-incorporates the principle of sufficient reason: "everything happens for a reason, and therefore somebody is responsible for the untoward thing that happened." It is not about what is true, but about who's to blame.

45 Stephen P. Turner & Paul A. Roth, *Introduction. Ghosts and the Machine: Issues of Agency, Rationality, and Scientific Methodology in Contemporary Philosophy of Social Science,* in BLACKWELL GUIDE, *supra* note 19, at 10–11.

46 MOORE, *supra* note 32, at 261–63.

47 In Chapters 14–20 of *Causation and Responsibility,* Professor Moore undertakes a theoretical consideration of singular and general causal relationships as they impact legal causation, splitting the inquiry into the consideration of: (a) causal relata, i.e. what is it among candidates like facts, events, tropes, objects, or states of affairs that we mean by the "cause" and the "effect", and (b) the relationship itself, the causal "glue" as it were.

48 MOORE, *supra* note 32, at 25–26, 472–73.

Alternatives to blame

One good reason to get beyond legal reasoning is that, particularly outside of the arenas of advocacy, law, like all reductive models and all systems of rules, hits a limit. Contemplation of law's limits, like all contemplation of paradox, inconsistency, and the infinite, is an uncomfortable business. We can put our figurative fingers in our figurative ears when it comes to contemplating our ultimate inability to understand everything, notwithstanding the seemingly irreducible paradoxes attributive and scientific causation. If we conceive of law as science, we are bound to want to think of the normative result of advocacy we call justice as something that can be explained, as Professor Moore seemed to hope, with the cause-and-effect of scientific knowledge.

I suggested in Chapter 1 that some aspects of post-modern thought appealed to me. It surfaces when I think about the problem of causation and blame. The inimitable Pierre Schlag's prediction seems more likely to bear out than Professor Moore's. According to Schlag, causation is an issue that a *science* of law has to "encounter, address, and resolve" so as to be entitled to the "epistemic mantle of knowledge." That is because a scientific discipline needs to

> specify its domain (its boundaries, depth, objects of inquiry, etc.) and . . . offer[ ] some reason to believe that its claimed intellectual dominion over this domain does not turn upon extraneous considerations that escape its control. That's one of the requirements of the project. Pretty hard to achieve. Probably not going to happen soon.[49]

To be clear, I am perfectly willing to attribute blame when it's warranted morally, but I have tried not to deceive myself that "blame" really fits the mundane (even if highly valuable) business disputes I've encountered. As I have said, pure lawyering is in itself amoral and agnostic as to the truth or moral value of its outcomes. I agree with those who believe that the legal system depends on an illusion among its participants that there is an objectively discoverable justice that arises from its processes.[50] Anybody looking at the system from the outside can see that there is no justice, just a lot of people using rules, axioms, conditions, statutes, and principles to further their self-interested ends.[51] To believe internally that a legal system produces a just result when it is clear to anyone looking at it that the participants use it solely for instrumental purposes, you have to adopt some kind of metaphysics.[52] I prefer Derrida's unsettling philosophical

---

49 Pierre Schlag, *Four Conceptualizations of the Relations of Law to Economics (Tribulations of a Positivistic Social Science)*, 33 CARDOZO L. REV. 2357, 2371 (2012).
50 Gunther Teubner, *How the Law Thinks*, 23 LAW & SOC'Y REV. 727, 742 (1989).
51 *Id.* at 736–38.
52 For a detailed treatment of this issue, see BRIAN Z. TAMANAHA, LAW AS A MEANS TO AN END (2007).

critique that law and justice are not equivalent. Law is a human institution and therefore finite. Justice is an unreachable ideal.[53] Hence law will never map on justice "in part because language is always too general, rules too rigid, but also because one must act, in the end, without knowing everything."[54] Yet I know so many people, particularly law professors, who seem to have the idea that there is objective justice, they know what it is, and they can demonstrate it by thinking like a lawyer.

In the purest form of pure lawyering, advocacy, we don't have to confront these issues. The game is nothing more than attributing blame. Being right is the same thing as winning. Causation in criminal and tort is a pure normative assessment that points the finger at the defendant and says, "Shame on you." It shows up as well in business and contract litigation. One of my former partners and esteemed mentors coined an earthy thesis: "In any commercial case, it doesn't matter who the plaintiff or defendant is. That just tells you who got to the courthouse first. The real issue is who is the f**er and who is the f**kee. Your job as a trial lawyer is to establish your client is the latter and the other side is the former." Even in business litigation, the other party is an opportunist, and maybe even a greedy pig, or a free rider, and maybe even a freeloader. And as most litigators know, if you can't manage to stir up a zealous fervor about the dastardly plaintiff or defendant, you can usually work up an intense dislike of the other side's lawyers.

But what kind of lawyering requires an understanding of the tension between legal causation and cause-and-effect in the real world? In other words, where do we need to get beyond the part of thinking like a lawyer that involves winning the game by establish the other side was to blame? I suggest two kinds: planning and counseling.

Planning

I want to return to the subject of contract lawyering, because it has both an after-the-fact and before-the-fact context. As noted above, tactics in business litigation may involve real or fake high dudgeon about morality. The actual law of contracts still incorporates the blaming aspect of legal causation, but it is a little subtler than the pure normativity you find in criminal or tort law. First, when it arises in litigation, it is still normative in a blaming sense, in that the putatively innocent party is trying to remedy a breach that ought not to have occurred. Second, the empirical elements of contract litigation are pretty much the same as those in tort or criminal litigation—both sides need to establish what happened

---

53 Leonard Lawlor, *Jacques Derrida*, STANFORD ENCYCLOPEDIA OF PHILOSOPHY (Spring 2014 ed.), Edward N. Zalta (ed.), http://plato.stanford.edu/archives/spr2014/entries/derrida/.
54 Linda Ross Meyer, *Catastrophe, Plowing Up the Ground of Reason*, in LAW AND CATASTROPHE 23 (Austin Sarat, Lawrence Douglas, & Martha Merrill Umphrey, eds. 2007).

and that what happened fits the "if *p*" of the rules, even if those facts of the matter are in dispute.

What makes the pure lawyering of contract cases subtler has to do with the nature of the "if *p*, then *q*" rules themselves. The rules that decide a contract case will be either: (a) the rules (i.e. the law) the parties created between themselves expressly or by implication, or (b), in the absence of such evidence, contract law doctrine, consisting of a body of rules derived inductively from what *usually* happens in similar circumstances.

In private contract and business law, the set of all law like that described in clause (b) of the preceding paragraph constitutes "default rules." The set of all law like that described in clause (a) constitutes the permissible activity of the parties in contracting around the default rules. A default rule reflects the subtle normativity of descriptive explanation: in most circumstances, the relevant community would expect, in the absence of evidence to the contrary, that the parties meant to abide by the default rule. A default rule is not based on anything that arises from the particular facts, whether expressly or "implied in fact." Default rules are "implied in law," which means that they are a kind of empirical judgment about what happens *as a rule*. In contract litigation, the dispute often involves a determination of the private law arising from the objective manifestations of the parties to the transaction. The result likely turns on this hybrid descriptive-normative imputation of "what should have been" based on our experience of the world.

Another good example of default rules is the law of descent and the transfer of property from generation to generation. If you die without a will, i.e. intestate, the law provides a will for you. The law is based on a certain experience of the world, for example, that you meant to leave something for your spouse, that you valued all your children equally, that if you meant to treat a non-natural child as your own, you would have gone through an adoption process, and so on. If you don't want your estate to pass that way, you need to do something about it and, subject to certain limitations, the wills and trusts you set up will contain the operative rules for distribution of your property.

We can test intuitions about default rules with a quick thought experiment. Partnership law is really just a specific and detailed subset of contract law. Every jurisdiction in the United States has adopted a set of statutory default rules that serve as the partnership contract in the absence of one expressly created by the parties.[55] The partnership statutes provide that two or more persons carrying on a business for profit as co-owners are partners whether they mean to be or not.[56] The reason is that our communities have concluded that the foregoing sentence describes something that *ought* to be considered a partnership, with all

---

55 Uniform Partnership Act (1914) ("UPA"); Revised Uniform Partnership Act (1997) ("RUPA").
56 UPA § 6(1); RUPA § 202.

the attendant consequences of being a partnership, because usually conducting business in that way means that the parties meant to be partners.

Here's the test. Knowing that much and not knowing anything else about partnership law, what do you think the default rule is for sharing profits in a partnership with x number of partners, assuming there has been no express or implied agreement otherwise? I am willing to bet that 100 percent of you answered something like, "share and share alike" or "even-steven." Why? It has to be because we don't need the law to tell us that the basic rule of being partners is that you split the pie evenly in the absence of any other mitigating circumstance. And you would be right. The partnership act in effect in each of the United States provides that, subject to any agreement between them, each partner shares equally in the profits.[57]

Default rules create a very gentle kind of substantive "blaming." They don't incorporate rules of *what ought to be* morally. Instead, they are rules based on community-wide understandings of *what ought to have been* because things happen like that as a rule. It is the basis of an entire economic approach to the study of contract law.[58] Assume there is a default rule that incorporates the community view of how things normally get done, like the 50–50 profit sharing rule in partnership. In the economic jargon, that rule is "bargain-forcing." If partners don't say anything else to change it, the profit split will be 50–50. If you claim after the fact that you are entitled to sixty, not fifty percent, of the profits, the onus is on you to show that the partners did something to change the default. If you can't, in the context of the litigation, you are to blame for the outcome.

That's contract law practice in the after-the-fact dispute resolution mode. Contracts are planning devices as well.[59] As we have explored, they are models intended to chart a future course of events, and to dictate legal consequences (i.e. to allocate the risk of the events occurring or not). My critique of pure lawyering doesn't deny the salutary effect of this modeling. It only draws attention to its limits. The sociology-influenced contracts casebook by Stewart Macaulay and his co-authors has already traveled this road. It largely eschews theoretical justifications of the doctrine and focuses instead on what business lawyers really do.[60] The authors are correct in asserting that "there are large gaps between the law school law of contract, what happens in courts, and what practicing lawyers do" and that "contract doctrine clearly is only one part of what lawyers need to understand to serve their clients."[61] They rightly warn students against the

---

57 UPA § 18(a); RUPA § 401(b).

58 *See, e.g.,* Ian Ayres & Robert Gertner, *Filling Gaps in Incomplete Contracts: An Economic Theory of Default Rules*, 99 YALE L. J. 87 (1989).

59 For a scholarly justification of the institution of contract law itself as a means of planning, *see* Curtis Bridgeman, *Contracts as Plans*, 2009 U. ILL. L. REV. 341.

60 *See generally* STEWART MACAULAY, ET AL., CONTRACTS: LAW IN ACTION (3d ed. 2010).

61 *Id.* at 15.

expectation "that your professors are going to hand you a beautifully worked out, consistent, and coherent system called 'contract law.'"[62] And yes, contract law is, instead, "a tool that you can use to try to solve your client's problems, rather than a set of answers to all your questions."[63]

The reason the last assertion is true is because a contract, by its very nature, can't be a set of all answers to all questions without being as complete as the reality it is trying to map.[64] The process of interaction between clients and lawyers does at least two things: (a) it helps produce a better understanding of what the deal actually is (i.e. a better map) and thus reduces the risk of future conflict, and (b) it can cause the express allocation of risk. As an example of the former, imagine a business selling mass market products to large retailers like Kmart and Wal-Mart. The supply contracts are long-term and complex. A sales manager says to the lawyer, "Price are to be escalated for inflation based on changes in cost of living." The lawyer asks a bunch of questions to figure out what "changes in the cost of living" means. Is it determined by the Consumer Price Index or the Producer Price Index? Is it to be the index for all products or just the products being sold? Is it to be the index for the entire United States or a regional index? The client ends up with a contract that has a precise formula for price increases. We'll never know if it avoids a dispute but, in the lawyer's mind, it is a better contract than one with an ambiguous or vague reference to cost of living adjustments.

The irony of being on the planning side of contract lawyering is that we assume that what we do makes a difference, but there really is no way of proving it. It would mean showing the counter-factual of what would have happened if we didn't write that agreement. Because we can't prove it one way of the other, there is nothing stopping us from believing, particularly after the fact with the 20–20 hindsight rampart among us contract litigators, that better lawyers doing a better job of planning would have written an agreement that was clear enough to avoid the present dispute. That's thinking like a lawyer, and transposing the lawyerly concept of causation as blame to an interpretation of how the world actually works in practice.

Getting beyond thinking like a lawyer if you are a planner means adopting a kind of resignation or fatalism about causation and blame. Before-the-fact lawyering isn't standard-less. It can be done well or it can be done poorly. But the fact that the before-the-fact lawyering didn't predict or adequately deal with the present dispute isn't in itself conclusive evidence of the quality of the work. Stuff happens, and chances are whole chunks of a contract are obsolete very shortly after the signatures go on it.

---

62 *Id*. at 18.
63 *Id*.
64 *See* Ayres & Gertner, *supra* note 58.

Counseling

One of the most satisfying aspects of being a lawyer is acting as someone's counselor. Somebody comes to you and wants your advice about how to deal with a problem. My thesis here is that your conceptions of causation and blame are going to have an impact on how you counsel others. To come up with advice, you need to theorize. You will do a better job if you are able to reflect on how you, as a lawyer, filter the client's narrative through your normative and descriptive theories. It's entirely possible that the advice you ought to be giving is that stuff happens, even when the skills of pure lawyering would allow you, on behalf of the client, to ascribe blame.

At the risk of oversimplification, here are two anecdotes, reflecting prototypes (even caricatures) at opposite ends of the metaphoric continuum of the lawyer's professional interaction with clients. At one end of this polarity resides the single-minded zealous advocate within the adversarial justice system. This evokes the metaphor of lawyer as warrior. A number of years ago, I participated in an interview with a candidate for a law school juvenile justice clinic. The subject turned to counseling the accused juvenile about confessions. The candidate, an experienced criminal lawyer within the juvenile justice system, said, in so many words, "Even if confession were good for the soul it is not good for the body. My only concern is the body (i.e. keeping the body free from incarceration)." I translated this into the following statement of the lawyer-client relationship, "Client, I am not your therapist, I am your lawyer. I have only one mission and that is either to beat the rap or to reduce the rap to its most benign juridical consequence. As to any other physical, psychic, emotional, or life needs, please see the appropriate allied professional."

At the other pole lies the transactional lawyer-counselor. This evokes a wholly different metaphor for the professional encounter. Many years ago, I represented a buyer (call him Joe) in his acquisition of a small business.[65] The seller was not a trustworthy character in a business in which there was a distinct possibility of side deals, payoffs, commingling of personal expenses with business expenses, and so on. Joe's business judgment was that, as long as the business's revenues could be verified, he would rely on industry standards rather than the seller's disclosures as the basis for valuation of the business. But even though we lawyered the usual panoply of contractual protections against the possibility of undisclosed liabilities—for example, structuring the deal as an asset sale rather than a stock sale, extensive representations and warranties, indemnities, escrowed purchase price holdbacks—there was still the possibility, despite best efforts at due diligence, that buying this business meant taking on some undisclosed skeleton in the closet.

---

65 I have altered the details to preserve confidentiality, but the story is accurate, to the best of my recollection, having occurred well over twenty years ago, in all material respects.

Shortly before Joe signed and simultaneously closed the deal, Joe and his wife (call her Jane) visited me. She had been crying, and began crying again in my office. She was afraid. Even for this wealthy family, it was a significant commitment of assets. She was not involved in due diligence or the decision-making. She might have a nice seat in first-class, but Joe was still flying the plane into what might be stormy weather. "Jeff, should we being doing this deal?" Reflecting my feelings about the limits of pure lawyering, I said something like the following: "I can't answer that question for you. I can tell you that we have responsibly and professionally documented the deal to give you a reasonable amount of legal protection. But I also know that there are limits to how much the contracts can protect you. There's always some amount of good faith and trust in the seller that goes into this, and Joe and his associates have to make the call on that. I think I'm more risk averse than Joe is, which isn't good or bad, but it means we might make different decisions about whether the risk is worth taking. Ultimately, you have to decide with Joe that you either trust what he's doing or not, and he has to decide what to do in light of your uneasiness. That's between you two."

The gold standard text on lawyer as counselor makes it clear that offering one's personal view in connection with a final decision is firmly within what is called the "client-centered" philosophy when the client requests it,[66] and sometimes even when the client does not.[67] The text is replete with examples of how to go about offering those opinions. What the text does not do is help the lawyer sort through his own conscious or unconscious separation of objective prediction and subjectivity normativity. For example, I do not like litigation, despite or perhaps because I spent the first ten years of my career as a litigator. I can recall at least two instances where as general counsel I was skeptical, as a matter of pure lawyering, about the merits of proposed litigation. Nevertheless, I deferred to the predictive judgment of lawyers on my staff that these were claims with a significant likelihood of good outcomes. Both matters went to trial and resulted in significant monetary recoveries. I have wondered since then about my luck or good judgment in deferring, because on my own I would likely have not allowed the cases to go forward. Certainly, my normative predilections would have affected how I communicated with the client.

Clients *will* ask me what they should do. I *will* have a subjective view that influences my view of the merits. I *will* bring my pre-existing theories of the "Deal" or the "Problem" to the client's hopes and aims for the transaction or dispute. Rather than merely mouthing a standard of neutrality, are we better off thinking about our own subjectivity in the counseling interaction, and dealing with it explicitly, whether to control it or to use it as a means of making progress? I think

---

66 DAVID BINDER, PAUL BERGMAN, PAUL R. TREMBLAY, & IAN S. WEINSTEIN, LAWYERS AS COUNSELORS: A CLIENT-CENTERED APPROACH 417–20 (3d ed. 2011).
67 *Id.* at 427–28.

so, taking the advice of another counseling profession: psychotherapy.[68] We bring the effects of thinking like lawyers to the relationship just as a psychoanalyst brings her pre-existing theories of human psychic development to the therapeutic inter-action. In each case, our success depends on our ability to employ our own professional theory-making as against the realities with which the clients, the adversaries, and interested third parties confront us. The difference is that thera-pists are professionally obliged to spend more time than lawyers thinking about their own thinking, and relatedly the effect of the influence of their own theoreti-cal orientation on their assessment of the patient's problems.[69] Psychoanalysts, for example, have to be patients to get licensed; nothing obliges a lawyer ever to have been a client![70]

There is a parallel to psychoanalytic theory and practice that my friend, the psychologist Steven Cooper, has explored. Cooper has written about psychoana-lytic theory in the following senses: (a) putatively scientific descriptions and explanations to which the academic or research side of the professional discipline aspires; (b) the way ordinary people make sense of what's going on in their lives (i.e. theory as a source of personal meaning); and (c) the means by which the professional assists the client in practice. My view is that lawyers as counselors need to do the same thing. Cooper identifies something he calls "a kind of return of the repressed positivistic."[71] I read it to mean that, as professionals, we want to be able to fit what we are observing in the professional encounter within the idealizations—the theories, constructs, and models—we have learned during our professional training. The point is that every theory is reductive in the sense of being less than all of life (or one's life). Practice, as opposed to academic specula-tion, necessarily involves some aspect of theoretical indiscipline or promiscuity, even at the cost of disdain from disciplinary theorists.[72]

What is true in the application of disciplinary theory to practice for psychoanalysis is true *a fortiori* to the relationship between lawyer as counselor, on one hand, and client, on the other. Non-lawyers generally do not express their aims and desires in terms of the algorithms of pure lawyering any more than analysands express their hopes and fears in psychoanalytic theory. The dark side of lawyerly thinking and acculturation is the lawyer-centeredness of pure lawyering. Theory (whether that of the practitioner or the academic) tends to trump therapy.

---

68 STEVEN H. COOPER, OBJECTS OF HOPE: EXPLORING POSSIBILITY AND LIMIT IN PSYCHOANALYSIS 381 (2000).

69 *Id*. at 266.

70 Once admitted, a psychoanalyst-in-training must undergo her own psychoanalysis "with a training analyst usually conducted with the analysand on the couch at a frequency of at least four sessions per week on separate days." Board on Professional Standards of the American Psychoanalytic Association, *Standards for Education and Training in Psychoanalysis* (June 9, 2010).

71 COOPER, *supra* note 68, at xiv–xv.

72 *Id*. at 262.

Cooper observes for psychoanalysts that "[w]e begin with a particular view of therapeutic action and define our focus or points of observation in order to detect the process we are hoping to achieve or, at least, observe." Within his profession, there are disputes about theory, but in practice, "[w]here is the place for unpleasant observations—things that we observe that do not fit our theories?"[73] Cooper uses the term "courting surprise" for the psychoanalytic clinician's experience in applying theory to the real life patients bring to the office. What he means is that life has a way of failing to adhere to our aspirations of scientific theorizing; nevertheless, "[w]e are deeply attached to our theories, for they follow us around, for better and worse, like our character, our adaptation. They seduce us and force us to see things through a particular lens."[74] For the analyst, one of the problems of theory is that it is not merely an objective tool used to interpret and classify the patient's symptoms, but it is the analyst's very means of conceptualizing the patient's information and structuring how the analyst might go about influencing the patient.[75]

Therein lies the conundrum. If the analyst's theory is powerful, but life has a way of not following theory, what should the analyst do? Cooper's answer is that the analyst is obliged to reflect on his "own resistance to learning from new experience in revising theory." This is because objectivity in the clinical encounter is an unobtainable ideal.[76] In analysis, as elsewhere, we cannot suspend our theories, our ways of making sense;[77] rather theory is "the guide who leads and determines the analyst's formulations and interpretive activity through shifting foci on past, present, and future threads within the patient's associations and the interaction between patient and analyst."[78]

Compare this to the observation in *Educating Lawyers* of the extent to which students separate what I call pure lawyering from the common sense understandings of the layperson.[79] We need to take care that our reflection on the client's problem is not simply another return of the repressed positivistic—the fixation on objectivity and reduction—that underlies both the thinking of pure lawyering and our professional self-selection as lawyers. Hence the answer, ironically, is to do more to educate our students in thinking about thinking inside *and* outside the disciplinary idiom, i.e. thinking about what it means to be a lawyer who gets beyond legal reasoning.

---

73 *Id*. at 262–63.
74 *Id*. at 265.
75 *Id*. at 266.
76 In the Freudian ideal, the analyst merely listened in the manner of a scientific investigator. Freud said, "I consider that one should not make theories. They should arrive unexpectedly in your house, like a stranger one hasn't invited." *Id*. at 268, quoting a letter from Freud to Sandor Ferenczi.
77 *Id*. at 269.
78 *Id*. at 271.
79 WILLIAM M. SULLIVAN, ET AL., EDUCATING LAWYERS: PREPARATION FOR THE PROFESSION OF LAW (SUMMARY) 5 (2007).

This is not easy stuff. For professionals steeped in a disciplinary ideal, as we steep lawyers from the first day of law school, suggesting that they think another way is uncomfortable. Counseling isn't just fitting facts into "if *p*, then *q*" rules. Sometimes we need dispassion, and sometimes not, and it's hard to decide. That is the lesson of the Joe and Jane story. It was not my money, and I could not make the decision for Joe and Jane. I was not comfortable telling her whether she ought to do the deal with her husband. Nor was I prepared to say that I thought the seller was a lying scumbag: (a) because I did not know if that was right, and (b) I decided that would not be helpful in their decision-making process. All I could do was my best to help them overcome the gap between non-legal uncertainties, fears, consequences, on one hand, and the limits of the legal documentation, on the other.

I do not believe, however, that the lawyer as counselor always *must* be dispassionate, any more than the psychotherapist must always be a backboard to the patient's tennis ball. If the lawyer is external, assimilation of the decision-making process, the ultimate integration of legal and non-legal meaning, may be subtle. When I was a law firm lawyer, most of my clients still seemed to want me to say something to the effect, "*It's your decision and your money, not mine, but if it were mine, this is what I would do.*"

If you believe, as Cooper does for analysts and I do for lawyers, that we want to influence, then we are better off countering the repressed positivistic with explicit thinking about our theories and our disciplinary ideals, particularly about causation and blame, in the context of our real-life counseling.[80] In other words, we need to be able to think about the "stuff happening" that we cannot address through pure lawyering.

---

80 COOPER, *supra* note 68, at 273.

6 Action, Authority, Rationalization, and Judgment

If it isn't clear by now, lawyering requires technical mastery of a certain kind of rigorous rationality, namely, the modus ponens sequence in which we convert real-world circumstances into legal consequences through rule application. We will deal here with the relationship of that technical mastery to action, authority, rationalization, and judgment.

If you consider decision-making from the inner experience of the decision-maker, rigorous rationality hits a very real limit, inviting at least three untoward consequences. The first shows up colloquially as the mental gridlock of the two-handed ("on one hand, on the other hand") lawyer. The opposite colloquialism is that somebody is simply too stupid to get worried. If you are smart and prescient and can see around metaphoric corners, understanding all the risks can make acting seem perilous. As a lawyer so consumed, you become the "Vice President of 'No.'"

The second consequence is the ultimate appeal to authority. Even if there is no sovereign issuing commands, what makes something law is that there is some source of authority, whether social or transcendent, and a corresponding sense of obligation to obey it.[1] If rationality lends itself to two-handedness, or if there are two of us with conflicting but rational views, we could submit our arguments to somebody else and let that authority do the deciding. That is what adjudication is meant to do. The problem is that we have simply begun an infinite regress in which *somebody else's* rationality won't be the same as deciding or choosing. If the third party authority can see both sides of the issue, he either has to make the choice himself or buck the issue to somebody else, and so on all the way down. The resolution of a dispute comes down to *some* authority's dictate, whether the dictate is couched in acceptable reasons or is arbitrary (like a parent saying "Because I say so"). At some point in the life of any lawyer, however, there is no authority and one becomes the parent. Then you have to decide and live with the consequences of the decision.

1 H.L.A. HART, THE CONCEPT OF LAW 79–91 (2d ed. 1997).

The third consequence is after-the-fact rationalization. Once we (or our clients) have made a decision or acted, we can rationalize or deceive ourselves into believing just about anything. The kind of thinking that characterizes pure lawyering is a handy tool for doing just that.

I invite you to engage with me in considering from the inside out, rather than the outside in, how you and I think rationally, decide, and then commit to action. When we are faced with hard decisions, whether it is a matter of giving business advice, starting a lawsuit, deciding on trial tactics, or deciding whether to settle a case, we can use the skills of pure lawyering to make arguments pro and con. But precisely because they are hard decisions and capable of pro and con argument, no single line of legal reasoning provides the definitive answer.

In this chapter, I want to take that one step farther. Doing rational analysis, as one would as a lawyer, ought to be tremendously helpful in making decisions. It is. Without that kind of rationality, we often can't get to the nub of what we have to decide.[2] Deciding and then doing is something quite different. Being rational is a little like making sure we have trained ourselves adequately and correctly packed our parachutes. But deciding and doing is like leaping out of the airplane. And what if we decided not to leap? Being rational also helps us rationalize that choice after the fact.

As I described this to a fellow law professor with extensive transactional experience, one of the hardest things about thinking like a lawyer is overcoming the very desire to be rational in the face of uncertainty. It is only a slight hyperbole to generalize that when I was counseling business people about tough decisions, there were always at least three or four good legal and business arguments either way. The proposed merger may have wonderful cost synergies, but we will spend $2 million in legal fees merely to have a chance at getting antitrust clearance. Do we buy or not? The entire value of the acquisition target depends on the strength of several patents, and it is hard to say whether the courts will uphold their validity. Do we invest or not? After we have completed an acquisition, we realize we can draft a nice complaint about how the seller breached its warranties and might have even defrauded us, but in doing so are we telling the markets that we didn't perform adequate due diligence? Do we file a lawsuit or not? The terms of the settlement are draconian, but if we go to trial and roll the dice with a judge or jury, it could be worse. Do we settle or not? In instances like this, I (the lawyer!) would often say, "Now it's time to hold hands, take a breath, and all jump out of the airplane together." That is the nature of uncertainty. We may think and choose correctly and still be wrong, and it will only be natural to second-guess or rationalize afterward.

---

2 The rational analysis includes gathering data. It would be foolish to suggest in this era of big data and sophisticated analytics that one not use them. But the inferences from the data are still, and always will be, the product of the kind of theory-making discussed in Chapter 3. And neither the data nor the analysis is the same as the decision.

At the core of all three consequences is the fact that reason and rationality—the essence of thinking like a lawyer—really are something different than deciding and then acting. To make a judgment involves traversing that lawless and rule-less domain akin to the leap of hypothesis discussed in Chapters 2 and 3. This is even scarier, because once we make the judgment about the parachute jump, we will be responsible for stepping out of the fuselage and into the air. That is the last subject for this chapter—what is judgment and how does it differ, if at all, from thinking like a lawyer? If a student were to ask me, I would respond that the answer is not a happy one. Judgment occurs in a lonely place, your head, and when the chips are down, chances are that there is no authority to tell you what to do, either in the casebooks, the treatises, or online, or your professors, your parents, or anyone else. On the other hand, much of what lawyers do may be replaceable by artificial intelligence, and what makes you irreplaceably human (and a good lawyer) will be your ability to make those judgments.

Rationality, decisions, gridlock, and action

The internal limits of rationality

Using legal reasoning, the deductive, inductive, and abductive processes we have discussed so far, is a way of being rigorously rational. What I want to establish is that, apart from any external critique of the value of rationality, being rational (as such) has its own internal limits when it comes to figuring out what we ought to do.

Robert Nozick, one of the great 20th-century American philosophers (colleague of John Rawls at Harvard and libertarian critic of his theory of justice),[3] described rationality as the human ability "to investigate and discover anything and everything; it enables us to control and direct our behavior through reasons and the utilization of principles."[4] Rationality is the basis for understanding that observed data yield generalizations that are more than merely accidental. They thus "constitute our license to travel from given data to predictions or expectations about further data."[5]

Being rational isn't hard to understand when it comes to making scientific predictions. What does it mean, however, to be rational in normative judgments, that is, about what we ought to do? In Nozick's conception, when we are normatively rational, we apply previous decisions to new cases based on a perception that they "all fall under a normative general principle."[6] Our principles are the "transmission devices for *probability* or *support*, which flow from data or cases . . .

---

3 ROBERT NOZICK, ANARCHY, STATE, AND UTOPIA (1974).
4 ROBERT NOZICK, THE NATURE OF RATIONALITY xi (1993).
5 *Id.* at 4.
6 *Id.* at 5.

to judgments and predictions about new observations or cases whose status otherwise is unknown or less certain."[7] In short, we have *principles.*

A principled judgment thus isn't merely a brute assertion or demand based on personal whims or desires. "Principles can guide us to a correct decision or judgment and to control for personal factors that might lead us astray."[8] Being normatively rational in the form of a set of coherent principles has a salutary effect. It can guide interpersonal dealings,[9] allow one to define one's own integrated and coherent personal identity,[10] aid in overcoming temptations to short-term action that have long-term negative consequences,[11] and provide symbolic meaning to actions (in which the nature of the decision itself and not just its consequence has utility).[12]

Deriving principles, and living by them, seems important to us, and guides us to some end (Nozick calls this the teleological function of principles) that we would not achieve merely by acting randomly.[13] The problem, of course, is that life is complicated. Even in our own efforts to live principled lives, it can be difficult to apply principles coherently.[14] For example, is there a principle for standing on principle? My wife and I have disagreed in principle on many things over the course of a thirty-seven-year marriage. A subject currently under discussion, for example, is whether I should own my own horse. I believe in the principle that owning (rather than leasing or merely using) a horse leads one to better riding, contentment, and a longer, happier life. My wife believes in the principle that it is too damned expensive to own a horse in the Boston metropolitan area. Both of us believe in the principle of marital peace. I am not sure about her, but I know I believe in the principle that one ought to compromise to achieve marital peace. Is willingness to compromise one's principles in this way, to value getting along above being right or getting what you want, a principle? If so, is that a contradiction in terms? If you are so sure that something you believe is true, why should you compromise? Nozick observed the same problem, asking, "Does [being rational] mean, then, that we must employ some principle to decide when to employ a principle: And what makes that situation one to be guided by principles rather than something else?"[15]

This is the internal problem of rationality and principle when applied both to making decisions about what is (i.e. the descriptive or positive) *and* about what we ought to do (i.e. the normative). If you try to reason back to some foundational principle, you end up with what the philosopher Hans Albert, a student of

---

7 *Id.* (emphasis in original).
8 *Id.* at 8.
9 *Id.* at 9–12.
10 *Id.* at 12–14.
11 *Id.* at 14–26.
12 *Id.* at 26–35.
13 *Id.* at 36–37.
14 *Id.* at 39–40.
15 NOZICK, *supra* note 4, at 37.

Karl Popper, called the Münchhausen Trilemma. It is "the thought that any attempt to justify a belief must end in one of three unsatisfactory ways: a vicious regress, a brute assumption, or circular reasoning."[16] As we've seen, this is the regress at the heart of judgment: there is no rule for the application of a rule. Or it is the circularity of choosing: there are alternative principles of reasoning, and the choice among them could depend on which principle of decision to apply.[17]

In other words, you can have reasons for deciding or doing, but having reasons isn't the same thing as either deciding *or* doing. And it works the same way no matter how momentous or trivial the decision. If the question is whether to disclose or not to disclose something in the Form 10-K, the annual report that a public company files with the Securities and Exchange Commission, lawyers will likely be able to muster arguments on both sides. But not to decide is to decide. You either disclose or you don't, even if the final arbiter is a coin flip. My wife and I, with our multiple Harvard, Michigan, and Stanford degrees between us, can muster brilliantly rational arguments on both sides of the horse issue. At this point, peace has prevailed because, as much as I want to own a horse, it's been all talk. Not to act is to act.

The essence of judgment in each case is a mental activity, undertaken by a subject whose own process of judgment must necessarily be affected by subjective factors. When we make a judgment, we have privileged access to our own minds vis-à-vis others. Even that privilege has its limits; we can never be objective about ourselves.[18] Do I really have free will? Or are all my decisions foretold by my nature and my nurture? Who knows? Despite the advancements in behavioral economics, which identify commonly used heuristics and biases that deviate from "maximizing" rationality,[19] assessing one's *own* judgment is irreducibly recursive. You can think about the extent to which your own bias, framing, heuristics, and so on have affected your judgment, but that analysis itself may be subject to the same bias, framing, heuristics and so on. Simon Blackburn made the same point about the interplay of biology and freedom.[20] Even if a scientist tells you what your hard-wired nature is, you still have the option, for example,

---

16 HANS ALBERT, TREATISE ON CRITICAL REASON 18–19 (Mary Varney Rorty, trans. 1985).

17 NOZICK, *supra* note 4, at 134.

18 Kant acknowledged the elusiveness of self-knowledge: "Indeed, even a human being's inner experience of himself does not allow him so to fathom the depths of his heart as to be able to attain, through self-observation, an entirely reliable recognition of the basis of the maxims which he professes, and of their purity and stability." IMMANUEL KANT, RELIGION WITHIN THE BOUNDARIES OF MERE REASON AND OTHER WRITINGS 82 (Allen W. Wood & George Di Giovanni, trans. 1998) (1793).

19 *See, e.g.,* SCOTT PLOUS, THE PSYCHOLOGY OF JUDGMENT AND DECISION-MAKING (1993).

20 Simon Blackburn, *Mind over What's the Matter*, N.Y. TIMES, July 27, 2008, at BR15 (book review).

of tipping the waitress you will never meet again or defending someone against an injustice even if it is contrary to your self-interest to do so.

This internal limit on rationality applies equally to legal reasoning. One of the most putatively objective rational calculations in law is Learned Hand's negligence algorithm: someone is negligent if the burden of precaution against an event is less than the probability of the event occurring times the magnitude of the resulting injury.[21] As Professor Oren Perez observed, even this formulation leads to an infinite regress.[22] As lawyers, we understand that courts have laid down rules of conduct (like what constitutes "due care"). Rational actors presume a relationship between the outcome of cases and the before-the-fact calculation in respect of that outcome that lawyers are supposed to make. For the model to work, it has to assume that potential tortfeasors and judges are perfectly rational and have perfect information. Hence, a hypothetical potential tortfeasor will be perfectly informed by the case holdings. She will know that she will be liable for any injury she causes if the cost of precaution is less than the probability times the magnitude of the accident.

But information and deliberation are not costless. Therefore, if she is fully rational, she will have to make a decision about whether to invest costs in doing the case research to obtain the necessary information and in deliberating about the choice. That decision would itself not be costless; she'd need to gather information about whether gathering information and deliberating is a fruitful way to spend her maximizing time. And so on to the infinite regress. The point is that the judgment must, at some point, necessarily reduce to something other than rationality. Perez's conclusion is that this is why there exist rules of thumb for deciding what to do—they sit somewhere between unsatisfying calculation and pure brute intuition.[23] It is another example of the Münchhausen Trilemma.

The development of professional lawyering since Dean Langdell took over at Harvard is an example of what Donald Schön, in his iconic work on professional "reflection-in-action," called Technical Rationality.[24] Professionalism through most of the 20th century has meant "instrumental problem solving made rigorous by the application of scientific theory and technique."[25] Law was no exception.[26] Schön's thesis was not about lawyers in particular. He observed practitioners in all professional fields who successfully negotiated the "irreducible element of art in professional practice" and found "ways to make sense of complexity and reduce

21 United States v. Carroll Towing Co., 159 F.2d 169 (2d Cir. 1947).
22 OREN PEREZ & GUNTHER TEUBNER, PARADOXES AND INCONSISTENCIES IN THE LAW 22–26 (2006).
23 *Id.* at 25.
24 DONALD A. SCHÖN, THE REFLECTIVE PRACTITIONER: HOW PROFESSIONALS THINK IN ACTION (1983).
25 *Id.* at 21.
26 *Id.* at 29 (citing Arlene K. Daniels, *How Free Should Professions Be?* in THE PROFESSIONS AND THEIR PROSPECTS 56 (Eliot Friedsen, ed. 1971)).

uncertainty to manageable risk."[27] He concluded that the essential issue of Technical Rationality in all professions isn't *problem solving*, that is, the tools professionals learn to use. Rather, the mark of expertise is *problem setting*, that is, deciding which tools to use. Schön recognized in problem setting the same issue as in all theory-making. There is a moment for the professional that is irreducibly non-technical.[28]

The rules of law we teach our students are what Schön would call the disciplinary foundation "grounded in systematic, fundamental knowledge, of which scientific knowledge is the prototype."[29] The student who reads the torts exam question at the beginning of Chapter 2 faces, on the other hand, the "swampy lowland where situations are confusing 'messes' incapable of technical solution."[30] For Schön, professional mastery of technical knowledge is necessary but not sufficient. To be a complete professional, you have to employ judgment beyond pure rationality. He called this "reflection-in-action:" "the 'art' by which practitioners sometimes deal well with situations of uncertainty, instability, uniqueness, and value conflict."[31] It is the art of legal issue-spotting that some students develop quickly while others lag behind.

Over thirty-seven years of professional and academic life, I have come to agree with Schön. In the end, the moment of judgment, of decision and choice, is not a matter of scientific reduction. I am not sure what it is. All I can reach for are metaphors like my leaping out of an airplane, taking the plunge, or, more classically, Kierkegaard's leap of faith.[32] Nor am I optimistic that a reductive answer is even possible. First, there is the regress of rule-application (there is no rule for the application of a rule). Second, there is the regress of the subjectivity of the decision-maker. The person undertaking the judgment can never be objective about herself, and that is a conceptual problem, not an empirical one capable someday of resolution. It is a reason to be humble, something to which I will return in the next chapter.

Choice rather than rationality

What I've been discussing so far are the limits you come to understand about decision-making when you start pondering rationality itself. As rational as I think I am, I have come to terms with the idea that merely being rational, or understanding what it means to be rational, can't account for the leap we experience when we move from thinking about something to doing something.

---

27 SCHÖN, *supra* note 24, at 18.
28 *Id.* at 40.
29 *Id.* at 23.
30 *Id.* at 42.
31 *Id.* at 50.
32 SØREN KIERKEGAARD, FEAR AND TREMBLING 34 (Sylvia Walsh, trans. 2008) (1843).

If lawyers will need to decide and act, but there are limits to thinking like a lawyer when it comes to deciding and acting, then we need to start thinking about ways of getting beyond thinking like a lawyer. This is not about assessing the leap out of the plane, or weighing the risks, costs, and benefits of taking the plunge, but about what it takes to step off the edge and into space. I said in Chapter 1 that there were aspects of existentialism and the critical studies movement that appealed to me, and this is where I examine why.

I am certainly not original in offering a critique of the kind of rationality that thinking like a lawyer entails. Before I was born, the European existentialists were most famously criticizing the contributions rationality and positive science could make to decisions about what we ought to do. Let's use the term "positivism" for this modern idea that we ought to be able to figure everything out. Existentialism was a reaction against positivism. It stressed decision with its free and undetermined nature, and emphasized its irrationality. It declared scientific knowledge uninteresting because of its objectivity. Positivism exalted rational analysis of facts; existentialism exalted choice and responsibility.[33] As Sartre said famously, "That is what I mean when I say that man is condemned to be free: condemned because he did not create himself, yet nonetheless free, because once cast into the world, he is responsible for everything he does."[34]

Despite years of education, three years of law school, mastery of thinking like a lawyer, and a career now spanning thirty-seven years, how can I be sure about what to do? The answer is that, in really hard cases, I still can't be sure, and that is discouraging. The existentialists used a stronger word when confronting the limits of rationality, the two-handedness of most problems: "despair." Here's the circularity again: it is up to us in the face of some considerable despair about the limits of our knowledge, to do the best we can. As Sartre said, "[Despair] means that we must limit ourselves to reckoning with only those things that depend on our will, or on the set of probabilities that enable action."[35]

Two contemporary analytical philosophers have, in my mind, helpfully confronted this despair of analysis in the face of the need to act. I have extensively discussed knowledge and belief, and the difference between figuring out what is and what we ought to do. Allen Gibbard, a philosophy professor at the University of Michigan, arrived at a kind of existentialist resignation to the limits of thinking but from a naturalist's perspective. In his view, humans have evolved to think and to plan, so thinking and planning how to make decisions about what to do must be part of the natural order.[36] Normative concepts arise out of the natural fact that we make plans. But what we come to believe we ought to do, rather than having some metaphysical genesis, really is no more than what we actually do. Hence,

33 ALBERT, *supra* note 16, at 75–76.
34 JEAN-PAUL SARTRE, EXISTENTIALISM IS A HUMANISM 29 (Carol Macomber, trans. 1997).
35 SARTRE, *supra* note 34, 34–35.
36 ALLEN GIBBARD, THINKING HOW TO LIVE xii (2003).

"[t]he notions of plan and belief have their limits."[37] If you think you've been wronged, should you complain? Personally, I don't give myself a break when it comes to making a lot of decisions. I don't like the way the service advisor at the car dealer just treated me. I don't like the fact that colleagues make more money than I do. If I don't complain, I feel like a sucker. If I do complain, I feel like a jerk. I'm willing to contend that conundrum also characterizes every decision about filing a lawsuit that I've ever encountered.

Gibbard framed the issue in the context of deciding whether to confront or defy a bully (perhaps an apt metaphor for many a lawsuit). He said,

> For a crucial sense of 'ought,' I say, the following holds: if you do accept, in every relevant aspect of your mind, that you ought right now to defy the bully, then, you will do it if you can. For if you can do it and don't, then some aspect of your mind accounts for not doing it—and so you don't now plan with every aspect of your mind to defy him right now.[38]

To Gibbard, as to Sartre, there really is no "ought" in a manner of mental calculation or planning that intervenes between the natural world and your decision. Your decision *is* your action. Both are natural facts, but reason doesn't have a lot to do with it.

Kent Bach, a philosophy professor at San Francisco State University, reached a similar conclusion. There is a field of study called rational decision theory. Bach called it an idealization of how people decide. He asked whether decision is the product of any reflection at all. Bach observed, "My eleven-year-old daughter appreciated this when I asked her, 'What problem is everyone faced with at every waking moment?' She immediately answered, 'The problem of what to do next.'"[39] In short, philosophers, psychologists, cognitive scientists, and others give much thought to dissecting the decision-making process in terms of the evaluation of alternatives, but in real life we are always settling what to do next because we are always *doing* something next.[40]

The distinction between positivism's rationality and existentialism' choice is helpful in thinking about the rationality of pure lawyering. The caricature of a positivist two-handed lawyer can come up with a dozen reasons why and why not to act, but can't decide. The caricature of an existentialist "ready-fire-aim" executive or entrepreneur doesn't think very much, but manages to act. This is not to say that even my caricature of a business person never reflects before making decisions. I am not making any empirical claim about the extent of reflection in C-suites. The critical point is not to be the caricature of the rational

---

37 *Id.* at 153.
38 *Id.*
39 Kent Bach, *(Apparent) Paradoxes of Self-Deception and Decision*, in SELF-DECEPTION AND PARADOXES OF RATIONALITY 185 (Jean-Pierre Dupuy, ed. 1998).
40 *Id.* at 186.

lawyer so committed to thinking like a lawyer that he or she fails to understand the limits of evaluation. Evaluation is a thought process. But not to decide is to decide, not to choose is to choose, and not to act is to act.

Critical rationalism

I've spent too much of my career being rational on behalf of clients and businesses to suggest one shouldn't be rational. Thinking rationally or thinking like a lawyer is a good thing. It means that any choice I make will be informed. Going beyond thinking like a lawyer means understanding that thinking isn't the only thing. The philosopher Hans Albert observed in regard to positivism and existentialism, "These are orientations that hardly differ at all on the dichotomy between knowledge and decision, but adopt radically different points of view in their evaluation of it."[41] The colloquialism is that you have to do both—to walk *and* to chew gum.

Albert was a student of Karl Popper, and one of the "critical rationalists" who tried to mediate between the dichotomies of positivist knowing and thinking, on one hand, and existentialist believing and choosing, on the other. If, like me, you want to be confident in what you know, but humble in what you believe, and wise enough to be able to discern the difference, this is an attractive philosophy. In this orientation, there are far more questions than answers. Popper's own answer was not to give up on truth, but to live with an agnosticism about *any* truth, to reject any assertion that truth is or can be manifest by *any* authority, to regard the sources of truthful assertions as manifold and unfathomable, to take refutation of plausible assertions as more helpful than the source of their truth, and to remain open to the possibility of such refutation.[42]

The core proposition of critical rationalism is that classical rationality is ultimately a search for an Archimedean foundation or justification of one's beliefs. Even in science, this creates a fruitless drive for certainty over truth.[43] In Kant's epistemology, this is reason's demand to seek the conditions of any state of affairs, and then the conditions of those conditions, and so on in an infinite regress to the "Unconditioned," the point "at which the given would appear as self-explanatory and hence necessary."[44] Yet we can't reach the Unconditioned without encountering one of the endpoints of the Trilemma. Hence, critical rationalism acknowledges the limits of justification and discourse, opting for a kind of modest and self-critical rationality.[45] Any belief not subject to criticism is

41 ALBERT, *supra* note 16, at 75–76.
42 KARL POPPER, CONJECTURES AND REFUTATIONS: THE GROWTH OF SCIENTIFIC KNOWLEDGE 11, 32–38 (1963).
43 ALBERT, *supra* note 16, at 12–16.
44 SUSAN NEIMAN, THE UNITY OF REASON: REREADING KANT 63 (1994).
45 John R. Wettersten, *Karl Popper and Critical Rationalism*, INTERNET ENCYC. PHIL. (2010), http://www.iep.utm.edu.

dogma, and the point of critical rationalism is to avoid dogma, whether in the empirical realm of science or in civil discourse.[46]

The paradox and elusiveness of having a commitment to rational thought yet still understanding its limits is evident from Albert's assertion that even critical rationalism itself is a *fallible hypothesis* (rather than a justified first principle).[47] In other words, one needs to consider whether the ultimate presupposition of critical rationalism is itself a dogma that deserves criticism. Critical rationalism is not without its own ultimate presuppositions, whether or not it calls them that. Critical rationalism still takes as foundational the idea of truth, but views truth as something that can only be "ever more closely approximat[ed]" by the process of criticism. "To do that," wrote Albert, "we must sacrifice the drive for certainty which lies at the root of the classical doctrine, and accept the price of permanent uncertainty about whether our theories will continue to be confirmed, and thus maintained, in the future."[48] That is an appealing but difficult agnosticism, as Albert himself demonstrated.[49] As humans, we seem to be hardwired to value structure over disorder, even if it means taking some foundational presupposition on faith for the sake of having any structure at all.[50]

Walking the critical rationalist line is no mean feat. It requires one to believe that truth is beyond human authority. At the same time, you have to believe that even inspired attempts to find the truth carry no divine or metaphysical authority.[51] You don't reject the idea of truth in either science or morality; you just treat it very, very gingerly and respectfully. That is particularly the case when it comes to moral absolutes that are matters of belief rather than knowledge. Even calling it "reflective equilibrium" gives it too much credit because it suggests a concrete solution to the Münchhausen Trilemma.[52] To me, being a critical rationalist simply means stepping back and reflecting when my reasoning takes me to a conclusion that induces either my own internal tickling of misgiving, or engenders a negative response from somebody else whose judgment I respect. It's my philosophical home for balancing both thinking like a lawyer and getting beyond it.

Rationality and the appeal to authority

Recall that being rational in making "ought" decisions means basing the decision on principle and not on personal whim (like "dammit, I want a horse"). That sounds a lot like one of the justifications for resolving matters under a rule of

46 ALBERT, *supra* note 16, at 47–48.
47 *Id*. at 47.
48 *Id*. at 44.
49 *Id*. at 69.
50 *Id*. at 67.
51 *Id*. at 39.
52 Norman Daniels, *Reflective Equilibrium*, STANFORD ENCYCLOPEDIA OF PHILOSOPHY (Edward N. Zalta, ed. Winter 2013 ed.), http://plato.stanford.edu/archives/win2013/entries/reflective-equilibrium.

law in a civil society. We would employ the tools of law, legal reasoning, rather than violence, as the basis for the resolution. But the very idea of law rests on there being a source of authority, the very thing as to which Popper counseled agnosticism.[53]

Imagine what it would look like if my wife and I were to apply the rule of law rather than social norms on the subject of buying a horse. We would make valid arguments to each other whether or not to buy it. When we came to an impasse, we would appeal to a third party (maybe a marriage counselor) to make the final decision. We'd agree to abide by the final decision, not resort to violence, and not engage in the marriage equivalent of secession or insurrection. The Münchhausen Trilemma has shown itself again. We will have submitted to the authority of a third party whose own ultimate justification for belief in the correct answer will turn on brute assertion, regress, or circularity.

In law, of the three, brute assertion is the most likely candidate. Resolutions under the rule of law come by way of the argument from authority. Why is something the answer? Regardless of the reason that putatively underlies the adjudicative result, and the custom that reasons may be given, the operative rationale is "Because I say so." Judges often give reasons for their decisions, particularly on important matters, but they don't always. In arbitration, regardless of the importance or value of the matter in dispute, the default rule is that the arbitrator need not render a reasoned award.[54]

When a legal decision-maker faces the possibility of applying different rules to a fact situation, the argumentation may call down merit in the form of policy or logic or equity. The arbitration may give reasons for the decision. But it is really just a softer authoritarianism. As Professor Geoffrey Samuel observes, policy or merit arguments are merely a basis for adopting one source over another within the theology-like "authority" paradigm that characterizes law.

> Lawyers work with texts that can be criticized but never questioned in terms of their authority. A law is a law, and so the scope of reasoning about laws is always going to be limited in comparison to work in other, what might be called enquiry paradigm, disciplines.[55]

Appeal to authority and the authority's power to enforce a resolution, by violence if necessary, are arguably what turn mutually understood norms into law.[56]

---

53 The ultimate source of that authority—whether in God, nature, a Grundnorm, or a Rule of Recognition—underlies some of the fundamental questions of jurisprudence.
54 AMERICAN ARBITRATION ASSOCIATION, COMMERCIAL ARBITRATION RULES AND MEDIATION PROCEDURES 37 (2009). (Rule R-42: "The arbitrator need not render a reasoned award unless the parties request such an award in writing prior to the appointment of the arbitrator or unless the arbitrator determines that a reasoned award is appropriate.")
55 Geoffrey Samuel, *Legal Reasoning and Argumentation*, INTERNATIONAL ENCYCLOPEDIA OF THE SOCIAL AND BEHAVIORAL SCIENCES 776 (2015).
56 *See* Robert M. Cover, *Foreword:* Nomos *and Narrative*, 97 HARV. L. REV. 4 (1983).

The untoward consequence of pure lawyering occurs when lawyers see the argument from authority as appropriate not just in the metaphoric war that is adjudication, but in other contexts as well.

It isn't stretching the war metaphor very far to see the vanquishing aspect of adjudication as the substitution of intellectual brutishness for physical brutality. Pure lawyering is a weapon. Litigation is the iron hand behind the velvet glove of more amicable resolutions; there is only a difference in degree, not kind, between warfare and litigation. Negotiating anything in the context of litigation, from the resolution of a discovery dispute to the case itself, barely clears the stink of power. As long as the parties have the safety net of saying "forget it, see you in court," the brutishness of the argument from authority will hold sway. Compare what happens when two equally motivated and non-coerced parties are negotiating a deal. After I moved from being a litigator to a transactional lawyer, I described this as "negotiating without a net." That is, the only thing you could do was appeal to whatever influenced the other party's judgment, and no authority in the world could compel a happy result.

Professor Samuel has questioned whether this prevalence of the authority paradigm should allow academic lawyers even to think of themselves as social scientists.[57] It returns us to the issue of transcendental illusion: when you are reasoning to a conclusion, how do you distinguish what you know from what you believe? To be internally valid, normative reasoning doesn't necessarily need to correspond to what it is; it only needs to be internally coherent. As Professor Samuel observed, within the framework of the discipline, law depends upon practitioners accepting that there is a coherent model of rules and concepts. And he invoked the possibility of illusion: "There may be disagreement about the elements of the model (rules, rights, remedies, or whatever) but there is consent that there is a model 'out there' that governs. It is arguably all a fiction, but that is another story."[58]

Professor Peter Goodrich at the Cardozo Law School, building on Samuel's authority thesis, made the same point about the conflation of advocacy and theory in the legal academy itself.

> Too often we meet the figure whom Doderidge nicely terms the legal temerist, the professor in a blind rush to judgment, intent only on proving his point, his worth and so conforming rather too easily to the almost comical persona of the 'authority paradigm', the dogmatist who cannot stay to explain in any sustained way why she thinks that philosophy, theory, hermeneutics, literature or deconstruction or some imagined spectre bearing that name should be banished, branded, destroyed. As if their opinion somehow

---

57 Geoffrey Samuel, *Interdisciplinarity and the Authority Paradigm: Should Law Be Taken Seriously by Scientists and Social Scientists?* 36 J.L. & SOC'Y 431 (2009).

58 Samuel, *Legal Reasoning*, *supra* note 55, at 783.

carried an unreal and unreasoned weight. Which, of course, is the problem with the authority paradigm.[59]

The critique of pure lawyering echoes Kant's critique of reason in that both are potentially illusion-creating. If you consider your rationality, your innate ability to figure out that something "makes sense" as a route to truth and knowledge, you really have no means of establishing your view as superior to another without working your way back to some authority whose reason is "Because I say so." That is fine if you have the safety net of an adjudicator to make the decision. In contrast, when you negotiate as a lawyer to make a deal, you are operating without a net. It means you have to address the other side directly in the second person, rather than speaking to an adjudicator about the other side in the third person. That is a subject to which we will return in Chapter 7.

Rationalization and self-deception

So far we have been discussing the problems of rationality in moving from thinking to making decisions and then acting. You can see both sides of an issue and go into mental gridlock. You can reason your way to a brute and authoritative conclusion that requires arbitrary enforcement rather than agreement. Here, we want to examine a third consequence of rationality—our lawyerly ability to convince ourselves of just about anything. How do we know that we been thinking reliably? Conversely, when, as characterized most famously by Sartre, have we been lying to ourselves?[60]

The literature of self-deception in philosophy, psychology, and behavioral sciences is rich in part because there is no universal consensus about what self-deception is or if it is even possible.[61] Behavioral science itself arises from the illusion that in making decisions we understand things that we really don't. As the Nobel Prize winning economist Daniel Kahneman observed, "The core of the illusion [of understanding] is that we believe we understand the past, which implies that the future should also be knowable, but in fact we understand the past less than we believe we do."[62] The benefit of tapping the *philosophical* rather

---

59 Peter Goodrich, *Intellection and Indiscipline*, 36 J. L. & SOC'Y 460, 477 (2009).
60 *See* JEAN-PAUL SARTRE, BEING AND NOTHINGNESS (Hazel E. Barnes, trans. 1984) (1943).
61 For those interested in that subject, sources include PERSPECTIVES ON SELF-DECEPTION (Brian P. McLaughlin & Amélie Oksenberg Rorty, eds. 1988); SELF-DECEPTION AND SELF-UNDERSTANDING: NEW ESSAYS IN PHILOSOPHY AND PSYCHOLOGY (Mike W. Martin, ed. 1985); MIKE W. MARTIN, SELF-DECEPTION AND MORALITY (1986); ALFRED R. MELE, SELF-DECEPTION UNMASKED (2001); SELF-DECEPTION & PARADOXES OF RATIONALITY (Jean-Pierre Dupuy, ed. 1998); Robert Audi, *Self-Deception, Action, and Will*, 18 ERKENNTIS 133 (1982); W.J. Talbott, *Intentional Self-Deception in a Single Coherent Self*, 55 PHIL. & PHENOMENOLOGICAL RES. 27 (1995).
62 DANIEL KAHNEMAN, THINKING FAST AND SLOW 201 (2011).

than *behavioral* work on self-deception is that it starts from the inside of the subject and works its way out. It does not merely seek to describe behavior that appears to be at odds with objectively rational conclusions. Instead it addresses the question how the subjective mind could be both believing and not believing the evident objective truth at the same time. It is about the very illusion of validity itself, which arises from "our tendency to construct and believe coherent narratives of the past."[63]

I don't want to get bogged down here in the philosophical debates about whether self-deception is even possible.[64] I am persuaded from my own life experience that we are capable of self-deception and that it is not necessarily irrational. That is especially the case if rationality is the application of principled and coherent thinking, like the kind we learn in our professional training and use in our practice, to the objective facts of the world. Self-deception is no more than the formation of a creative hypothesis for the purpose, as Kent Bach describes it, "of giving up or replacing the unpleasant belief, at least as far as one's ongoing thinking is concerned."[65] I accept that there is a phenomenon we have all experienced in which we manage to keep ourselves from thinking about something we believe is true, but do not want to face.[66]

The point is that self-deception is another way of approaching the subjective and motivated processing of objective data. Deceiving oneself is at the heart of the problem-setting process that Donald Schön described. When we encounter a problem to be solved, we need to come up with an explanatory hypothesis and then test it. As we explored in Chapters 2 and 3, something very hard to pin down in the thinking process is the source of our ability to develop the hypotheses we use as the bases of alternative explanations. As Robert Nozick conceded, "There is no mechanical (algorithmic) procedure for generating the most promising alternative—none that we know of anyway."[67] If our desires, rather than rationality, impact the processing of information and the justification of a course of action that we tell ourselves are our reasons for acting, it is not surprising that we might have a reason to question our own rational conclusions.[68]

---

63 *Id.* at 218. One of the leading thinkers on self-deception, Alfred R. Mele, illustrates the construction of such a narrative. Sid, who is fond of and regularly lunches with Roz, theorizes that Roz's refusal to go out with him, and her insistence that she loves her steady boyfriend, is instead "playing hard to get." Alfred R. Mele, *Two Paradoxes of Self-Deception*, in SELF-DECEPTION AND PARADOXES, *supra* note 61, at 37, 44.

64 Sissela Bok, *The Self-Deceived*, 19 SOC. SCI. INFO. 923 (1980); Donald Davidson, *Who is Fooled?* in SELF-DECEPTION AND PARADOXES, *supra* note 61, at 1, 5; Ariela Lazar, *Division and Deception: Davidson on Being Self-Deceived*, in SELF-DECEPTION AND PARADOXES, *supra* note 61, at 19.

65 Bach, *supra* note 39, at 167.

66 *Id.*

67 NOZICK, *supra* note 4, at 172–73.

68 MELE, *supra* note 61, at 25–46.

The question is how, when we persuade ourselves that we know something to a theoretical or moral certainty, do we know we are not fooling ourselves? The philosopher David Sanford explains self-deception as rationalization.[69] To justify his pleasure in having bought it, a man told himself his new car is a bargain. The pleasure is beyond rationality, but it is honest. The justification comes from what Sanford calls a "thirst for rationality [that] is a major source of lies."[70] The invented and purportedly rational reasons are *ostensible*, which Sanford distinguishes from the more paradigmatic view of self-deception:

> The car buyer invents the belief that his new car is a bargain. The lie, which here has the thirst for rationality as a source, is the second-order belief that one believes the car to be a bargain. The car-buyer somehow really knows that the car is not a bargain, but he deceives himself into thinking that it is.[71]

In contrast, what makes a reason ostensible is not that it is necessarily false (in Sanford's example, we are to assume that the buyer can in fact demonstrate support for his belief that the car is a bargain); rather, it is ostensible because the reason is a rationalization to cover for other more honest reasons (like I just *want* it!).[72]

Often, self-deception may consist not of persuading oneself that the false is true, or vice versa, or even of holding inconsistent belief. I contend the very process of rationalization, whereby we adopt anticipating and ostensible beliefs (versus the honest but perhaps irrational ones), constitutes self-deception. Sanford claims there can be no self-deception that is free of rationalization, but notes his qualms about the role of rationalization in making that very assertion:

> Those who defend theories often provide striking examples of rationalization. Although the defender of the theory thinks he regards the theory as adequate because he thinks there are no genuine counterexamples, his treatment of putative counterexamples is actually heavily biased by his fondness for the theory.[73]

Justifying past conduct is a large part of what lawyers do. The very nature of that justification often creates precisely the gap between invented and ostensible reasons that Sanford identified. When I was a young lawyer in Detroit, I represented a large corporate client in a commercial lawsuit that the in-house counsel thought was meritless. I agreed though it was likely we could get out by way of a summary

69 David Sanford, *Self-Deception as Rationalization*, in PERSPECTIVES ON SELF-DECEPTION, *supra* note 61, at 157.
70 *Id.* at 157 (quoting T. Penelhum, *Pleasure and Falsity*, 1 AM. PHIL. Q. 81 (1964)).
71 *Id.* at 158.
72 *Id.* at 158–59.
73 *Id.* at 163–64.

judgment motion after a minimal amount of discovery. The in-house lawyer, however, wanted to punish the plaintiff by making it engage in extensive (and expensive) discovery. The case was being litigated in Detroit (the plaintiff's place of business). The corporation was headquartered in a city less than an hour away by commercial airline (back in the days before airport security existed). At some point, the plaintiff served a notice of deposition for one of our client's employees whose office was back at the headquarters. The notice specified that the deposition was to take place in Detroit. The in-house counsel instructed me to file a motion for a protective order objecting to the location of the deposition, despite the fact that the corporation's employees traveled back and forth to Detroit all the time. I was able to find a case holding that the proper location of the deposition was the corporate headquarters, and that was the ostensible legal basis for the motion. I still dreaded going to the hearing because I knew the honest reason was simply to impose more inconvenience and cost on the plaintiff.

Let's assume your company holds a patent. You have a weak but colorable claim that a competitor has infringed the patent. One of the possible remedies for infringement is a permanent injunction against infringement. Filing the case would allow your sales representatives, if they do it carefully (and, as a practical matter, even if they don't) without concern for trade defamation, to imply that the competitor may not be a viable long-term supplier if the patent gets upheld. Assume the claim has a 10 or 20 percent chance of succeeding. The ostensible basis for the lawsuit is the pure lawyering of the patent claim; the honest reason is that the lawsuit serves as a marketing tool.

A well-publicized incident from the 1990s struck me as the prototypical consequence of a kind of professional self-deception. Bernard Nussbaum, a senior partner at Wachtell, Lipton, Rosen & Katz in New York City, became Counsel to the President in 1993. He resigned in March, 1994, due to the political fallout after having counseled President Clinton and First Lady Hillary Clinton to resist the Justice Department's attempt in the so-called "Travel-gate" affair to search the office of Vincent Foster immediately after Foster's suicide. In later testimony before Congress, "he professed bewilderment at the fuss his obstruction had provoked. Virtually any lawyer would have done as he did, he said, with unfortunate plausibility."[74] Nussbaum claimed his resignation was the "result of [a] controversy generated by those who do not understand, nor wish to understand the role and obligations of a lawyer, even one acting as White House Counsel."[75]

There was nothing wrong with Nussbaum's pure lawyering. The issue instead was that he saw the world through the eyes of a lawyer, and moved immediately to the conclusion that legal justification would serve as general justification of an

---

74 William H. Simon, *The Confidentiality Fetish*, ATL. MONTHLY, Dec. 1, 2004, at 113.

75 *Id.*; Letter from Bernard W. Nussbaum, White House Counsel, to the Honorable Bill Clinton, President of the United States (Mar. 5, 1994), http://www.presidency.ucsb.edu/ws/?pid=49763.

action. Arguably, within the four walls of the East and West Wing offices where he and his clients discussed the response to the controversy, he was reasoned, persuasive, and truly believed himself to act within the legal and ethical bounds of a lawyer's professional canons. In my view, his fundamental failure was not a legal error. He may have been entirely correct. The real problem was that he persuaded himself he was right, because his reason told him what ought to be the legal result. That effort was an exercise in self-deception, not because he was wrong about the law, but because he was wrong about the relationship between legality and politics. The correct legal answer led to a political miscalculation.

My concern is about how legal reasoning assists you in undertaking that subtle journey from justification to rationalization to self-deception. Philosopher Marcia Baron noted the ubiquity and even the necessity of self-deception:

> self-deception is, for most of us, virtually indispensable. And this is the case not merely because there are episodes in most lives in which we cannot bear to face the truth; it has more to do with the opacity of self-knowledge.[76]

Perhaps that should have been the answer to my angst about the discovery motion: ignore what you perceive as the truth and proceed ahead regardless. But if you justify and rationalize as a core of your profession, it seems to me at some point you have to rationalize the rationalization and justify the justification. As Professor Baron observed, "we pick a story, though not *just* any story, to make sense out of our lives."[77]

Thinking like a lawyer is capable of exacerbating difficult decisions or disputes. Although rationality is capable of allowing us to solve problems, it is also capable of rationalization, justification, and, in the end, self-deception. The problem is particularly acute when we are negotiating the line between legality and ethics. The point of business is utilitarian: to maximize something we have concluded is a good—profits, productivity, sales, or share price, to name a few. But the business game has rules, and companies often espouse moral values which include playing the game by the rules. The question is whether we're capable, in thinking like lawyers, of justifying whatever conclusion we want when there is a tension between what we want and what is right.

I don't believe there's a cure for self-deception other than to understand that there is a distinction between what you know and what you believe, and to be relatively humble about your ability to draw the distinction. None of us can help but let our rationality morph into rationalization and self-deception. As I thought about my rationalization thesis in terms of entrepreneurs (say, versus other professionals like bankers or lawyers), my visceral reaction was that perhaps entrepreneurs were the more self-deceived, and ought to be, because they are

---

76 Marcia Baron, *What is Wrong with Self-Deception?* in PERSPECTIVES ON SELF-DECEPTION, *supra* note 61, at 431, 441.
77 *Id.* at 442.

visionaries, and bankers and lawyers are rational technocrats. After all, entrepreneurs are supposed to be affected by those "irrational" behavioral characteristics of over-confidence and over-optimism. There is something to the idea that creativity or innovation itself requires taking leave of what really is in favor of what could be.[78] The opposite side of the self-deception coin is the heart of creative endeavor capsuled by the idea of the willing suspension of disbelief.[79] In this way, self-deception aids decisiveness.

But I have come to think, consistently with my intuitions expressed here, that lawyers and business people, to the extent they are thinkers rather than doers, are each self-deceived in their own way. One of the great things about lawyering in litigation when it is based on rationalizing a client's conduct is the objective finality of the adjudication. Nothing mitigates one's self-deceptive belief in the rightness of one's cause quicker than an adverse decision. But even if the business of being a lawyer means at times justifying and rationalizing after the fact, of presenting ostensible (yet colorable and ethically permissible) reasons rather than honest ones in pursuit of clients' instrumental ends, going beyond thinking like a lawyer also means learning how not to fool yourself.

The loneliness and irreducibility of judgment

This is where I contest the idea that computers or robots will ever replace great lawyers, notwithstanding the recent announcement that a large law firm has hired "Ross" to assist in its bankruptcy practice.[80] Judgment is an irreducible exercise of a single mind, regardless of the influences and information that come

---

78 On the morning I originally wrote this paragraph, the *Wall Street Journal* had run an interview with Paul Simon about his new album. The interviewer asked, "What's your success rate with songwriting? How often do you hit a dead end?" It seemed to me that Simon's response evoked a certain self-deception underlying creativity—you proceed believing what you know is not good in the belief that it also is good:

> [O]ccasionally, I'll be in the middle of a song and drop it if it doesn't feel true. It's not a fun thing to do. You tend to fool yourself as you go along, because you're working hard at it. In a sense it's good, or competent, but it doesn't pass the test.

John Jurgensen, *A New Tour and a New Audience at 70*, WALL ST. J. (Oct. 14, 2011).

79 SAMUEL TAYLOR COLERIDGE, BIOGRAPHIA LITERARIA, Chapter XIV (1817); *see* Alan Singer, *The Self-Deceiving Muse: Fiction and the Rationalistic Dictates of the Present*, 12 SYMPLOKĒ 77 (2004).

80 Michal Addady, *Meet Ross, the World's First Robot Lawyer*, FORTUNE (May 12, 2016), http://fortune.com/2016/05/12/robot-lawyer. Ross isn't really a lawyer; it's a highly sophisticated legal research computer. For a more sophisticated discussion of this issue, *see* Kevin Ashley, Karl Branting, Howard Margolis, & Cass R. Sunstein, *Legal Reasoning and Artificial Intelligence: How Computers "Think" Like Lawyers*, 8 U. CHI. L. SCH. ROUNDTABLE 1, 18–21 (2001); Eric Allen Engle, *Smoke and Mirrors or Science? Teaching Law with Computers—A Reply to Cass Sunstein on Artificial Intelligence and Legal Science*, 9 RICH. J.L. & TECH. 6 (2002); Eric Allen Engle, *An Introduction to Artificial Intelligence*

from others. It is the closest practical embodiment of what is known in philosophy of mind as "the hard question of consciousness," that is, coming to terms scientifically with the apparent reality that we have privileged access to our own mental inner lives. In the exercise of that professional inner life, when the businessperson or lawyer incorporates the legal and business conditions to draw a practical conclusion, it is still, in the words of the bromide, "lonely at the top."

Here is an illustration. We were representing a company in a sensitive piece of litigation. The problem was not whether the company's legal position was solid but the adverse publicity the very existence of the claim was generating. The legal issue had to do with whether certain business arrangements were really the company's responsibility, i.e. was an intermediary between the company and certain customers an agent of the company or of the customers? While we might have been able to demonstrate that the company had no legal responsibility, the public impression was going to be that it let its customers hang out to dry. I recall a conference room with a large square table and at least a dozen people, inside lawyers, outside lawyers, the chief financial officer, the vice-president of bank operations, and others arrayed around the company's CEO. The CEO asked each person to state a view on the question of "fight or settle?" After hearing each person's response, she paused for a moment and then said, "I think we have to settle." What struck me at the time was that every person there had a rule, a truth, or an authority to which he or she could appeal—whether it was law, a sense of justice, sound banking, or customer relations. Despite all of the discussion, when the time came to make the decision, the CEO had no authority to fall back on except her own.[81]

Sublime legal judgment is the analog of what the CEO did. It involves a kind of thinking that goes beyond legal reasoning. When we consider what it means to think, we begin with consciousness itself because thinking seems to be at the heart of whatever a conscious mind is. The so-called hard issue of consciousness deals with scientific explanations (or the difficulty of finding any) for the empirical fact of the subjective inner life of the mind. Our mental states have an associated feeling of being our own experience; as one philosopher noted, "These qualitative feels are also known as phenomenal qualities, or qualia."[82] I can show you a dish of guacamole or play Rachmaninoff's Second Concerto or mow your lawn, but only you can experience the taste, the melody, and the smell. The natural sciences

---

and Legal Reasoning: Using xTalk to Model the Alien Tort Claims Act and Torture Victim Protection Act, 11 RICH. J.L. & TECH. 53 (2004).

81 In an essay on the loneliness of the United States Presidency, Nancy Gibbs quoted Dwight D. Eisenhower: "[O]ne [person] must conscientiously, deliberately, prayerfully scrutinize every argument, every proposal, every prediction, every alternative, every probable outcome of his action, and then—all alone—make [the] decision." Nancy Gibb, *Obama After One Year: The Loneliest Job*, TIME, Jan. 25, 2010, at 64, http://www.time.com/time/magazine/article/0,9171,1953705,00.html (deliberately made gender-neutral by me).

82 DAVID CHALMERS, THE CONSCIOUS MIND: IN SEARCH OF A FUNDAMENTAL THEORY 4 (1996).

have not so far been helpful in explaining that phenomenal experience. Much of the debate is about whether science will ever be able to explain it.[83]

The philosophical question at the very edge of the development of artificial intelligence is: can a computer have a mind that observers would regard as conscious (i.e. that it is thinking as a human being would think)? Alan Turing, one of the pioneers of computing, proposed the most famous test of whether a machine can be said to think.[84] If a questioner poses sustained questions to a hidden responder and cannot tell whether the responder is a human being or a machine, and the responder is a machine, then, for all intents and purposes, the machine thinks.[85] The most famous response to the Turing test was John Searle's Chinese room problem, the point of which is that the mere carrying out of the steps of an algorithm does not logically require that the entity so carrying it out actually understands it.[86] I haven't met Ross, but I feel quite confident that he/it won't pass the Turing test.

There are many hypotheses about consciousness, but one that resonates with me comes from the renowned mathematician and physicist, Roger Penrose. He explicitly linked the issue of consciousness and judgment, claiming that judgment-forming is itself the *hallmark* of consciousness.[87] His premise was that consciousness is likely to have conferred some selective evolutionary advantage on those possessing it. He asks what that advantage might have been.[88] What consciousness permits is figuring out how to deal with new problems not previously faced.[89] Humans, unlike computers, have non-algorithmic capabilities, particularly as to judgments of understanding, truth, common sense, and artistic appraisal. That is a selective advantage over non-conscious or wholly pre-programmed beings. If one knows which algorithm is necessary for the solution of a problem, then one must have seen the problem before.[90] But what happens when the problem is wholly new, and we must decide which algorithm to use? Penrose said, "Somehow, consciousness is needed in order to handle situations where we have to form new judgments, and where the rules have not been laid down beforehand."[91] What Schön called problem-setting, Penrose described as the issue that so frustrated us in middle-school algebra: "Once an appropriate

---

83 COLIN MCGINN, THE MYSTERIOUS FLAME: CONSCIOUS MINDS IN A MATERIAL WORLD 4–5, 28–29 (1999).
84 A.M. Turing, *Computing Machinery and Intelligence*, 59 MIND 433, 433–34 (1950).
85 *Id.*
86 John R. Searle, *Minds, Brains, and Programs*, in THE MIND'S I 353 (Douglas R. Hofstadter & Daniel C. Dennett, eds. 2000).
87 ROGER PENROSE, THE EMPEROR'S NEW MIND: CONCERNING COMPUTERS, MINDS, AND THE LAWS OF PHYSICS 532 (1998).
88 *Id.* at 529.
89 *Id.* at 530–31.
90 *Id.* at 534.
91 *Id.* at 531.

algorithm is found, the problem is, in a sense, solved."[92] If our teacher gives us the algebraic equivalence, the process of solving for *x* is far easier than if we are given a story, and it is up to us to determine the algebraic equation that will solve the problem of the number of apples Mary will be able to eat in June.

Hence we don't need to get to complex business decisions, like the one facing the CEO, to encounter the loneliness of a lawyer's judgment-making. A law student will experience it in class or while taking an exam. Even before we get to the modus ponens application of a rule to the facts (the "A" in the famous IRAC or TREAC method of answering law school and bar examination questions), we need to decide that there is a legal issue buried in the problem and select a rule to be applied (the IR or TRE portions of the method). These problem-setting judgments "themselves . . . are the manifestations of the action of *consciousness*."[93] But they are lonely judgments that "one continually makes while one is in a conscious state, bringing together all the facts, sense impressions, and remembered experiences that are of relevance, and weighing things against one another—even forming inspired judgments, on occasion."[94]

Perhaps science will someday be able to conclude the naturalistic basis for consciousness. Perhaps technology will allow tracking of the substance and not just the electric impulse of thought. For the time being, however, it remains that each of us has privileged access to our own inner lives, and we have either irreducible free will or an inability to unravel the complexity of determinism. Something is going on in there, but we have no way of knowing precisely what it is. Like consciousness, our experience of judgment is wholly our own and is capable outwardly of being replicated by an automaton or zombie with no inner experiences whatsoever. We will simply never know whether anything compelled the bank CEO to say, "I think we have to settle."

Sometimes it appears that judgment is a collective undertaking; for example, in a faculty vote on a pressing issue or in the vote by which a law firm partnership admits new partners. That is different. Judgment still occurs in the mind of the voter. For example, our faculty recently took a vote expressing the sense of the faculty on an issue facing the university. The individual decision of the faculty member proposing the resolution was an act of conscience. Each individual decision to speak at the meeting, and even the decision to attend the meeting, was an act of conscience, as was each instance of casting a vote. The collective expression resulting from the vote, however, was a political act, not an act of conscience.

As Hannah Arendt suggested, conscience, in the sense of the ethical judgment one makes as in the faculty vote, is a mental activity closely linked to consciousness

92 *Id.* at 534.
93 *Id.* at 531.
94 *Id.* at 533.

in the sense of inner awareness described above.[95] Thinking, she observed, is the soundless dialogue we have with ourselves; it is like a wind that sweeps away "the implications of unexamined opinions and thereby destroys them" and manifests itself in judgment.[96] She further observed that judgment is "the faculty to judge *particulars* without subsuming them under those general rules which can be taught and learned until they grow into habits that can be replaced by other habits and rules."[97]

Whether the judgments are ethical, as opposed to merely practical, they occur in our minds, are privileged to us, and are beyond influence, authority, external truth-justifications, and power, regardless of whether we accede, knowingly or unconsciously, in the solitude of our own minds, to influence, authority, justifications, and power.[98] If, as lawyers, we are going to act rather than merely consider and advise as to the options, if we are going to cooperate or compromise rather than vanquish through the assertion of authority, if we are going to temper the inclination to self-deception, we alone are going to have to do it. Understanding that takes us a long way past merely thinking like lawyers.

---

95 Hannah Arendt, *Thinking and Moral Considerations: A Lecture*, 51 SOC. RES. 7, 34–35 (1984).

96 *Id*. at 36.

97 *Id*. at 35–37.

98 In a discussion of this point, my colleague Pat Shin directed me a number of years ago to the "plural subject theory" developed by the philosopher Margaret Gilbert. *See, e.g.*, MARGARET GILBERT, SOCIALITY AND RESPONSIBILITY: NEW ESSAYS IN PLURAL SUBJECT THEORY (1999). Her central thesis is that a joint commitment is fundamentally different than an individual intention and "cannot be analyzed [solely as] . . . the sum or aggregate of the individual commitments" or intentions. *Id*. at 3. That seems consistent with my position. A commitment, whether individual or joint, is a *doing*, even though it involves the minds of the committers. In contrast, a judgment is a thought process that precedes commitment, whether individual or joint.

7 Beyond Legal Reasoning

O wad some Power the giftie gie us
To see oursels as ithers see us.[1]

In the previous six chapters, we've looked at "thinking like a lawyer" and its implications for better or worse. The thesis in Chapters 2 and 3 was that: (a) the core of pure lawyering is the reasoning process by which we theorize legal consequences from antecedent factual conditions, and (b) the process is agnostic as to truth or the moral value of the outcomes. My critique of pure lawyering has not been an attack on legal reasoning. It has been an assessment of its limits. We've seen there is a lawless or ruleless moment within the process of what Donald Schön called problem setting. For lawyers, that begins with issue-spotting on a first-year exam. One intuits the possible rules that could apply, and then fashions a legal theory based on the one that best fits the circumstances. In pure lawyering, the client's gold standard is the lawyer who, when the chips are down in a hard case, comes up with a clever theory that wins the litigation or solves the business problem. Once past that first leap to a rule that fits, induction and deduction take over, and the lawyer is well into the reasoning process. But the hard part, and the hardest part to explain, is over.

The insight from Kant has been that legal reasoning, like all exercises of reason, is merely a regulative process, and not in itself the source of constitutive truth. Even if there were truth to be found, that one has merely engaged in the process is no guarantee one has found it. But the question of truth, when considering legal reasoning, is a red herring. The legal conclusions a lawyer reaches are normative, not descriptive, in that they are the logical inference of what the consequence *ought to be* if the operative facts are present. There is no way to prove, as in scientific theorizing, that the conclusions are either true or false by way of empirical testing. Yet the similarities of the reasoning process as between

---

1 Robert Burns, *To a Louse*, BURNS COUNTRY, http://www.robertburns.org/works/97.shtml (last visited Aug. 21, 2016).

description and normativity can have untoward consequences, particularly for lawyering outside of the litigation arena. We explored some of these: illusions of moral certainty, cynical instrumentalism, inappropriate game-playing or modeling, focusing on blame instead of causation, mental gridlock, arguments from authority, and self-deception. All are potential consequences of the failure, at some point in one's lawyering career, to step back and take stock of what is substance and what is form in the lawyerly thinking process.

My goal has been to give philosophical cover to a less traditional and more nuanced professional self-conception beyond that of the metaphoric zealous warrior-advocate. It has not been to suggest that using the sublimated violence of litigation—of engaging in pure lawyering as a last resort—is necessarily wrong. War is hell, but sometimes generals are forced to go to war. The warrior-lawyer metaphor is well developed. It would be easy simply to end by saying that the metaphor for lawyers can be as well for diplomats, peacemakers, counselors, policy-makers, or deal-makers. But I want finally to suggest a means of thinking beyond the thinking weapons of the warrior-lawyer.

If there is a continuity between teaching pure lawyering and getting beyond it, it lies in that murky area of problem-setting. Recall the conclusion from *Educating Lawyers* that lawyers need to be able to connect the law's models (and their inherent simplifications) to the complexity of real life. Legal relationships, the ones lawyers get trained to see, do not exist in a vacuum. Certainly in business transactions, but even when litigation is part of a broader strategy, lawyers need to understand that legal meaning—the anticipation of legal consequences from antecedent conditions—can be significantly less than the whole of meaning that the non-lawyer participants take from the encounter. Our challenge as lawyers who don't litigate is to escape the cocoon of law school, law firms, continuing legal education, and bench and bar activities. We need to understand not just legal conditions and consequences, but also to understand the meaning created by the law and the work lawyers do. When, as *Educating Lawyers* notes, the doctrines and rules of the formal and rational systems of laws diverge from the common sense understandings of the layperson, it is often that the law has to give.

The profundity of that particular insight is that people derive meaning about the world around them often by means other than the purely rational. They certainly find meaning other than by thinking like a lawyer. Understanding and dealing with meaning is not just a matter of being smart and analytical as though we were behavioral scientists. We probably deceive ourselves if we believe we are always making cool and objective assessments of someone else's behavior. Instead, we filter what we perceive through our own subjective experience of translating desires into results. If you want to be a litigation-warrior, you will almost certainly worry about the subjective reactions you provoke in a judge or a juror. There's usually no reason to worry about your opponent's subjective reactions other than as a matter of strategy and tactics. But if you want to solve problems with your adversary rather than vanquish him, it may pay to: (a) see yourself a little more objectively, (b) see the other with whom you are transacting as having subjectivities like your own, and (c) understand that we are each using imperfect objective signs including but not limited to, the rationality of pure lawyering to convey subjective meaning.

This last chapter presents several modest suggestions about reflection on these particular topics. Even if my discussion of them is rational and theoretical, I acknowledge that the tools are, in practice, far more affective than rational. I have little hope that I will persuade you by way of argument. Rather, mull them over and see if they speak to you. The first is a consideration of the cognitive science of meaning. The thesis is that human beings have a unique ability to "blend" concepts and thus create new meanings. Just how do we and others go about attaching significance not just to rationality like the fruits of pure lawyering, but to other manifestations? How might that occur in circumstances in which lawyers are involved?

The second is about the second-person perspective. This means understanding there isn't an object on the other side of the transaction, but somebody who has a subjective inner life, just like you do. When you combine the second-person idea with the blending idea, you end up with what I call empathetic blending, a willingness to understand meaning as conveyed to others.

The third is my attempt to deconstruct wisdom. It involves a funny paradox. One side of it is the adoption of an attitude of epistemic humility—being conscious of the affective underpinnings of wisdom and learning versus knowledge and analysis—when considering the reasons that others act. The flip side is epistemic courage: being willing to take the leap or the plunge and to accept responsibility for the consequences of one's decisions in an uncertain world.

The creation of meaning

My theoretical speculations about the relatively narrow scope of *legal* meaning stem from my observed experience as a business lawyer. For example, why do venture capital term sheets exist even though there is almost no real-world legal force to them? Why do most real-world contracts exist even though they are rarely litigated? Why do business people tend to have a far more fluid reaction to contract terms than the lawyers? A lawyer's first obligation is to focus on how the language of the document creates rights or structures or allocates risk. Nevertheless, the documents can convey meaning beyond their semantic content. Language can, for example, be performative. As the philosopher of language J.L. Austin observed:

> to utter the sentence (in, of course, the appropriate circumstance) is not to describe my doing of what I should be said in so uttering to be doing or to state that I am doing it: it is to do it.[2]

2 J.L. Austin, How to Do Things with Words 6 (1965).

The sentence, "I take thee to be my wedded wife," is not, when recited in a ceremony, a description of one's action but the performance of the act of marrying.[3] Or the document can have symbolic or ritual meaning. The Jewish marriage contract, or *ketubah*, that my wife and I signed is neither truly legally binding on us nor a performative, but part of the ritual we undertook. I have attended enough closings of multi-million and multi-billion dollar corporate transactions to believe that the documents, while obviously having legal effect by way of their semantic content, also exude meaning as custom, symbol, or ritual.

It is this last symbolic or ritualistic aspect on which I want to focus. A number of theorists have in recent years tried to assess meaning as an aspect of cognitive science. Whether or not it ultimately succeeds as science, it is nevertheless thought-provoking. Professors Mark Turner and Gilles Fauconnier coined the term "conceptual blending" to describe the process of the creation and descent of meaning. They are *not* addressing meaning in the interpretive sense familiar to lawyers, as "the textual scholar who takes it as given that a particular text is meaningful and . . . who regards it as his task to interpret the text for us."[4] The issue instead is "[h]ow it is possible in the first place for meaning to arise and descend."[5] Turner and Fauconnier contend blending or "cognitive integration" is the process by which humans derive new meaning from influencing spaces.[6]

An example is the meaning of the sentence, "the surgeon is a butcher." We have a fairly clear idea of what a surgeon is: a doctor who cuts into human bodies for the purpose of curing ailments. We also have a fairly clear idea of what a butcher is: someone who cuts up animals for consumption by human beings. One can understandably be a competent surgeon or a competent butcher. Turner says:

> [T]he essence of conceptual integration is its creation of a new mental assembly, a blend, that is identical to neither of its influences and not merely a correspondence between them and usually not even an additive combination of some of their features, but is instead a third conceptual space, a child space, a blended space, with new meaning. This new meaning is "emergent" meaning, in the sense that it is not available in either of the influencing spaces but instead emerges in the blended space by means of blending those influencing spaces.[7]

---

3 *Id*. at 8–9. As Austin notes, the performative utterance need not be the only way in which a particular act is undertaken. The act of marrying could be the silent hopping over a broom or the smashing of a wine glass.

4 MARK TURNER, COGNITIVE DIMENSIONS OF SOCIAL SCIENCE: THE WAY WE THINK ABOUT POLITICS, ECONOMICS, LAW, AND SOCIETY 11 (2001).

5 *Id*.

6 *Id*. at 16 (setting forth Turner's own compendium of the articles in which he and Fauconnier expounded the theory).

7 *Id*. at 17.

There is nothing about being a doctor or being a butcher that suggests incompetence, but a butcher-doctor means something: the doctor is not competent.[8] We could string combinations together, each of which creates a new meaning. Tom Brady, an American football quarterback, is a surgeon when he picks apart defenses with his passes. "Surgeon-quarterback" means something: an expert quarterback. We could go on. A faculty committee could have a quarterback, but the "committee-quarterback" probably does not have anything to do with football. "Committee-quarterback" means the leader of the committee but in a particular fashion—a leader who is not merely titular but is involved in getting things done.

The creation of meaning is not just a matter of semantics nor even of a single mind's integration of influencing spaces to generate new meaning. I once sent an email to my friend, the late (and beloved) Dan Markel, the founder of PrawfsBlawg, a website originally intended to highlight the work of relatively new law professors (hence "Profs" combined with "raw" contributing to a "blog" about "law"). Working with the TypePad, a blogging program, can be tricky, and I was pointing out several mechanical mistakes a new guest blogger had made. I wrote to Dan: "You are the Johnny Carson of new bloggers." That was a conceptual blend. One influencing space was mentoring new stand-up comedians. The other influencing space was law professor blogging. The blend of the two suggested a new kind of mentor: one whose job it is to introduce neophyte law professor bloggers.

Turner's core example of blending arose out of a wholly non-semantic social ritual: Clifford Geertz's iconic anthropological observations of the rituals surrounding a traditional Balinese cockfight.[9] There is no particular consequence to my projection of Johnny Carson to a Florida State University law professor, but as Turner observes, for the Balinese cockfight, "there is a lot at stake; there will be a winner and a loser," and a complex governing structure has arisen.[10] In Bali, winning and losing takes on a meaning well beyond the mere entanglement of two fighting chickens. Turner quoted Geertz:

> [To the Balinese,] [f]ighting cocks . . . is like playing with fire only not getting burned. You activate village and kin group rivalries and hostilities, but in "play" form, coming dangerously and entrancingly close to the expression of open and direct interpersonal and intergroup aggression . . . but not quite, because, after all, it is "only a cockfight."[11]

The idea of blending is an avenue for coming to terms with the paradoxes of business lawyering I posed at the beginning of this section.

---

8 *Id.*
9 Clifford Geertz, *Deep Play: Notes on the Balinese Cockfight*, in THE INTERPRETATION OF CULTURES 412 (2000).
10 TURNER, *supra* note 4, at 42.
11 *Id.* at 44 (quoting Geertz, *supra* note 9, at 440).

A contract, however, is one particular way in which human beings make sense (or attempt to control) a highly contingent and uncertain future. Contracts create private law using the syllogisms of pure lawyering to anticipate future antecedent conditions and dictate the legal consequences if they occur. For example, assume a store owner is renting space in the mall. She may need the space beyond the one-year term of the lease. Thus, she asks for and receives the following provision in the document: if Tenant notifies Landlord in writing at least ninety days before the end date of the lease that Tenant wishes to extend the lease for another year, then the legal consequence will be that the lease is extended. But for this private law, Landlord would be entitled to evict Tenant at the end of a year. This is a relatively simple and mundane way of using a contract to impose the kind of formal linguistic model on the world we observed in Chapter 4.

The critical lesson for somebody getting beyond pure lawyering is the potential divergence between the meaning of the words as logical or coherent constructs within the law (i.e. the documents and structures the business lawyer creates on behalf of clients) and the possibly unrelated meanings of those words and other acts within the custom or ritual that constitutes executing a document. If I understand conceptual blending as a source of meaning to others and myself, does it help me make judgments beyond pure lawyering? I am positive it does not help to *explain* in naturalistic terms the leap we have already explored that is the making of the judgment. It simply does not eliminate the irreducibility of (i.e. the mystery in trying to explain) judgment. Turner himself denies any such metaphysical ambitions. To give blending its explanatory "oomph," all we have to be able to observe is that, given two existing influencing spaces, they are capable of producing a blend that does not necessarily correspond with the original meanings or empirical reality.[12]

The concept of blending is a powerful image for the non-algorithmic aspect of judgment. Blends are metaphors. They shake up the existing categories (the influencing spaces) and create new ways of interpreting the world. Turner explains:

> Blends let you do what you cannot do, be what you cannot be, not always so you can escape your situation, but instead, often, so you can learn about, make decisions about, and develop consequences for your situation, especially your mental and social reality, through events in a blend that, sometimes, for one reason or another, cannot or will not in fact be real.[13]

Light beams have nothing to do with surfing or sailing a boat; however, blending the influencing space of chasing a wave and the known property of electro-magnetic

---

12 What makes this "cognitive science" rather than philosophy is the hypothesis that conceptual blending is the key differentiator between modern human minds and all others. At least in concept, that is a testable proposition. TURNER, *supra* note 4, at 52–54.

13 *Id.* at 44.

radiation led Einstein to believe he could never catch up with the light wave but instead that, as he approached its speed, time itself would slow down.

If we understand blending as an ongoing engine for the creation of meaning, we will better understand how we create meaning beyond the rational content of the legal maneuver. Professor Turner says, "We often take our cues for action, feeling, or belief from these blends. We assemble blended futures and choose between them, or blend counterfactual presents and grieve at their counterfactuality."[14] In counterfactual blends, we have to imagine what might have happened, but didn't, as the result of a particular choice.

For example, in business acquisitions, lawyers negotiate the text that allocates liabilities created by the selling business. The buyer of the business assumes some of the liabilities. The seller retains those liabilities the buyer does not assume. Third parties, however, may not be legally obliged to honor that allocation. Lawyers cure the problem (assuming both parties are collectable) by providing cross-indemnifications. The seller will indemnify the buyer if a third party asserts a non-assumed liability and vice versa. Generally, the parties limit those indemnification rights—there are deductibles called "baskets" and agreed limits on total indemnification called "caps." Moreover, the indemnification rights do not extend to the statute of limitations; the parties negotiate a "survival period."

The Fauconnier-Turner model of counterfactuals accords with my intuition about the non-textual meaning implicit in this bit of lawyering. In qualitative research, the preliminary descriptive question is, "What if X had never happened?" It is a means of getting to the normative policy decision, "Should we ban future instances of X?" The question "asks us to blend conceptual structure from different mental spaces to create a separate, counterfactual mental space."[15] We make choices by composing, completing, and elaborating from the mental influencing spaces we have thus created. Composition is a matter of selectively bringing meaning back from the influencing image to the blend. Completion involves introducing other specific or general knowledge that might bear on the result. Elaboration "develops the blend through imaginative mental simulation according to principles, logic, and dynamic patterns in the blend."[16]

Let's apply that to the particular text of the acquisition agreement. We are lawyers in a conference room negotiating the indemnification provisions. We are creating emergent meaning out of multiple counterfactual possibilities. We compose the blend by thinking about all the things that could go right or wrong in connection with the operations being sold. One influencing space is the image of the products the business makes. Who is in the best position to deal with defective products that were manufactured before the closing but for which claims were not made until long afterward? We might imagine all of the liabilities as a pool that is capable of being divided. That is another influencing space. We complete the blend

14 *Id.* at 54.
15 *Id.* at 70.
16 *Id.* at 74.

by calling on cycles of experience in similar deals, for example, the actual likelihood that third parties assert claims more than one or two years after a closing. We elaborate by imagining how we might fairly classify or divide the pool into different tanks, perhaps each with different rules governing the allocation of liabilities or the survival of the indemnification rights.

Even this description of a small (but important) part of the deal-making process understates the complexity of the "meaning making" that is going on as among all of the actors—individuals within the corporate clients, the lawyers for the parties, and others not involved but who may be affected by the transaction. For example, when a large corporation sells a division, it commonly wants to include in the acquisition agreement a post-closing covenant under which the purchasing corporation agrees to maintain the salaries, perks, and job positions of employees for a period of time (e.g., one or two years). There is a meaning to this provision from a purely legal standpoint: the covenant significantly reduces the legal risk that employees will assert employment termination or discrimination claims against the selling company arising out of the sale. Whether or not that really is a significant risk, the provision also has separate and non-legal important purpose. What the provision says, not to the departing employees, but to the employees who remain with the unsold divisions of the selling corporation, is that they too will be protected in a similar way if the time comes when the corporation determines that its portfolio requires that their division be sold. That is, the selling corporation is less concerned here with either the economics of the sale as it relates to the currently transferred employees or the marginal legal risk than with the meaning that descends to other non-transferred employees.

There are myriad other examples of a divergence between the semantic content of a lawyer's utterances and the meaning of the utterances. The filing of a lawsuit against the seller for breach of representations and warranties (or worse yet, fraud) after the closing of the business acquisition may make perfect sense from a litigation standpoint. It may, however, mean something wholly different in the investment community—namely, that management was not competent in its pre-closing due diligence or in the post-closing integration of the company. Aspects of employee relationships, like incentive compensation or perks of office (e.g., access to the company plane, even if the executive pays for it out of her own pocket) may create meanings and atmospherics in the workplace only marginally related to the economics or legalities of the situation.

Moreover, my long experience of deal negotiations is that there is the equivalent of ritualized cockfighting among the lawyers, wholly apart from the interests of their clients, and it creates meaning beyond the mere reduction of a business transaction or structure to words. I recall a large firm lawyer I had hired to negotiate the representations and warranties in an acquisition whereby we were acquiring another company. The firm on the other side had a reputation of being tough and aggressive. She told me that it was well understood that if you were a lawyer in that firm, you simply "had" to win a majority of the negotiating points, regardless of their importance to the deal. One of the business people observed to me that the battle between the two young lawyers over the document had taken on a life of its own. I have done no empirical work on this point, but I am willing to suggest that any survey of transactional lawyers will indicate that this is a discouragingly common phenomenon.

The profession—academic and practicing—reflects blending that has been reified as concretely as the social norms of Balinese cockfighting. The lesson to be learned is that even high-powered lawyers, trained in pure lawyering, begin to provide exquisite judgment when, consciously or unconsciously, they understand the blending by which they create emergent meaning not necessarily congruent with the rational words they use in undertaking legal acts.

The second person

Conceptual blending is a powerful description of the process by which we continuously create meaning. What strikes me about its application to professional judgment beyond pure lawyering is the combination of empathy with that understanding.[17] We cannot control the blends by which others create meaning, but we can think about blends as we might make them ourselves, and try to anticipate the ones that others create.

I thus want to extend the assessment of exquisite judgment to include the ability to distinguish between "I," "You," and "It." That is, my judgments will be better if I understand how others with whom I deal create meaning by way of conceptual blending. To do that, I must undertake a further blend in which I project myself into the counterfactual circumstance of being that person, with that person's needs, and the meanings that person will create out of the mutual circumstance in which we find ourselves. But another subject is not merely something, an "It," in the environment. She is another consciousness like "I." That is, she is a "You," who is simultaneously creating meaning. To exercise judgment, I must empathize with her, and I cannot reason my way to empathy.

Empathy is an emotional, not a rational, response to another. One of the most significant statements about empathy comes from Martin Buber's *I and Thou*.[18] Buber, one of the foremost philosophers and theologians of the 20th century, has a reputation as a mystic. Yet he is circumspect in his "mystical" claims and concerned not so much about any person's relationship with God, as about relationships with each other. Ironically, *I and Thou*, the primary statement of Buber's philosophy, is not revered as a Jewish document. Its fame spread as the result of acclaim by Protestant theologians.[19] Moreover, it claimed no access to mystical insight. His translator, Walter Kauffman, observed,

---

17　*See* Patrick McKee, *Toward an Epistemology of Wise Judgment*, 10 PHILO 136 (2007) for another philosophical approach to the role of shifting one's perspective in making wise judgments.

18　MARTIN BUBER, I AND THOU (Walter Kauffman, trans. 1970) (1923).

19　Walter Kaufmann, *I and You: A Prologue*, in BUBER, *supra* note 18, at 20.

[w]hat is much more remarkable is that a sharp attack on all talk about God and all pretensions to knowledge about God—a sustained attempt to rescue the religious dimension of life from the theologians—should have been received so well by theologians.[20]

Buber understood our interaction with the world and others not as it or they acting upon us, but in the very pairing of us with the world or others.[21] Hence, a third-person relationship is not merely "I" and "It." Instead, a word pair "I-It" symbolizes it in language. Similarly, a second-person relationship is not "I" and "You." The relationship itself is a basic word composed of "I-You."[22] Our experience of the world occurs in our mental processing of the those I-It and I-You relationships. In the simplest case, my relationship with a taxi driver may not be significantly different than my relationship with the subway. It is I-It. The taxi driver is an instrumentality, not another person like me. It is possible to live a life defined entirely by the "I-It" relationship. That is a life in which our reason (of which pure lawyering is a subset) is paramount.

In contrast, the "I-You" relationship is the unmediated second-person relationship.[23] It is the pure *encounter* between two beings.[24] I'm not sure the encounter even has to involve explicit communication between them. I was walking the dogs the other day and passed a little girl sitting on a step with a table on the sidewalk, and a sign in child's printing that said "Bake Sale $1.00." I had this welling up of emotion that had to do with my memories of my children undertaking projects and their grief when disappointed by the outcomes. That is, my relationship with her, even though I was on the other side of the street, transformed from I-It to I-You because I could feel her possible subjectivity in the same way I could feel that of my own children.

In Buber's philosophy, the theory of the "I-You" relationship becomes practical through what he calls dialogue, a process he described in his book *Between Man and Man*.[25] Buber himself expressly extended the concept to the process of making difficult business and legal judgments. He wrote, "You ask with a laugh, can the leader of a great technical undertaking practise the responsibility of dialogue?" and answered his own question: "He can."[26] The essence of dialogue is rooted in a relationship between one person and another, and that relationship transforms the nature of the communication. "Moreover it is completed not in some 'mystical' event, but in one that is in the precise sense factual, thoroughly

---

20 BUBER, *supra* note 18, at 20–21.
21 *Id.* at 53.
22 *Id.* at 53–54.
23 *Id.* at 62.
24 *Id.*
25 MARTIN BUBER, BETWEEN MAN AND MAN (Ronald Gregor-Smith, trans. 2002) (1947).
26 *Id.* at 44.

dovetailed into the common human world and the concrete time-sequence."[27] Dialogue does not occur when one person perceives another in his capacity as observer or onlooker: the person observed "is for them an object separated from themselves."[28] In dialogue, he perceives in the other person "something, which I cannot grasp in any objective way at all, that 'says something' to me."[29] That describes my reaction to the bake sale child. Buber posits an intuitional sense, derived from a second-person relationship, that the world is something other than what the subject, the "I," has rationalized and justified it to be.[30]

Our ability to make excellent judgments arises not just from pure lawyering but as well by the intuitive insight we obtain only by hearing and accepting what someone says to us. It may well be that, in a particular negotiation, we cannot satisfy what the other side wants. To be able to make that decision, however, we first have to be able to hear: "[t]he basic movement of the life of dialogue is the turning towards the other."[31]

Note how pragmatic Buber, the mystic, is on the subject of dialogue, particularly as contrasted with monologue. The problem with monologue is not a failure in the ability to create rich meanings. Rather, "[h]e who is living the life of monologue is never aware of the other as something that is absolutely not himself and at the same time something with which he nevertheless communicates."[32] Dialogue is a relationship in which we hear the questions of another; it is not altruism, and it is not love.[33] But neither is it a reasoning process, like thinking like a lawyer.[34]

Buber's lyricism about the I and the You itself blends with the idea of conceptual blending to create a different way of understanding empathy in action. When I undertake empathetic conceptual blending, I am operating affectively, not rationally. By imagining that I *am* my adversary, I may be able to see that the world is something other than what I have rationalized and justified it to be.

---

27 *Id.*
28 *Id.* at 11.
29 *Id.*
30 *Id.* at 14.
31 *Id.* at 25.
32 Id. at 23.
33 *Id.* at 24.
34 I need to distinguish another second-person concept that has had some academic currency but does not get beyond the boundaries of law and lawyering. Professor Robin Bradley Kar, building on the work of philosopher, Stephen Darwall, undertook an ambitious re-conception of legal positivism. Robin Bradley Kar, *Hart's Response to Exclusive Legal Positivism*, 95 GEO. L. J. 393 (2007); Robin Bradley Kar, *The Second-Person Standpoint and the Law*, 40 LOYOLA L.A. L. REV. 881 (2007). His claim was that law is best understood as a second-person relationship, under which we address one another with claims and grievances, or respond to those claims with apology, excuse, or justification. That is a fundamentally different point than I am making here. Professor Kar's casting of the second-person relationship as one of the right to make claims and demands on another is essentially *legal*. He has focused on the other's *rights* as against the actor, not as I am here, on the actor's inter-subjective *understanding* of the other's needs.

I have resisted the tendency to rationalization and self-deception but not by think-ing like a lawyer. Rather I have heard and attempted to consider meaning, at least for the empathetic moment, in what you and I do or say to each other.

Wisdom

Wisdom as a subject of inquiry goes back at least to Aristotle. Recently, it has been the subject of investigation in groups such as the Berlin Wisdom Project, estab-lished by Paul B. Baltes at the Max Planck Institute for Human Development in the 1980s.[35] As Baltes and others concede (not surprisingly) wisdom is a difficult subject to pin down systematically, as its acquisition "requires time and effort and that it involves some combination of education, practice, apprenticeship, personal experience, and deliberate reflection about life matters."[36] So I am not going to try to be systematic but merely thoughtful about it.

I have come to think of wisdom as a combination of epistemic humility and epistemic courage. Like empathetic blending, both of these attributes are affective or emotional, rather than capable of rational reduction.[37] Epistemic humility deals with the knowledge side of things—to be wise I need, like Socrates, to be aware there are so many things I do not know, and to be skeptical of any assertion of a foundational truth. It is not to reject candidates for foundational truth out of hand, but it is likely to leave them for all time as candidates without ever allowing them to be elected. The first step in the translation of knowledge to action, then, is an understanding of the subjectivity inherent in knowledge and humility about *any* analysis in the face of the need to act.

One of the observations in the Summary to *Educating Lawyers* was that the young lawyer in practice often continues to think "like a student rather than an apprentice practitioner, conveying the impression that lawyers are more like competitive scholars than attorneys engaged with the problems of clients."[38] My first epiphany on the subject of engagement with clients and humility took place early in my career. The firm entrusted me with an unsupervised assignment to handle a lawsuit Conrail had filed against a client in the scrap metal industry. The client had shipped material to a customer, and paid the rate quoted by Conrail's

---

35 *See* Paul B. Baltes & Jacqui Smith, *The Fascination of Wisdom: Its Nature, Ontogeny, and Function*, 3 PERSP. ON PSYCHOL. SCI. 56 (2008).

36 *Id.* at 57.

37 Some have attempted empirical studies of wisdom. I recognize that the game in such studies lies in the definition of wisdom. Nevertheless, one conclusion they reach is that intelligence alone is not the most powerful predictor. "Instead, high predictive value comes from a combination of psychosocial characteristics and life history factors, including openness to experience, generativity, cognitive style, contact with excellent mentors, and some exposure to structured and critical life experiences." *Id.* at 60.

38 SUMMARY OF WILLIAM M. SULLIVAN, ET AL., EDUCATING LAWYERS: PREPARATION FOR THE PROFESSION OF LAW 6 (2007), http://archive.carnegiefoundation.org/pdfs/elibrary/elibrary_pdf_ 632.pdf.

sales agent. Conrail's subsequent audit revealed that the client had underpaid the rate applicable to the route the traffic had taken. Conrail sued for the difference, citing the longstanding principle that carrier rate misquotations are not a defense against legal actions by carriers seeking to collect undercharges.[39]

My contact at the client was the grizzled old freight manager, who insisted that the appropriate defense came from something he called the "Red Book." He insisted there was an exception to the rule when the carrier had misrouted the traffic contrary to the shipper's instructions. I looked high and low in the usual case reporters for any indication that such a rule existed, and simply discounted what this "school of hard knocks" graduate was telling me. I had another pure lawyering strategy anyway: "if you want to collect, you must have a record of the debt." I requested the shipping records in discovery and, when Conrail did not produce them, kept filing discovery motions. In a way I was justified in doing so, because Conrail eventually agreed to dismiss the case when it couldn't find the records of the shipment routing.

In the meantime, the old traffic manager, no doubt with some amusement, tried to persuade this bright young whippersnapper that there really was a dispositive answer to the issue. And it turns out he was right. There *was* a Red Book, and the answer to the issue was in I.C.C. Conference Ruling 214.[40] But for the longest time, I simply could not see it because of what the behaviorists call the *bias blind spot*:

> The tendency to believe that one's own experiences afford a particularly enlightened perspective on the conflict, and that one thereby sees the relevant issues more clearly than anyone else, can lead individuals to reject proposed solutions not only when offered by members of the opposing side but also when suggested by neutral third parties.[41]

39 Louisville & Nashville R.R. v. Maxwell, 237 U.S. 94, 97 (1915). ("Deviation from [the applicable rate] is not permitted upon any pretext . . . . Ignorance or misquotation of rates is not an excuse for paying or charging either less or more than the rate filed. This rule is undeniably strict and obviously may work hardship in some cases, but it embodies the policy which has been adopted by Congress in the regulation of interstate commerce in order to prevent unjust discrimination.")

40 CHARLES F. WALDEN, FREIGHT TRAFFIC GUIDE (1921), http://archive.org/stream/freighttrafficgu00walduoft#page/n9/mode/2up. Ruling 214, adopted in 1907, acknowledged that "[t]he lawful charge on any shipment is the tariff rate via the route over, which the shipment moves. No carrier can lawfully refund any part of the lawful charge except under authority so to do from the Commission or from a court of competent jurisdiction." Nevertheless, there was an exception to the rule if the traffic moved on a higher cost route not specified by the shipper, as long as there was no attempt to evade the correct tariff. *Id.* at 216–17.

41 Joyce Ehrlinger, Thomas Gilovich, & Lee Ross, *Peering into the Bias Blind Spot: People's Assessment of Bias in Themselves and Others*, 31 PERSONALITY & SOC. PSYCHOL. BULL. 1, 11 (2005).

I recently had a dialogue with a close friend about data he had discovered regarding the comparative ability of adults and children to collaborate in finding solutions to difficult problems. His view was that collaboration could be taught. I thought not. The source of difference between the adults and the children was that the children *learned* naturally. It was because they were already learners (an epistemic orientation) that they collaborated. Again, the infinite regress surfaced. Can you teach an adult non-learner (one who resists learning) to learn? It seems obvious that someone who resists learning will also resist learning how to learn. Teaching is an activity from the outside in; learning is an activity from the inside out. Teaching is equivalent to disclosure or information; learning is equivalent to judgment or decision. My accession to wisdom in the Conrail case, it seems to me, was less cognitive than affective. I simply reached the point through utter frustration where I was prepared to listen to someone I did not think knew as much as I did about the systems of the law.

Even the most dyed-in-the-wool evidence-based management gurus have no reductive silver bullet for wise decision-making. Stanford management professors Pfeffer and Sutton wrote a book called *Hard Facts, Dangerous Half-Truths & Total Nonsense: Profiting from Evidence-Based Management*.[42] In a section entitled "Wisdom: The Most Important Thing," they still fall back on attitude and state of mind rather than intellectual horsepower. The most important characteristic of managers and advisers is the *attitude* they have toward knowledge. "The idea that wisdom is reflected in the attitude people have toward what they know, not in how *much* or how *little* they know, goes back at least to Plato's writings." Wisdom, however, precedes the conceptual framework used to organize the data. Wisdom is the mental act of "striking a balance between arrogance (assuming you know more than you do) and insecurity (believing that you know too little to act). This attitude enables people to act on their present knowledge while doubting what they know."[43]

There is an opposite side of the coin to epistemic humility. Sometimes you have to decide and act rather than merely reflect. This is epistemic courage. That is, one needs a certain amount of epistemic courage either to face the world as it is, or to insist that the world can be changed by way of action in accord with one's beliefs, and then to act on the belief. That is the leap or the plunge explored in the last chapter. It takes confidence and courage, not humility, to do that. That's the paradox.

The last step in epistemic courage is the idea of taking responsibility for the decision to leap and the leaping itself. Responsibility is really a function of how we think about our actions in relation to time. The objective reality of having chosen and acted in the past is fixed, but how we conceive of it is not. One aspect of epistemic courage is not reconstructing the past in an effort to rationalize or

42 JEFFREY PFEFFER & ROBERT I. SUTTON, HARD FACTS, DANGEROUS HALF-TRUTHS & TOTAL NONSENSE: PROFITING FROM EVIDENCE-BASED MANAGEMENT (2006).
43 *Id.* at 52–53.

avoid responsibility for decision. Did we make a commitment in the past or not? That is tricky territory for lawyers, since after-the-fact rationalizing or justifying is at the core of what lawyers do. There is always room for after-the-fact opportunity depending on how we hypothesize the problem. "Well, we did have a contract. There is no doubt about that. And we did make commitments. But the question now is whether the commitment really means what the other side is now saying it means."

The "sunk cost" problem is one demonstration beyond the rationality of pure lawyering in which wise lawyers might counsel their clients to face reality, accept consequences, and not engage in a reconstruction of the past. The behavioral psychologists tell us the sunk cost problem is a "behavioral trap," one form of which is the "investment trap." People regularly make poor decisions about exiting from activities, like investments, because they feel attached to what they did in the past by way of expenditures of time, money, or resources."[44] Once we have ridden this metaphoric horse (or share of stock) from its peak value down to the bottom, why should it matter whether we ride it or another back up to the top? The rule of rational action in these kinds of decisions is that the past shouldn't influence us. Just because I lost money on Yahoo stock doesn't mean I have to recoup it on Yahoo stock.

Here is a mundane little example. In 2005, my wife and I invested in a small rental property in the Michigan town where we spend our summers. Our plan was to rent it out at the prime summer weekly rates. The financial crisis and the ensuing depression hit Michigan and that market dried up. By 2011, the suggested listing price if we were to sell was about 60 percent of our equity in the house. Rational choice would tell us that as long as the house were merely an investment, the lost equity was a sunk cost, and there was no rational reason to prefer recouping the loss with the house or an alternative investment. But in fact we resisted selling. That was not rational. The past simply should not have mattered.

Robert Nozick, whose views on rationality we explored in Chapter 6, argued nevertheless that a principled (and therefore rational) decision might take account of the past. His reason was that not all expected utility from a decision is tangible; symbols can be meaningful as well and have value in a rational calculation.[45] We might find a reason for not selling the house or not changing investment horses or not giving up on an entrepreneurial enterprise, for example, in commitments that we have made to others (or, I suppose, to ourselves). But is the reason mere justification or self-deception? What is the principle for deciding when our decision to take account of the past is not an instance of commitment or endowment bias,

---

44 SCOTT PLOUS, THE PSYCHOLOGY OF JUDGMENT AND DECISION-MAKING 241–44 (1993) (citing H.R. Arkes & C. Blumer, *The Psychology of Sunk Cost*, 35 ORG. BEHAV. & HUMAN DECISION PROC. 124) (In experiments, 85 percent of respondents choose to complete the last 10 percent of a multi-million research investment, even though the product of the research had already been made obsolete by a competitor's product).

45 ROBERT NOZICK, THE NATURE OF RATIONALITY 22–26 (1993.).

but is in objective truth a rational decision? We are back to the infinite regress. Is there a principle for deciding when to be unprincipled? It seems to me that we cannot think our way out of the sunk cost conundrum because there is no "thinking" solution.

It may well be that my professional responsibility as lawyer-advocate is to use the tools of the law to recreate the past the best I can on behalf of the clients who are paying me. I accept that. But a fully formed lawyer-counselor, it seems to me, needs to keep some Sartre in mind. Getting things done is a "no-whine" zone. Rationality and knowledge hit their limit, and we simply have to decide. As counselor, I can hardly claim this to be an absurd world—it is not completely indeterminate and there is a place for reason, principles, and theory. Putting myself in the shoes of my client-actor, however, those processes of thought hit a limit. At that point the actor takes whatever information the world provides and makes a decision, and the actor is responsible. And the actor's commitment must be now not to lie to himself, i.e. not to deceive himself that the past was anything other than what it really was. That is taking responsibility.

Toward a conclusion

It ought to be clear by now that I have a reasoned skepticism about our ability to navigate through life on a wholly reasoned and rational basis. Sometimes being wise means understanding we just have to conclude, to decide, to act, to pay our money and take our chances. I recognize fully the abstraction of much of what I have said here. But I have wanted to counter the underlying rational, objective, and scientific underpinnings of much of the professional mindset: we can figure it all out and control it if we just think hard enough. More practically, as some have suggested, there is a real question whether any of this state of mind can be taught in school.

My life as a lawyer has been too rewarding, intellectually and otherwise, to denigrate the orderliness and rigor of thinking like a lawyer. The essence of the lawyer's contribution to a business decision is the processing of knowledge under some coherent theory. The lawyer can create a theory of success, a theory of risk, a theory of liability, a theory of failure. But our legal analysis is but another rational path through a complex world. As in the case of the CEO's decision to settle described in Chapter 6, every expert and every discipline had a view on either the ultimate issue or how various permutations of the ultimate result could affect his or her particular disciplinary responsibility. For the CEO, the thought process when integrating all of those points of view could have gone something like this:

> If we do X, the tax people are thrilled, but the environmental people are worried. If we do Y, we will be giving up a valuable real estate asset, but if we don't give it up, we won't get Z, which we need to make the business work going forward. Yes, we can stand on our contract rights and litigate until the cows come home; but the opposing party is a customer, and we are likely to

win the battle and lose the war. Yes, I understand the logic of the tax scheme you have proposed, but let's step back and do a sanity check.

This kind of decision-making may be less heroic or inspirational than crusading for justice, but I am firmly convinced that great lawyers in the mundane milieu of making money bring something more than keen analytical skills to the table. They bring some kind of wisdom—a metaphorical creativity—that transcends disciplinary boundaries, both within the law and without. Beyond that, even non-legal rationality has its limits. Creating and innovating products and solutions in the real world turn out not to be something we can model in any form of decision theory, simplified or complex. Those problems invoke decision, and are problems of action, of what to do next. They are not solely problems of knowledge or reason.

To the authors of *Educating Lawyers*, the work-a-day need in the curriculum including a retaking of the sense of justice from the beating it took during the first-year inculcation in rational analysis. I'll leave the idea of justice to somebody else but agree that something else takes a beating in law school. That is the notion of judgment as an aspiration that sits above smarts or cleverness (the stuff of mere reasoned analysis). More bluntly, I have said many times that every time I thought I was being amazingly smart or clever (and, trust me, I can be) in a business or legal situation, it invariably came around to bite me in the behind.

Is it possible to teach that kind of wisdom in law school? In part, it will take the courage not to be coolly rational and technical but to employ the techniques of Donald Schön's reflection in action, of knowing intuitively without knowing analytically, and of overcoming the lawyer's dependence on words and deductive logic. The bane of our profession, it seems to me, is what Schön describes as practitioners divorced from the theoretical mindset it takes to be reflective, who are "locked into a view of themselves as technical experts," who "have become too skillful at techniques . . . which they use to preserve the constancy of their knowledge-in-practice," and for whom "uncertainty is a threat; its admission is a sign of weakness."[46]

There is, moreover, a link between judgment, learning, and leadership. For academics (and legal ones particularly), the challenge is discovering that "scholarship" is just a term of art for a particular product of people who ply their trade in academia. I began with F. Scott Fitzgerald's dictum about holding opposing opinions, being able to function, and its relationship to intelligence. Being truly able to learn means that you have to force yourself to understand why someone would hold an idea that is opposed to yours; thus, in that moment of empathetic conceptual blending, you hold both ideas. Somebody can be a "scholar" for fifty years and never have one of those epiphanies.

---

46 DONALD A. SCHÖN, THE REFLECTIVE PRACTITIONER: HOW PROFESSIONALS THINK IN ACTION 69 (1983).

Real learning is related to a certain kind of leadership, the idea of coach-mentor-inspirer that modern leadership theory extols over old-fashioned command-and-control. While the first Fitzgerald quote is widely known, the sentence that follows suggests an even more profound insight: "One should, for example, be able to see that things are hopeless yet be determined to make them otherwise."[47] We can always analyze our way to hopelessness (that is a lawyerly specialty), but the determination to make things otherwise calls on—I hate to say it—a kind of faith, even if it is no more religious than a vague sense of purpose or ends, or a recognition that our determination to make things otherwise is what makes us want to get out of bed in the morning and face another day in lives that in the scheme of things do not mean anything.

Like Balinese cock-fighters, law students come to internalize from their teachers, mentors, and employers a model for describing what they do, as well as how they might ascribe meaning to what they do. The challenge is to learn to teach learning, which may well be nothing more than the willingness to see the metaphors and analogies that disturb our complacent categories. Here is an analogy: wisdom is to judgment as justice is to law. Law and judgments are subject to wide-ranging disputes about what they are but they are undoubtedly of this practical world. Justice and wisdom, on the other hand, are aspirations. But, as we aspire to and fall short of perfect justice in law, we will also aspire to and fall short of perfect wisdom in our judgments. But that is no reason not to aspire.

---

47 F. Scott Fitzgerald, The Crack-Up 69 (Edmund Wilson, ed. 1993).

Index